Conceptual and applied approaches
to self in culture in mind

Edited by
Tia G. B. Hansen
Kristine Jensen de López
Peter Berliner

SELF IN CULTURE IN MIND, VOLUME 2

Conceptual and applied approaches
Self in culture in mind (SICIM), volume II
Edited by Tia G. Hansen, Kristine Jensen de López & Peter Berliner

SICIM series editors:
Tia G. Hansen, Kristine Jensen de Lopez & Manuel de la Mata Benitez

© The authors and Aalborg University Press, 2015

Layout: akila v/ Kirsten Bach Larsen
Printed by Toptryk Grafisk ApS, 2015
ISBN: 978-87-7112-101-8
ISSN: 2245-1528

Cover painting: Casper Kjærsgaard Christensen
Language editor: Chris Cummins
Assisting proof reader: Bjarke Kronqvist Kristiansen

Published by:
Aalborg University Press
Skjernvej 4A, 2nd floor
9220 Aalborg
Denmark
Phone: (+45) 99 40 71 40
aauf@forlag.aau.dk
forlag.aau.dk

This book is financially supported by The Department of Communication and Psychology, Aalborg University, Denmark.

All rights reserved. No part of this book may be reprinted or reproduced or utilized in any form or by any electronic, mechanical, or other means, now known or hereafter invented, including photocopying and recording, or in any information storage or retrieval system, without permission in writing from the publishers, except for reviews and short excerpts in scholarly publications.

Contents

1. Conceiving and applying the self-culture-mind triangle   5
   Peter Berliner, Tia B. Hansen, Kristine Jensen de López

2. Self and others in autobiographical narratives. A study of German and Iranian students' first memories, early non-remembered events and remembered smells/feelings   23
   Monika Abels, Shahrenaz Mortazavi, Heidi Keller

3. Making one-self   53
   Ole Michael Spaten

4. Self-serving bias and psychological health. A cultural approach   87
   Pilar Sanjuán

5. Weddings, funerals and other important activities. Playing the Zapotec way   105
   Kristine Jensen de López

6 Culture, self, and symptom. Perspectives from cultural psychology 137
Andrew G. Ryder, Lauren M. Ban, Jessica Dere

7 Identity construction in narratives of migration 177
Beatriz Macías Gómez-Stern, Olga A. Vásquez

8 Intercultural family work An inclusive paradigm for psychosocial intervention 201
Rashmi Singla

9 Self-positionings and voices in identity reconstruction of women after suffering gender violence 233
Manuel L. de la Mata Benítez, Mercedes Cubero Pérez, Andrés Santamaría Santigosa, Francisco Javier Saavedra Macías

10 The cultural self in mind and action 257
Qi Wang, Jessie Bee Kim Koh, Yang Yang

Author list 271

Peter Berliner
Tia B. Hansen
Kristine Jensen de López

Conceiving and applying the self-culture-mind triangle

The topic of the second volume of the book series *Self in Culture in Mind* (SICIM), *Conceptual and Applied Approaches*, views the theme from two distinct but complementary perspectives. One is the development of new conceptual frameworks – whether these are purely theoretical or purely methodological or a combination of both – in order to reach a better and more detailed understanding of how human beings are inherently cultured and how self-construal becomes possible. The other is the idea that application and execution of relevant conceptual frameworks is an important and necessary scientific contribution to society.

Background and context

In our first volume Carpendale and Lewis considered how humans are created in culture within reciprocal processes including the social-cultural niche and historical processes (Carpendale & Lewis, 2011). They focused on the underlying interpersonal processes that support humans' ability to become able to conceptualise and sense oneself, leading to a self. Culture and self were addressed in relation to phylogeny, ontogeny and language. Following this notion of culture emerging within interpersonal relationships, we proceed in expanding our conceptual understanding of culture and self-construal in different settings and different social contexts.

A commonly acceptable definition of culture might run along the following lines:

> A group that can be characterised as having a culture base is seen not as a fixed or static entity but as one that is constantly changing in environmental interaction with other groups. However, members of a cultural group tend to reinforce certain attitudes and behaviours in one another, and those become identifiable features that are constant over time and space. Culture might thus be described as the totality of learned, socially transmitted behaviour of a group that emerges from its members' interpersonal transactions (Axelson, 1993, p. 3).

This definition is useful as it states that culture emerges from processes of interaction, i.e. group processes at the community level. Nevertheless, the definition also asserts a process of crystallisation such that the cultural patterns and norms may become fixed and immobile. Thus, these two aspects of the definition may seem slightly incongruent. It seems to us that both of these definitions of culture – as a background, and as an ongoing process of understanding the interaction between people in a community – are included within most approaches to culture.

The main consequence of the first aspect – the crystallisation assertion – is that the widespread use of "culture" as a concept may prevent us from meeting each other with an open mind and a sense of curiosity. Another consequence of the use of this concept in an abstract manner is that it ignores and maybe even conceals the socio-economic situation in which a person is situated. This situation may involve unemployment, low-standard housing, inadequate finances, lack of a social network, and scarcity of other resources. Thus, the concept may encompass or allow an ideological bias. By this criticism, we do not mean to challenge the concept of culture as such, but to warn against the use of "culture" as a fixed explanation of individual behaviour. In this respect, using the concept of "culture" would interfere with the necessity of meeting others with respect for their individual differences as well as possible group-wide similarities. Rather than allowing for such shortcuts and stereotyping, the essential endeavour of this volume is to understand how "the other" – any other – is part of their context, and how s/he makes use of her/his social network.

As seen above, the concept of culture could be used in a highly political way, overtly or more subtly. And it frequently has been. Sometimes it is an essential part of ethnic revival movements. In other contexts it is employed for segregation and oppression of groups within a population.

In summary, "culture" has become part of our everyday vocabulary. This has had a noteworthy impact on the language of social science and psychology. The concept of culture has been transformed into a proposition, as if culture existed in itself. Culture is sometimes used as an explication of the final cause of behaviour. Another kind of understanding of culture sees culture as a kind of map. Thus, "culture" is a very abstract concept and is applied in various ways.

Some researchers argue that globalisation leads to less cultural differences than before – and to other definitions and criteria for culture than merely place and ethnicity (Scollon and Scollon, 1995).

Whereas culture might be considered a suitable explanation of behaviour, it may be better understood as a movement, a way of changing perspectives and making references within a multitude of options and understandings. As an ongoing emergence it is perpetually built through discourses, interactions and distributions. Culture is in the making – which calls for a theoretical framework informed by complexity theory and network theory (see Bergendorff, 2009, and Braidotti, 2013).

An example from the first author's supervision of staff in Danish day-care institutions may illustrate this understanding of culture:

A Muslim father complains to the director of a preschool. His complaint centres on disappointment regarding his son's use of the same cutlery as the other children. The problem is that the cutlery is cleaned in the dishwasher. And in the dishwasher the cutlery is exposed to small pieces of leftovers, including pork. Because of this, the father demands that his son's cutlery must be washed separately. The director focuses on the cultural dimension and replies that he must accept the procedures in this Danish preschool, or take care of his child at home. The father gets upset and it all ends up in a quarrel and threats.

In another preschool a similar situation is handled quite differently. The director meets the father with appreciation of his concern for the nutrition of his son. Then she explains that the best solution to the problem is that he brings his son's cutlery back home every day and washes it himself. The father reconsiders the problem and concludes that the respectful treatment he receives from the director assures him that she is a very committed person – and because of that he is sure that the dishwasher at the institution is very good and cleans the cutlery well. Thus, his son's cutlery has been properly cleaned in the dish-washer in the preschool. He just wants the director to assure him that his conclusion is correct, i.e. e. that the dishwasher is new and functioning well.

This simplified example may illustrate – with inspiration from Bateson's theory of learning (1972) – that:

- Every situation as experienced may be defined through a multitude of contexts. The problem with the cutlery may be seen in the context of impurity of food. But it may also be seen in the contexts of control, of director-parent communication in public preschools, of work tasks, or of the different roles of males and females. There is no simple relation between the components, the experience and a cultural system. Culture is the movement of decisions.
- Culture may be understood as the course of the communication that provides value to particular aspects of the challenge – as we see when the second director in the example views the father as a

father rather than as a Muslim, and specifically a father who genuinely worries about the well-being of his child.
- The behavioural pattern, the interpretation and the social use of interpretations form another context in which the outcome of the social interaction might be understandable to an observer – or even to the participants.

Culture may be understood as a very flexible concept describing a network of discourses, social interactions, and material distribution. In this process the system may implode into rigid procedures and understanding or may emerge into diversity, creativity and innovation – or both at the same time in diverse sections. This is understood as complex adaptive systems with focus on the importance of desires, visions and vitality - as reflected in current approaches to culture, which suggest that culture is symbolic and that ethical aspects are drivers of sustainability and innovative change in all cultures (Bergendorff, 2009). Bleichmar (2011) speaks of the ethical self and of the subject as a part of citizenship with social responsibility. Social responsibility may expand the systemic or socio-ecological concept of social resilience, in that social responsibility includes a desire for mutual support, dignity, and respect as formulated in the Declaration of the Universal Human Rights (cf. Anasarias & Berliner, 2009).

We find that such an approach opens the way for looking at experiences through diverse theoretical lenses. The researcher and the practitioner in a cross-cultural setting may select and combine understandings and theoretical frameworks to achieve more inclusive understandings – a theme which is addressed by, among others, de la Mata et al., Ryder et al., and Singla in this volume. The following case taken from the first author's clinical and community based interventions for supporting psycho-social healing in traumatised refugees and refugee families in Denmark illustrates the need for diverse understandings of the intersection between culture, living conditions, family dynamics, and political context.

A refugee family from Eastern Asia, now situated in a large town in Denmark, suffers from violent confrontations between the father and the teenage son. For the first year in Denmark the son had to be very responsible as the father was confined to prison and tortured in their homeland. The problems occurred shortly after the father was reunited with the family in Denmark. The father is unemployed, socially isolated and dependent on the welfare system. The family is living in a small apartment, which has been allocated to them by the local municipality.

In trying to understand the problems in this family, we may draw on several different theoretical frameworks within psychology, such as:

1. Theories of post-traumatic stress and symptoms of crises – in a contextual and culturally adaptive way. Cultural traditions, values, and practices profoundly influence how people understand trauma, individual and social suffering, and social support and social resilience. Cultural practices provide a means of coping with crisis and show how the dominant individualistic and biological focus of Western psychiatry may be supplemented by more collectivistic and collaborative healing practices of cultural groups and local communities – including the local context for people living in exile. Otherwise people in crisis may find themselves isolated and uprooted and without access to stable social and economic structures, cultural values, and thus a socially supported identity and self-perception (see Henderson, Berliner, and Elsass, 2016 for documentation and further discussion).
2. Developmental psychology, which in this case focuses on the development of identity in adolescence. We suggest that a culturally sensitive understanding of the transition from child to young adult should be developed, including early adolescence as a period characterized by the beginning of an object-related sexuality, identity, a growing awareness of morality, and more reflective and abstract thinking. Neuropsychological research suggests that the brain, too, is developing rapidly in the early teens (Steinberg, 2014), in parallel to the development of self, self-efficacy, social decision-making, risk assessment. All of these characteristics have been suggested as significant factors in mastering peaceful conflict resolution, confident relationship formation, finding and engaging in developmen-

tal pathways, social resilience and demonstrating social responsibility in action (Jetha & Segalowitz, 2012; Reyna, Chapman, & Dougherty, 2011). In a globalised world the context may present a wide range of possibilities for choosing your identity. At the same time, a growing gap between rich and poor, and a deep influence on choices by the market and the media (see Putnam, 2014 for a summary of documentation) - may offer these options mostly to better-off children, while limiting options for poorer children, especially those of families with low income (Kieling et al, 2011; Friedl, 2009; Khanlou & Wray, 2014). In early adolescence the sense of citizenship grows (see Pancher, 2015 and Verhaeghe, 2014) and with increasing implementation of the United Nations' Convention on the Rights of the Child into institutional practice, in many countries it is now accepted that also children are citizens and thus the child's viewpoint should be taken into consideration in every decision impacting on the child's life, including research on children (see Paris & Winn, 2014; Wells, 2015; Lancy, 2015).
3. Educational theories of complex social learning, including cognitive and non-cognitive competencies in problem solving and collective intelligence in the everyday practice of the family (see van Merriënboer, 2013).
4. Community psychological theories about the impact of the socio-economic situation of the family, marginalisation, and limited social support (see Putnam, 2014, and Friedl, 2009).

All the theories may be combined in an effort to understand the family's situation and to support the family in building social resilience in the present context. This should be promoted through a composite effort to change the situation of the family, encompassing the dynamics of the relationship between the communication in the family and the opportunities the family encounters in the local community, such as access to education and work as well as to other economic, cultural and social resources of the community. The recovery processes and future stability of the family encompasses inclusion of the family into a supportive community with its institutions, civil society associations, and social network.

Our own Nordic model of organising the welfare state as a particular living culture illustrates this context. It is argued that this model of organisation of the society entails a high level of trust between people and between people and the state, as well as a high level of autonomy provided by the state to the individual (Trädgardh, 2012). Autonomy of the individual may not be individualism in a psychological sense as it is not seen as being in opposition to the state power but rather secured by the welfare state on a basis of fundamental rights and obligations.

In this way we see that identity is shaped through a particular organisation of the society and the community – which may imply that identity, and then maybe to a certain extent also self-construal, is outlined and made possible through this organisational process – a theme which is also addressed in different ways by both Jensen de Lopéz and Spaten in this volume. Thus, the self is made possible through a comprehensive system, which encompasses a discursive, a social, and a material (i.e. natural and economic) level (Anckermann et al., 2005, Berliner et al., 2011). When we conceive the system in that way, it becomes clear that self-construal and identity is not outside the organisation of the society and the local community but is an intrinsic part of that very process in itself. If so, that means that we can develop the system as a whole to make it more resilient (see Berliner et al., 2010). We can build societies and communities which are more capable of coping with challenges such as climate change and the high level of violence and poverty globally. Today, this perspective is reflected in theories of social resilience and community resilience.

Resilience is the result of a learning process – and this learning process is in itself part of the sustained resilience to change and adversity: *Research suggests that resilience pertains to the ability of a system to sustain itself through adaptation and occasional transformation. Resilient communities, hence, learn to cope with, adapt to and shape change* (Magis, 2010: 412). A resilient society or community takes action to increase the capacities of its members and institutions to respond to and influence the course of change. Community resilience is built through an ongoing process of strengthening social support and a sense of belonging (Maguire & Cartwright, 2008; Norris et al., 2008). Creating more supportive links between the individual, the family and the community is a means of sustaining these focal points in actions (Berliner et al., 2012 as well as Macías Gómez-Stern and Vasquez in this volume).

Culture is not a component in this process of promoting resilience – it is the very process. In this way we are building culture every day and in every moment in a learning process. The challenge today is to aim this learning process towards making us more resilient in the face of current and coming challenges to the global community, national societies, and thus to the local community.

Today, we see a growing interest in how culture and community form a unity, which sets the conditions for the understanding of the self at the collective and the individual level (O'Donnell & Tharp, 2012 and Sanjuán in this volume). This may be partly inspired by the seminal criticism by Foucault in his influential work *The Order of Things* (1971), which ended by proposing that our present focus on the human being as the centre of the world may vanish and disappear as just another kind of historically limited philosophy and epistemology. Currently, this may be further encouraged by climate change and the consequent understanding of the limits of human entrepreneurship, focalised in our present understanding, thus opening up the potential for the development of new understandings of collective reflection and ethical responsibility beyond humanism. Globalisation contributes to putting culture on the present agenda in politics, business, and research – both as a way of providing and sustaining international security and as a means of promoting national advances in the international economy. Cross-cultural psychology should contribute to this by looking at the present to understand how humankind can develop into a more knowing and thus a socio-ecologically more responsible component of the world as we know it, i.e. a more caring species.

Introduction to the chapters of this volume

The chapters in this second volume of the Self in Culture in Mind book series represent a range of perspectives on the concept of culture and self-construal in our present time of global challenges. The chapters are presented in two sections: conceptual approaches and applied approaches.

How might culture and society influence autobiographical memories of young people living in Germany and Iran respectively? This is the general research question posed by Monika Abels, Shahrenaz Mortazavi and Heidi Keller, the authors of the *second* chapter of this volume. These authors investigate narrative construction comparing early first memories and autobiographical narratives of German and Iran university students regarding their early life events. The study applies a mixed methods methodology through quantitative comparisons of the microstructures involved in the narratives of each group (numbers of words, sentences, language complexity, characters mentioned, emotionality, vocabulary), and the age at which the specific events took place, as well as through qualitative analyses of the content of the students' retrospective autobiographical narratives. The authors show how the narratives are linked to ecological and cultural factors, especially the characteristics of the participants' families of origin. The results of the qualitative analyses revolve around five different main topics, which were present in the narratives of both cultural groups, but in some cases with different magnitudes and content. The topics comprised the following: the role of the student's mother during early socialisation, meta-cognitive reflections on significant events, memories of events where the student felt he/she was "standing out", memories centred around aspects reflecting discipline and defiance during socialisation, and memories regarding episodes of death or funerals of a family or extended family member. Although the narratives from the two cultural communities resembled each other regarding most of the structural measures, the content of the narratives also differed with respect to the age of the students' first memories. Consistent with previous studies, the Abels, Mortazavi and Keller study shows that Iranian students' events are from a later age than the events remembered by the German students. This difference reflects the distinction between age of memories of Asian and Euro-American people. Among the interesting cross-cultural differences found in the Abels, Mortazavi and Keller study, it is worth pointing out that the Iranian students mention a large number of significant people in their narratives compared to the German students, reflecting the notion of a higher level of interdependency regarding self-construal than is the case for German students of this particular cohort. A second interesting cross-cultural finding is seen in the students' early metacognitive anchoring of early memories, where the Iranian students' memory clearly involve dialogues with other people or cooperative actions focusing on "we" whereas the memories of the German students act in social isolation focusing on "I".

The notions of self-construal and narrativity, along with self-esteem, are also the core concepts of the contribution of Ole Michael Spaten in chapter *three*. This study addresses the interrelationship between culture, family and peers in the self-construal of Danish school age children of low and high social economic status. Through use of qualitative interviews the children are asked to describe themselves, to reflect on whether their clothing plays a role in how they are accepted by others, what they would be like if they had had different parents, etc. The study shows that this development of self is formed through a complex pattern of relations between the children's activities and their narratives about these activities. The author also points to similarities between the Danish results and the general literature (Harter, 1999) on children's development of the concept of self that has showed that early concepts are based on concrete descriptions while later concepts build on more abstract descriptions. The children were interviewed at different ages and also requested to fill in a questionnaire about their self-esteem. Results were compared with results from American children collected in the 1980s and hence close to two generations earlier than the collection of the Danish data. Despite this confounding factor the author shows consistent gender differences in the children's reporting of elements of their self-esteem.

Pilar Sanjuán indirectly addresses the notion of self-esteem and self-construal by investigating concepts that are known to relate positively to this, namely self-serving attributional bias (SSAB) and well-being. SSAB is defined as the tendency of individuals to make more internal, stable, and global attributions for positive than for negative events. It was found that the sample did display this bias, which is explained by the changing of the Spanish culture from a rather collectivist, interdependent, and relatedness-oriented culture to a more individualistic, independent and autonomy-oriented culture. This particular bias also forms part of positive psychology and relates to the notion that individuals adopt a positive bias leading to a positive image of themselves. This self-enhancement could contribute to people's development of self-construal. On the other hand, individuals also judge themselves in a way that is culturally determined and following this self-serving attributional bias is predicted to be a characteristic of individualistic cultures, such as those of the United States or Western Europe. Interestingly, the magnitude of the self-serving attributional bias did not differ in this Southern European (Spanish) sample from what is seen in North American samples, suggesting it to be a universal characteristic in Western societies. Finally, she suggests that self-serving attributional bias could serve as a protective factor for individuals.

The contribution of chapter *five* consists of a cross-cultural comparison of the functionality of play in toddlers in two very different and geographically far apart indigenous communities in Mexico: a Southern Mexican Zapotec indigenous community and an Eastern Mexican Mayan indigenous community (studied by Gaskins, 1999). The study challenges traditional approaches to children's play, where pretend play has been addressed as *"a pedantic intellectualization"* (Vygotsky, 1978), by instead addressing children's play as an activity reflecting the child's specific needs and wishes, thereby understanding the socio-cultural settings of children's play at reality. This view allows for the inclusion of play as a feature of the child's zone of proximal development and in relation to the child's culturally specific awareness and self-construal rather than merely striving towards intellectualization. The study follows Gaskins' proposed cultural principles that are used to explain the child's engagement in specific play activities: namely the primacy of adult work, the importance of parental beliefs and the independence of child motivation within a child-within-context approach. Furthermore, the study sets out to show that despite the relative low level of play activities sometimes reported for *exotic* indigenous communities it is possible and also important to understand the child's play at reality as an expression of its desire to actively work through real-world embodied experiences in order to become an enmeshed participant of the specific culture. The study also stresses the way material cultural artefacts often set the stage for Zapotec children's spontaneous play activities. The comparison of the frequency of play activities across the Zapotec and Mayan Mexican indigenous communities sheds light on cultural differences between these two Mesoamerican societies, but also on some common universals of children's play, e.g. pretend play, which despite its overall universalism is clearly affected by culturally specific institutionalised rules and practices.

Turning to chapter *six*, here the Canadian psychologists Andrew G. Ryder, Lauren M. Ban and Jessica Dere introduce a theoretical and conceptual framework for understanding how culture, self and symptoms of psychopathology, by being closely intertwined, are actually able to "make each other up". They show that cultural variations in the self-concept set certain parameters around behaviour that constitutes normal and abnormal human functioning. It follows from this that symptoms of psychopathology are taken up and transformed within a culture's meaning system. The mutual constitution of culture and self shapes the interpretation, experience, and expression of symptoms, and does so in a dynamic way across persons, cultural contexts, and historical periods. The authors importantly stress that such approach requires that knowledge from the cultural psychology become integrated within clinical psychology. Self is viewed within the interactionist tradition of sociology, distinguishing the notion of self from the notion of self-concept, where the self is constituted dialectically, but it is also conceptualised differently in different cultural contexts. Drawing on the work of Markus and Kitayama (1991) the authors argue that a mutual constitution of culture and self is vital to understanding the cultural variations related to independent and interdependent self-construals in relation to humans' emotional expressions. The authors discuss different ways in which concepts of mental disorder, for example Major Depressive Disorder, can be characterised when taking into account important cultural variations such as beliefs about etiology and symptoms and the role they play in specific socio-cultural milieus. The overall aim of the authors is to illustrate how a cultural psychology perspective can be applied in order to provide an acceptable understanding of depressive symptoms, which is contextualised within a cultural framework and hence not necessarily the same experience in every culture. The authors cleverly show the need for such understanding by comparing differences in depression among Chinese compared to Euro-Canadian psychiatric outpatients and furthermore how these cross-cultural differences are influenced by the specific history and the concepts of somatisations and psychologisation.

In chapter *seven* Beatriz Macías Gómez-Stern and Olga Vásquez provide results from a participatory research action study of a group of Mexican immigrant women participating in La Gran Dimension, a community centre programme in Escondido, San Diego. Building on the theories of Bruner and Bamberg as well as the notion that narratives provide an interpretation of events, rather than an explanation, the authors provide ethnographic data illustrating the common structure of identity construction in the context of migration from Mexico to the United States. Their analyses of *narratives of migration* as self-defining memories serves to go deeper in the understanding of these narratives as an intertwining of cultural and personal identities. They state that the shared experience of migration leads cultural identity to play a leading role in the personal identity of the members of this group. This means that the cultural identity is constructed by personal narratives. They conclude that the study of *narratives of migration* constitutes a rich field of study that may help us understand how personal and cultural identities interweave with each other. The common characteristics emerging from the analyses relate to the notions of migration achievements, intertwinement of personal and cultural identification from past experiences, actual desires and future goals as opposed to homeland nostalgia and emotional responses related to their experienced difficulties in visiting their homeland. The results are compared to previous studies of narratives of migration in Andalusian participants illustrating cross-cultural differences in how different migrant groups construct their autobiographies, identity and self through narratives and become able to make sense of chaotic and unexpected situations in their lives.

Following the concept of culture, self and health, the contribution of chapter *eight* is by Danish clinical psychologist Rashmi Singla, who has an Indian cultural background. Singla delineates an inclusive paradigm for psychosocial intervention work with families across cultural boundaries. She shows how families actively negotiate categorisations such as gender, generation, and socioeconomic position to create their own culture as a meaning system. She argues that the practitioner and family members should pay attention to this broader context, i.e. the societal conditions in which the cultural practices take place.

The contribution of the Sevilla Activity Setting group consists of chapter *nine*, by Manuel de la Mata Benítez, Mercedes Cubera Pérez, Andrés Santamaría Santigosa and Francisco Javier Saavedra Macías. The study addresses the notion of (self-) positions and voices in identity reconstruction of women after suffering gender violence. The authors propose a dynamic and discursive view of identity, while challenging the essentialist perspectives of continuity and stability. Departing from Bakhtin's concept of *utterance* or *voice the* authors show how these voices are linked to a specific social, cultural and historical context and how communicative acts are constituted as exchanges of the voices that we reproduce, manipulate and quote. In this sense self is always essentially social and closely connected to voices of ventriloquation – the process whereby one voice speaks through another voice or voice type in a social language.

The final chapter of this volume consists of a general comment by Qi Wang, Jessie Bee Kim Koh and Yang Yang. The authors discuss the previous chapters and conclude that the overall message is that the self is cultural in nature. The cultural self is dynamic. It is not constituted by mechanical neural connections or networks as involves dynamic mental representations emerging through our making sense of our psychological, social, and cultural experiences. Culture takes shape in our actions and interactions through behaviour and language.

Together the ten chapters of this second volume in the series Self in Culture in Mind address different aspects of culture and how culture and the notion of self-construal come to be created through interactions. All the chapters aim to create a new understanding of culture in our time of globalisation, encompassing common challenges such as climate change, migration, socio-economic situations, poverty and violence.

When seen within a common array the contributions of this second volume of Self in culture in mind serve to remind us of the following:

- the autobiographical and the conceptual self together make up the "cultural self "
- the self-culture-mind triangle is potentially dynamic, adaptive, biased, multifaceted, psychopathological, part of play and resilient

Self in culture in mind: conceptual and applied approaches

The current and second volume of the Self in Culture in Mind series, Conceptual and Applied Approaches, constitutes an array of original theoretical, empirical and applied contributions to research on how our construal of self in culture in mind has implications for various areas of applied psychological science.

With this second volume of Self in Culture in Mind we hope to make clear the importance of taking into account different concepts of culture, and their relation to self-construal, when working within the areas of clinical or applied psychology.

References

Anasarias, E., & Berliner, P. (2009). Human Rights and Peacebuilding. In J.de Rivera (Ed.), *Handbook of Peacebuilding* (pp.181-196). New York: Springer.

Anckermann, S., Dominguez, M., Soto, N., Kjerulf, F., Berliner, P., & Mikkelsen, E.N. (2005). Psycho-social Support to Large Numbers of Traumatised People in Post-conflict Societies. *Journal of Community and Applied Social Psychology, 15,* 136-152.

Axelson, J.A. (1993). *Counseling and development in a multicultural society.* Pacific Grove: Brooks/Cole.

Bateson, G. (1972). *Steps to an ecology of the mind.* New York: Ballantine.

Bergendorff, S. (2009). *Simple Lives, Cultural Complexity: Rethinking Culture in Terms of Complexity Theory.* Lanham: Lexington Books.

Berliner, P., Anasarias, E., & de Casas Soberón (2010). Religious Diversity as Peacebuilding – the Space for Peace. *Journal of Religion, Conflict, and Peace.* Vol. 4. Retrived 28.7. 2015 from: http://www.religionconflictpeace.org/node/79

Berliner, P., Larsen, L. N., & de Casas Soberón, E. (2012). Case Study: Promoting community resilience with local values – Greenland's Paamiut Asasara. In M. Ungar (Ed.), *The Social Ecology of Resilience* (pp. 387-399). New York: Springer.

Berliner, P., Larsen, L.N., & de Casas Soberón (2011): A social action learning approach to community resilience: Our sharing of thoughts and feelings, our respect and trust should be passed on to the next generation. In Jensen de Lopez, K. & Hansen, T.B. (Eds.), *Development of Self in Culture in Mind* (pp. 197-221). Aalborg: Aalborg University Press.

Braidotti, R (2013). *The Posthuman.* London: Polity.

Bleichmar, S. (2011). *La construcción del sujeto ético.* Buenos Aires: Paidós.

Carpenter, I.M., & Lewis, C. (2011). Self constructed in culture. In Jensen de Lopez, K. & Hansen, T. B. (Eds.), *Development of Self in Culture in Mind* (pp. 25-40). Aalborg: Aalborg University Press.

Foucault, M. (1971). *The Order of Things – an Archaeology of the Human Sciences.* New York: Pantheon Books.

Friedli, Lynne (2009). Mental health, resilience and inequalities. Copenhagen: WHO.

Gudykunst, W.B. & Ting-Toomey, S. (1988). Culture and Interpersonal Communication. London: Sage.

Henderson, S., Berliner, P., & Elsass, P. (2016). *Disaster Mental Health: Research and Implications for intervention.* In R. Dahlberg, O. Rubin, and Thanning Vendelø (Eds.). Disaster Research – Multidisciplinary and International Perspectives (pp. 224-238). New York: Routledge.

Jetha, M.K., & Segalowitz, S. (2012). *Adolescent Brain Development. Implications for behavior.* Oxford: Academic Press.

Kieling, C., et al. (2011). Child and adolescent mental health worldwide: Evidence for action. *The Lancet, 378*(9801), 1515-1525.

Khanlou, N. & Wray, R. (2014). A Whole Community Approach toward Child and Youth Resilience Promotion: A Review of Resilience Literature. *International Journal of Mental Health and Addiction, 12,* 64- 79.

Lancy, D.F. (2014). *The Anthropology of Childhood: Cherubs, Chattel, Changelings.* Cambridge University Press. Kindle Edition.

Magis, K. (2010). Community resilience: An indicator of social sustainability. *Society & Natural Resources, 23*(5), 401–416.

Maguire, B., & Cartwright, S. (2008). *Assessing a community's capacity to manage change: a resilience approach to social assessment.* Canberra: Bureau of Rural Sciences.

Markus, H.R., & Kitayama, S. (1991). Culture and the self: Im-plications for cognition, emotion, and motivation. *Psychological Review, 98,* 224-253.

Norris, F. H., Stevens, S. P., Pfefferbaum, B., Wyche, K. F., & Pfefferbaum, R. (2008). Community resilience as a metaphor, theory, set of capacities and strategy for disaster readiness. *American Journal of Community Psychology, 41,* 127–150.

O'Donnell, C. R. & Tharp, R.G. (2012). Integrating Cultural Community Psychology: Activity Settings and the Shared Meanings of Intersubjectivity. *American Journal of Community Psychology, 49:* 22-30.

Pancher, S. M. (2015). *The Psychology of Citizenship and Civic Engagement.* New York: Oxford University Press.

Paris, D. & Winn, M.T. (2014). *Humanizing Research: Decolonizing Qualitative Inquiry with Youth and Community.* Thousand Oaks: Sage.

Putnam, R.D. (2014). *Our Kids. The American Dream in Crisis.* New York: Simon & Schuster.

Reyna, V.F., Chapman, S.B., & Dougherty, M.R. (Eds.). (2011). *The Adolescent Brain: Learning, Reasoning, and Decision Making.* Washington: American Psychological Association.

Steinberg, L. (2014). *Age of opportunity – lessons from the new science of adolescence.* New York: Houghton Mifflin Harcourt Publishing Company.

Scollon, R. & Scollon, S.W. (1995). *Intercultural Communication.* Oxford: Blackwell.

Trädgardh, L. (2012). Nordic Modernity – Social Trust and Radical Individualism. In K. Kjeldsen, J. R. Schelde, M. A. Andersen & M. J. Holm (Ed.). *New Nordic Architecture & Identity.* Louisianna Museum of Modern Art.

van Merriënboer, J.J.G. (2013). *Ten Steps to Complex Learning: A Systematic Approach to Four-Component Instructional Design.* New York: Routledge.

Verhaeghe, P. (2014). *What About Me?: The Struggle for Identity in a Market-Based Society.* Melbourne: Scribe Publications.

Wells, K. (2015). *Childhood in a Global Perspective.* Wiley. Kindle Edition.

Monika Abels
Shahrenaz Mortazavi
Heidi Keller

Self and others in autobiographical narratives
A study of German and Iranian students' first memories, early non-remembered events and remembered smells/feelings

In this chapter we will explore how university students in Germany and Iran construct themselves in narratives about early events in their lives. We will try to link these narratives to ecological and cultural factors, and to characteristics of the participants' families of origin, in order to make sense of the individual's autobiographical narrative in a national and cultural context. We approach the memories in an exploratory way, using a coding scheme for some aspects of the narratives and complementing this with qualitative analyses of aspects that are related to children's general experiences or traumas, or which connect to the cross-cultural literature.

Our samples of university students are small and no doubt selected in various ways, so this chapter is exploratory, intended to point towards future research. Nonetheless, we do find some useful patterns that can guide such future work.

In this chapter we consider three broad ways in which retrospective, autobiographical narratives might be influenced and patterned: by the cues used to elicit the narrative, by the cultural environment provided by the national context and by the content of the narrated event. The first exploration of this chapter concerns the cues that are used to elicit narratives about past events. Regardless of the community the participants are from, narratives about three different types of early life events are shown to differ systematically, for instance in terms of the length of the narrative and how emotions are treated. Iranian and German students' narratives differed in respect of the age they reported for their memories, the length of the narratives and the number of persons that were mentioned. Finally, the content of the memories regarding topics such as parents, defiance and death appeared in narratives in both communities and revealed some interesting patterns. For instance, they demonstrated the parents' roles in the families, which were experienced as fairly similar by narrators from both Iran and Germany. However, there were also interesting differences in the amount of control experienced in the described defiance situations. Though no doubt there are other influences on such narratives besides these three, we summarise each of them in some depth, using both qualitative and quantitative methods, in our report.

Development and Functions of Autobiographical Narratives

Autobiographical memory is defined as memory for facts and events of the past that are personally meaningful. Autobiographical memory develops in the context of past-event talk in the family, conversations that start developing when the child has acquired sufficient language competencies and has started using self-referrals (Nelson, 1993). These conversations are shaped both in structure and content by the narrative environment the child is exposed to (Reese, Haden & Fivush, 1993; Wang, Leichtmann & Davies, 2000). It has been shown that socialisation experiences shape the child's developing memory structures and self-construction (Greenfield, Maynard & Childs, 2003).

However, autobiographical memory is related to the self in a complex way. Not only do conversations and memories shape the self, but the self also can be explained, expressed and stabilised through autobiographical memories and narratives (Bluck, 2003; Nelson & Fivush, 2004). The narrative form incorporates the structure of events and perspectives, goals, temporal context, causal structure (landscape of action) and motivations, mental states, etc. (landscape of consciousness) (Bruner, 1986). Therefore, besides recounting events, autobiographical narratives can be conceived as self-making narratives in which the individual's life is reconstructed by the individual (McAdams, 2003).

Autobiographical memories help us to make sense of our environment as we experience it. We can derive rules about the world and use our autobiographical knowledge to solve problems and make predictions about future events (Bluck, 2003). In this way, autobiographical memories are linked to the present and also lend themselves to comparisons and connections between the past and the present.

The autobiographical narrative in its expressive character can also have social functions (Bluck, 2003). Autobiographical memories can be used as topics of conversations and they ease social interactions and teaching. By falling back on our own memories, we can understand others and empathise with them and express that through biographic self-disclosure.

To summarise: autobiographical narratives possess the following characteristics (Nelson & Fivush, 2004):

- They provide shape and meaning.
- They are ordered in a temporal-causal sequence determined by the personal past.
- The *Self* may be both an important character (the central protagonist in many cultures) and the story teller (dialogical view).
- They have both individual (identity) and social functions.

Autobiographical narratives and the socio-cultural context

The experiences that children have in their early lives and the way a family narrates autobiographical events are embedded in a wider environment (Bronfenbrenner, 1979; Whiting, 1981). Consequently, the national and socio-cultural context also influences autobiographical narratives and it does so for each of the characteristics of autobiographical memories described above. In this chapter, we report on German and Iranian participants' autobiographical memories. Studies that have included both Germany and Iran are rare, which leaves us to speculate to some extent on differences. Hofstede's (1980) groundbreaking study of value orientations among employees of a multinational company is one of the few studies including German and Iranian participants and placed them at different points along several cultural dimensions. We will try to formulate hypotheses as to how autobiographical narratives may differ based on these findings. While employees in Iran and Germany were fairly similar in terms of 'uncertainty avoidance', they differed in 'power distance' (in which Iran scored higher than Germany), 'individualism' and 'masculinity' (both of which yielded higher scores in Germany than Iran) (Hofstede, 1980).

Power distance is a measure of how hierarchically a cultural community is structured. In this case, when talking about childhood memories, this dimension may relate to how other persons and their actions are described in relation to the child. While children are generally dependent on their caregivers, there are differences in the perception and treatment of children, which can be conceptualised as related to differences in the accepted power distance. In ethnotheories of infancy, it has been shown that in some cultural communities the child is already treated as a (quasi-)equal interactional partner (Keller, 2007), which we consider as an indication of low power distance, whereas other communities consider children as apprentices whose caregivers have to structure their experiences for them (Keller, 2007), an indication of high power distance. Iranian employees reported more power distance than did German employees and this can be expected to be reflected in the family structures to some extent.

The individualism/collectivism dimension has been one of the most widely used concepts in cross-cultural psychology. High levels of individualism correspond to a sense of autonomous decision-making and personal agency (Kağıtçıbaşı, 2005). It is also connected to a model of the self in which the self is seen as independent and distinct from other persons, in contrast to a model of the self that is interdependent and has fuzzy self-boundaries in collectivist societies (Markus & Kitayama, 1991).

Masculinity refers to both an orientation of the whole society towards 'masculine' goals, such as ambition, dominance and aggression, and to larger differences between men and women (Hofstede, 1980), for instance between mothers and fathers when we consider families.

These cultural differences are expected to be represented in the socialisation of children in families and therefore to appear both in the memories of adults and in narratives they heard about themselves when they were children. Cultural differences have actually been shown to be reflected in the ways that people narrate their childhood memories (e. g. Wang, 2001). Among the aspects that differ are agency, the number of persons mentioned, emotions and the structural complexity of the narrative.

The narrator's awareness of his/her own and others' agency is expressed through activities, evaluations and the possibility of influencing events. The relation of the narrator's and the caregivers' agency can be interpreted as the child's reconstruction of hierarchical social structures (cf. power distance, as discussed above). That is, if narrators describe their caregivers as being the main source of agency, their early childhood environment can be assumed to have been characterised by a large amount of power distance.

The number of persons mentioned is on one level related to the actually experienced social environment: that is, how many persons were present at an event. This is reflective of family and social structures. However, cultural communities also differ in their socialisation practices concerning other persons, for instance in their emphasis on teaching children to address interactional partners correctly and relate objects to them (Ochs & Schieffelin, 1984). As a narrator can choose whether or not to mention persons, on a psychological level, mentioning other persons can be understood as an early interpersonal orientation on the part of the narrator.

Emotions are viewed (Kitayama & Markus, 1994) and expressed differently in different cultural communities (Matsumoto, 2006). From infancy onward, the expression of positive emotions is associated with independent cultural communities whereas the regulation of negative emotions is associated with interdependent cultural communities (Keller, 2007). The structural complexity of narratives has sometimes been taken as an indicator of a more elaborative narrative style, which in turn has been associated with independent cultural communities (Han, Leichtman & Wang, 1998).

As Germany and Iran have been shown to differ on the cultural dimension we wanted to know whether these differences are reflected in German and Iranian university students' narratives of autobiographical memories. We anticipate that:

- Iranian participants show higher deference to authority in their narratives.
- Iranian participants are more concerned with other persons.
- German participants focus more on their own volitions, needs and thought processes and perceive themselves as agentic.
- German participants perceive gender roles as more equal.

With economic and social developments in the two countries since the 1960/1970s when Hofstede's data were first collected, the cultural differences described above might have changed. Increasing individualisation has been found in many parts of the world, including Germany (e. g. Heitmeyer & Olk, 1995), and Iranian students have recently been shown to emphasise both in- and interdependent aspects of their self-concepts (Watkins, Mortazavi & Trofimova, 2000).

Eliciting childhood memories

There are different ways to elicit adults' childhood memories. We will focus our discussion on the earliest childhood memory, the first remembered smell and feeling, and a cued non-remembered event.

The participants' first remembered events have been elicited in several studies on childhood memories in the past (e.g. Mullen, 1994; Wang, 2001). They can be assumed to be a manifestation of the person's early self-concept. Accordingly they shed light on a person's way of constructing themselves and their relationship with others as a child. Furthermore, the way they narrate the event can illuminate their current perception of the event and of their childhood self.

The second type of narrative refers to smells or feelings that the person remembers. Smells have previously been used to elicit memories (Willander & Larsson, 2006, 2007). It is assumed that memories related to smells or feelings may differ from the first remembered events as evoked in the previous question. They can be expected to have a more sensual quality and refer less to an event with a temporal extension and plot. These are included in a rather exploratory way in this chapter.

The third type of narrative is on the topic of the first event that the participant knows about but does not remember personally. These events represent something that was told to the person or documented in a photograph, usually by his or her family members. That these events were preserved either orally or visually indicates that they were important events from the family's point of view. It can be assumed that they were either told to help the child stabilise his or her identity (possibly as a member of a family group), to socialise the child, or because the event was memorable because of other characteristics.

We will explore whether and how these three frames for eliciting narratives shape the narratives for German and Iranian students and whether the cue or type of narrative has an influence independent of the participants' cultural community or idiosyncratic narrative style. That is: would the cue determine the narrative, or would there be cultural characteristics that determine the way participants narrate any type of event? We expected a blend of these two influences. In particular, we expected the non-remembered event to differ vastly between the two samples as this can be expected to reflect parents' direct socialisation efforts and thus reflect the national differences found by Hofstede (1980) more closely than the present day student generation.

Finally, we wanted to explore themes that would emerge in the sample generally, and in the two national groups. This gives us an insight into both the environment and life events that the students experienced as children. Comparing these events across the samples will give us the opportunity to understand similarities and differences in students' and families' experiences in these different environments and the ways in which they make meaning of similar experiences.

Locales
Iran

The Islamic Republic of Iran was founded in 1979. It has an area of 1.6 million square km and is located between Turkey in the northwest, Armenia, Azerbaijan, Turkmenistan, and the Caspian Sea in the north, Afghanistan and Pakistan in the East, the Gulf of Oman and the Persian Gulf in the south and Iraq in the west (http://worldfacts.us/Iran.htm, retrieved 18 September 2009).

Iran's population was estimated to be approximately 66 million in July 2008, the vast majority being Shi'a Muslim (http://worldfacts.us/Iran.htm, retrieved 18 September 2009). The population has almost doubled since 1976 when it was 34 million (http://countrystudies.us/iran/32.htm, retrieved 18 September 2009).

Iran's capital is Tehran, a city of about 7.8 million inhabitants, located in the northwest of Iran. This is an area of the country with a high population density. Desert regions that have low population densities dominate the centre of the country.

Iran's economy is mainly dependent on petroleum and petrochemical products, although 30% of the workforce are occupied in agriculture. Approximately 80% of the population are literate (around 85% of men and 73% of women).

In Iran, marriages are traditionally patrilocal and often specific categories of relatives get married to each other (Abbasi-Shavazi, Morgan, Hossein-Chavoshi & McDonald, 2009). Few Iranian women are employed outside the home (Statistical Center of Iran, 2007) and there is a traditional emphasis on motherhood and domesticity (Abbasi-Shavazi et al., 2009). By their adolescence boys learn that they are considered superior compared to girls (Chavoshian, 1992). Family loyalty and self-denial and sacrifice for the family are highly valued in traditional Iranian culture and still upheld by many today (Hojat et al., 1999; Moghadam, Knudson-Martin & Mahoney, 2009).

The majority of Iranian participants in a study on family values feel that the mother should be home with a child during the first year of the child's life, otherwise the child is expected to become ruthless (Hojat et al., 1999). However the child and mother-child dyad are seen as part of a larger family system and the extended family are often involved in child care (Chavoshian, 1992). While dependence of young children is accepted and physically close caregiving preferred, middle class mothers also encourage their children's independence (Chavoshian, 1992). Discipline can take the form of verbal and physical punishment and is approved of by many parents (Oveisi et al., 2010), but children are also praised, particularly by extended family members (Chavoshian, 1992). Parents expect their children to be obedient and respectful towards elders (Chavoshian, 1992; Behzadi, 1994). Children are supposed to suppress their anger, but also to be fearless (Diener & Lucas, 2004). Accordingly, children learn to conceal their emotions (Novin, Bannerjee, Dadkhah & Rieffe, 2009).

Germany

The Federal Republic of Germany was founded after the Second World War in 1949. The current German state shares borders with Denmark, the Netherlands, Belgium, Luxembourg, France, Switzerland, Austria, the Czech Republic and Poland. It has an area of 349,223 square km. It has 82.7 million inhabitants; one third of the population are Catholic, another third of the population are Protestant (http://worldfacts.us/Germany.htm, retrieved May 30, 2010).

In Germany approximately 50% of the labour force work in the tertiary sector- that is they have occupations in service, finance and related domains. Only 2.2% work in agriculture (http://www.destatis.de, retrieved June 13, 2010). 10 years of school attendance is mandatory in Germany and 96.1% of the population have a school-leaving certificate. 24.4% of the population have a qualification for college/university entrance (http://www.destatis.de, retrieved June 13, 2010). 48.8% of the German population live in urban areas and 35.8% live in semi-urban areas (http://www.destatis.de, retrieved June 13, 2010).

The importance of marriage as the foundation of a family has decreased in Germany and children entitled to maintenance live in only 25% of German households (Lehmann & Wirtz, 2004). Birth rates in Germany are low and the government supports families with paid parenting leave during the first year of the infant's life and family benefits until the children finish their education. In Germany too, the mother is perceived as the ideal main caregiver for a young child.

More than 40% of men and women feel that a mother of a child under 3 years of age should not work outside of the home (Bertram & Spieß, 2010). Childcare institutions for children below the age of three are guaranteed by the German goverment.

German families highly value individualism and independence. For instance, they make efforts to select unique names for their children (Keller, Zach & Abels, 2005). As early as three months, German infants are expected to sleep on their own and through the night (Abels, 2008; Keller et al., 2005) and parents wish that their infants should play on their own (Abels, 2008). Education plays a great role in socialisation and children are enrolled in classes early in life (Keller et al., 2005). Germany has undergone dramatic changes in the late 1980s and 1990s with the reunification of the two German states that existed before. However, the first remembered childhood events of the participants took place before these changes and the majority of participants were born and raised in the Federal Republic of Germany.

Method

Students in Osnabrück, Germany and Tehran, Iran were asked to fill in questionnaires in German and Persian respectively. The questionnaires were translated into Persian by an Iranian psychologist and back-translated by an Iranian student who was fluent in German, had lived in Germany for several years and was writing her PhD thesis in German at the time. The content of the Persian version was identical to the German version. Students were recruited from psychology classes but also in public areas of the university.

In the questionnaires the participants were asked to fill out details of their age, educational history and their family background during the first 8 years of their lives. They were then asked to take some time to remember the first event in their life that they could recall and how they had felt during this event. They were then asked to describe an event in their childhood that they knew about from narratives by their parents, photographs or other sources but that they do not remember. A third question asked whether there were any smells or feelings that they recall from their childhood, what they were and whether they could remember and describe the situation in which they experienced this smell or feeling.

Nine questionnaires from the Iranian sample were translated into German by the student who also did the back-translation of the questionnaires. The translation retained the stylistic characteristics of the narratives rather than smoothing the resulting German sentences. Additionally, words referring to country-specific objects (e.g. food items) were not translated, but their meanings were explained by the translator. The first memories of the Iranian students (8 – one participant did not fill in this part of the questionnaire) were coded by topic and matched with 17 German questionnaires that contained the same topics in the first remembered event. This was done to ensure that possible stylistic differences were not due to differences in the events. For instance, a separation from a caregiver can be assumed to elicit more negative emotions than the exploration of the outside world.

We chose an exploratory, mixed methods approach to the data, which was guided by the research questions outlined above. Quantitative coding was done according to a coding scheme developed by Abels and De La Mata (unpublished manual). The data will be discussed qualitatively in terms of differences and similarities between the samples, including several aspects that arose from the data inductively. The topics of the discussion were chosen on the basis of either being relevant for children independent of the cultural community they live in (e. g. their relationship with their mother, discipline), being traumatic (e.g. death), or being traditionally associated with a particular cultural orientation (e. g. reflections on the self/theory of mind, standing out).

Coding

The following codings were used in the analysis of the data.

Topics

Each narrative was analysed to determine the main topic(s) of the event described. These topics consisted of the following:

- agency (having or gaining control over a situation or attempting to do so; this can also apply to being in control of one's thoughts)
- being separated (being separated from the primary caregiver or significant social partner, losing one's way)
- death/severe illness of others
- diseases/threats to the self
- family relations (memories in which family relations play a role; these may be positive or stressful)
- birth of a sibling
- nature/animals/exploration (interaction with or observations of animals or nature is described).

These topics were taken as the basis for matching the Iranian and German students' questionnaires.

Volume
The number of words and sentences in the narrative was counted.

Characters
Each new character mentioned in the narrative, besides the narrator himself or herself, was coded.

Structural Complexity
Each marker of structural complexity of the narrative was scored. These markers could be causal (e.g. *because, as*), temporal (e.g. *after, before, then*) or reflexive (e.g. *which, that*). Subordinate clauses that were not introduced with a complexity marker were additionally coded.

Emotionality
- Self-other: for all emotions mentioned it was coded whether these emotions were described for the self or other persons.
- Explicit: emotion terms were used to explicitly state the person's emotional state (e. g. happy, angry, sad, excited).
- Symptoms: bodily symptoms of emotions are described but the narrator does not label the emotion (e. g. crying, shouting, shaking knees).

- Absence: emotions are absent when they would be expected. 'Absence' is also coded if the narrators themselves state that they did not experience any/a particular emotion.

Vocabulary:
- Mental: vocabulary referring to cognitive or mental activities was coded. These include thinking, remembering, fantasising, knowing etc.
- Volition/preference: vocabulary referring to wanting or preferring one thing or option to another was coded here.
- Need: any reference to needs is coded here. Needs are either indicated by the narrator's use of the word "need" or if there is a reference to a bodily need such as "hunger".

Results
Analyses of variance were calculated with prompt and sample as independent variables. Separate analyses were calculated for each group of variables. Scheffé tests were used as post-hoc tests.

The three prompts for autobiographical narratives compared
As expected, overall the narratives about remembered (first memory and smell/feeling) and non-remembered events differ. Non-remembered events happened significantly earlier in the participants' lives than the first remembered event and the first remembered smell/feeling ($F(2, 52) = 28.12$, $p < .001$, partial eta^2 = .52). There is also a significant interaction effect of narrative * cultural community ($F(2, 52) = 3.28$, $p = .045$, partial eta^2 = .11), due to a more clear-cut and extreme pattern in the Iranian participants' responses (see table 1 for full data).

In terms of the length of the narrative, the non-remembered event and the remembered smell/feeling are more similar to each other than they are to the first memory. The first memory narratives consist of more words ($F(2, 56) = 6.77$, $p = .002$, partial eta^2 = .20) and more sentences ($F(2, 56) = 9.41$, $p < .001$, partial eta^2 = .25).

There are several aspects of mentioned emotions that differ across the three narratives. The narrations of the first memory contain more explicit mentions of emotions ($F(2, 56) = 15.97$, $p < .001$, partial eta^2 = .36) and more emotions of the self ($F(2, 56) = 14.66$, $p < .001$, partial eta^2 = .34) than the other narratives.

The number of characters does not differ across narratives ($F(2, 56) = 1.65$, $p = .20$, partial eta^2 = .06) but there is a significant interaction effect of narrative * cultural community ($F(2, 56) = 11.87$, $p < .001$, partial eta^2 = .30). While the German participants mention more persons in their first memories than the Iranian participants, they mention fewer persons in their narratives of the non-remembered event and of the smell/feeling. The Iranian participants, on the other hand, mention more persons in the non-remembered than in the remembered event and even more in the narrative of smell/feeling.

Table 1 Quantitative description of the memories (means, SD in brackets)

Sample	First remembered event			Non-remembered event			Smell/feeling		
	Iranian	German	Total	Iranian	German	Total	Iranian	German	Total
N	8	17	25	6	16	21	3	12	15
Age at event (yrs)	4.8 (2.2)	3.7 (1.5)	4.0 (1.8)	1.4 (0.8)	1.3 (1.2)	1.3 (1.1)	7.2 (2.8)	3.9 (1.2)	4.7 (2.1)
Volume (words)	79 (38)	70 (29)	73 (32)	62 (47)	29 (19)	38 (32)	60 (22)	28 (17)	35 (22)
Sentences	5 (1)	5 (2)	5 (2)	4 (3)	2 (1)	3 (2)	4 (1)	3 (1)	3 (1)
Number of characters	1.4 (1.5)	2.5 (1.5)	2.2 (1.5)	2 (1.5)	0.6 (0.9)	1.0 (1.2)	3.7 (1.5)	0.4 (0.8)	1.1 (1.6)
Complexity markers/sentence	0.4 (0.7)	0.7 (0.6)	0.6 (0.6)	0.7 (0.6)	0.5 (0.6)	0.5 (0.6)	0.3 (0.4)	0.4 (0.5)	0.3 (0.5)
Emotionality									
self	2.6 (1.3)	2.4 (1.1)	2.5 (1.2)	0.8 (1.2)	0.2 (0.8)	0.4 (0.9)	2.7 (3.1)	0.7 (0.9)	1.1 (1.6)
others	0.4 (0.7)	0.5 (1.2)	0.5 (1.1)	0.3 (0.8)	0.2 (0.4)	0.2 (0.5)	0.0 (0.0)	0.1 (0.3)	0.1 (0.3)
absent	0.6 (1.1)	0.4 (0.7)	0.4 (0.8)	0.2 (0.4)	0.2 (0.4)	0.2 (0.4)	0 (0)	0 (0)	0 (0)
explicit	2.1 (0.8)	2.0 (1.5)	2.0 (1.3)	0.2 (0.4)	0.1 (0.3)	0.1 (0.4)	2.0 (2.6)	0.4 (0.8)	0.7 (1.4)
symptoms	0.6 (1.1)	0.3 (0.6)	0.4 (0.8)	0.8 (1.2)	0.2 (0.5)	0.4 (0.8)	0.3 (0.6)	0.2 (0.4)	0.2 (0.4)
Vocabulary									
cognition	1.3 (1.2)	0.7 (1.6)	0.9 (1.5)	0.3 (0.5)	0.0 (0.0)	0.1 (0.3)	0.6 (0.9)	0.7 (0.6)	0.6 (0.8)
need	0.1 (0.4)	0.0 (0.0)	0.0 (0.2)	0.0 (0.0)	0.1 (0.3)	0.1 (0.2)	0.0 (0.0)	0.0 (0.0)	0.0 (0.0)
volition/preference	0.4 (0.7)	0.4 (0.6)	0.4 (0.6)	0.3 (0.5)	0.3 (0.4)	0.3 (0.5)	0.7 (0.6)	0.1 (0.3)	0.2 (0.4)

According to an inductive analysis, the answers to the question on remembered smell/feeling seem to fall into roughly three categories. There are memories that are described mainly in terms of their sensuous quality, as we had expected of this type of narrative (e.g. "the smell of spring", "my mother's smell", "pancakes", "feeling the sun on my skin"). Another category, which is comparatively rare, refers to fantasies (e.g. "the feeling when I fantasised being a squirrel or a horse" or "I always felt that I was an important person and the world has to know, like and adore me"). The third category is emotional (e.g. "anger, loneliness – I had the feeling that I didn't belong! – I had to go to daycare and my siblings didn't.") Some participants refer back to the remembered event that they described in the earlier question and elaborate upon it. Often these elaborations include further details of the context of the event or visual memories that were omitted in the first narrative.

While there are no statistical differences in the distribution of topics between the three types of narratives, this absence can probably be attributed to the small total number of narratives, as some topics seem to occur much more frequently in a specific type of narrative than in others. Others' deaths or severe illnesses are only mentioned in the narrative of the first memory, for example. Being separated is rarely a topic of the non-remembered event, but one's own diseases or threats to the self seem to be over-represented in this type of narrative.

In summary, the first childhood events that the participants were told about or shown photographs of are very early events in their lives. They occurred on average more than 2.5 years before the first event participants remembered themselves. Though these narratives can contain life-threatening events, the narratives about them are comparatively short and contain few emotions.

The first remembered childhood event occurred later in the participant's life and is typically narrated at a greater length including more of the participant's own and explicit emotions. Others' death or illness may be the topic of this memory.

Remembered smells or feelings share characteristics of both other types of narratives. On the one hand they, like the narratives of remembered events, refer to later events than the non-remembered events. But, like the non-remembered events, smells/feelings are conveyed in short narratives that contain fewer of the participants' own and explicit emotions.

The two samples compared

The Iranian participants remembered events at a later age than the German participants ($F(2, 52) = 9.93$, $p = .003$, partial eta$^2 = .16$). This becomes apparent in the difference of one year between the German and the Iranian participants' first memories. (Although the difference is even larger for the smell/feeling, this is somewhat unreliable because of the small number of narratives.) The Iranian participants' narratives contained both more words ($F(2, 56) = 8.34$, $p = .005$, partial eta$^2 = .13$) and more sentences ($F(2, 56) = 3.87$, $p = .054$, partial eta$^2 = .07$) than the German participants'. They do not differ significantly in terms of the complexity markers contained in the narratives. There are also no differences in terms of the emotions mentioned in the narratives.

Iranian participants mention more characters in the narratives than German participants ($F(2, 56) = 9.52$, $p = .003$, partial eta$^2 = .15$).

In summary, the Iranian participants narrate later events than the German participants. The narratives about these events are longer and contain more different characters but do not differ in other ways from the German participants' narratives. While it is possible that some of the differences in length are due to the differences between the languages, there also seems to be a stylistic difference, with the Iranian students providing more details and elaborating more on their memories than the German students.

We will now turn to the more qualitative analyses of the data. These will focus on the role of the mother, remembering thoughts, standing out, discipline and defiance, and death. As mentioned above, these topics were chosen because they can either be assumed to be important for children in most cultural communities, have been discussed as specific to one cultural community, or are potentially traumatic. We will examine examples from narratives from both samples and discuss how these can be related to the more general context of societal and economic conditions.

The role of the mother

Both in the Iranian and the German sample there are examples of the great importance of the mother to the child and that missing her causes emotional turmoil in the child.

One of the Iranian participants narrates how it became necessary for him to herd sheep, separated from his mother, when he "still needed her" at the age of seven. The separation was caused by a severe drought. The participant describes how he tried to resist being separated from his mother and returns to this event when asked about a smell or feeling and mentions that his father and older brother were present. Obviously they were not sufficient to support the participant emotionally. The father is described as "having or showing fewer emotions".

An example differing both in the cause and the duration of the separation is described by a German participant. She remembers that she wanted to show her mother a character from the children's TV series 'Sesame Street'. She went out of the house to search for her mother but could not find her. She went back feeling jealous of her brother who had gone shopping with their mother. Again the father is a rather distant figure who is described as "not having noticed anything" in this episode.

While it can be assumed that the mother is the primary caregiver of children in both cultural communities, families also seem to socialise their children to regard their relationship with their mothers as special. This can be seen from a German example of a non-remembered event. The participant writes about an event from the age of about 4 weeks old: "Mother went shopping. I was lying in the cradle and cried. I raged and kicked my legs till I reached the headboard, got half undressed doing this and could not be consoled." While in this example the reference to the mother is rather indirect she still seems to be the crucial factor in consoling the child.

An interesting aspect of the children's emotional relationship with their mothers is that it is not necessarily consciously represented, as they do not address their emotional state explicitly but only narrate indicators of emotional states. This can be seen in another German participant's narrative which describes being hospitalised at less than

2 years of age. While she explicitly describes feeling happier being with the nurses, she started crying when her mother left. The lack of an explicit representation of longing for the mother could be due to the young age at which the participant experienced the situation. However, she is quite elaborate on cognitive processes (see section "Remembering thoughts" below), and therefore an alternative conclusion may be that she developed a defensively independent strategy (cf. Rohner, 1999).

The mother in these examples is constructed as an important source of emotional support and events in which she was not available are remembered as stressful or sad. The separation is brought about either by economic factors (shopping, herding sheep) or by unfavourable health status (hospitalisation). When the father is mentioned at all in the memories studied here, he is described as either unaware of or unable to fulfil his child's needs or desires.

Interestingly, the German participants who narrate missing their mother were younger at the age when they recall such an event than their Iranian counterparts. While this may be an effect of the German narrators' earlier independence from their mothers, this could also just be an effect of the general tendency of German narrators to remember earlier events.

Remembering thoughts

There are several examples in which participants remember thinking about something; that is, their narratives refer to meta-cognitions. These examples exceed the cognitive vocabulary code by being comparatively complex. Three instances of remembering thoughts are provided in the following illustrations.

The first example is from the German participant whose first memory referring to hospitalisation was already mentioned in the section on the mother's importance. She writes: "Being in hospital at 16 months. I remember my mother behind a pane of glass, her clothes, her hat and that I could not say anything but that I understood everything that the nurses said to and about (!) me and that I knew that they assumed I hardly understood them."

A second German example refers to thoughts while having to jump to look out of the window. Part of the participant's response to the question about how she felt about the event is: "It was not a moment of particular joy, but after having jumped for the first time to look out the window, I thought that one day I would be tall enough so I wouldn't have to jump and that if windows were lower or larger that they would be too low for parents or would reveal too much of the inside of the house."

The third example is an Iranian participant's first memory in which she imagines that ants go to school, like human children: "When I was four years old I took my two year old brother's hand and together we went to the corner of the courtyard. I said to him: we will sit down here and wait until the ants come back from school and we will catch their school bags. In my fantasy I thought that that was a smart thought." She adds when asked about her feelings: "I was enthusiastic about this idea and felt very intelligent, because I could possess an ant's school bag. I was also not disappointed when I did not manage that but became more determined and thought that I would become my father's smartest child this way."

There seems to be a marked difference about the involvement with other people in the different memories. The Iranian participant is co-active. She takes her brother along with her and explains her thoughts to him. She also thinks about her father's reactions by hoping to "become my father's smartest child".

By contrast, the children in the German participants' memories seem to act in social isolation even though the topics of their thoughts include their social environment. In the first example the isolation of the child is highlighted by the fact that she only saw her mother through glass and that she "could not say anything". This may be due to medical procedures or may be due to little speech development at that age. However, her thoughts reveal a complex understanding of others' thoughts indicating a false belief understanding or a theory of mind. She writes: "I understood everything that the nurses said to and about (!) me and I knew that they assumed that I hardly understood them".

In the example in which the participant describes jumping up, she thinks about the future and the reference to parents could be another way of referring to adults in general and thereby possibly the future as well (when she herself is an adult). In contrast to the Iranian participant, neither of the German narrators describe sharing their thoughts with someone else. Their thoughts seem self-serving and do not lead to actions as the Iranian narrators' do. They also do not seem concerned about the approval of their social environment.

Standing out

The paragraph on remembered thoughts already contains one reference to standing out: the Iranian participant who wants to "become my father's smartest child". The same participant states that she "always felt that I was an important person and the world has to know, like and adore me. I wanted to be best in every respect." When asked about a situation in which she felt this way, she writes "for example at a wedding at which all of my cousins and friends had put on nice clothes, I thought that I was in the centre and that everybody would look at me and adore me. I am the most beautiful and best dressed."

While this Iranian participant does not seem particularly perturbed by failures and stated "I was also not disappointed when I did not manage", a German participant, however, describes a situation in which she felt humiliated by the failure to show a skill at a party at her grandmother's place. "It was an embarrassing experience: […] I wanted to show that I can recognise my father blindly and everybody was supposed to stand in a circle. I held my hand in front of my eyes and turned and peeked through my fingers, of course. My plan was to recognise my father by his shoes but unfortunately another guest at the party was wearing the same shoes and I did not run into my father's arms." When asked about her feelings, she writes: "I proudly wanted to show something and then I felt pretty embarrassed and I was disappointed in myself and angry."

Interestingly, there is also a German example in which a participant describes a non-remembered event in which the child stands out. "At the Christmas party at our shooting club children could recite poems which, however, was arranged in advance by the parents.

When asked who else wants to recite a poem, I came forward even though I had not practiced with my parents. I strutted to the front and recited my poem and got a present." While it is subtle, there is a certain connotation of inappropriateness in the participant's choice of the word "strut". It is unclear whether the behaviour is considered inappropriate by the adult narrator or whether the child's parents considered it as inappropriate and told her the story in this way as a means of socialisation. If it is the mere repetition of the parents' connotation it seems like an ambiguous story – telling the child about a self-promoting behaviour but at the same time conveying that this behaviour was somewhat inappropriate and possibly warning her of excessive pride by ridiculing it.

Discipline and defiance

More direct means of socialisation are remembered by some participants, and these often involved narratives of control and defiance. An Iranian participant narrates the event of how she was weaned from her pacifier at two years of age. This is a narrative produced when prompted to recount an event that the participant does not personally have a memory of. "During my childhood I was used to sucking on a pacifier and my parents tried to break this habit. One day when we had travelled to Mashhad with my aunt and her husband, my aunt's husband took the pacifier, dipped it in pepper and put it into his pocket. Only after I had searched and cried for a long time I found it and put it into my mouth immediately. After a few seconds I started crying and screaming and since then I never needed a pacifier again." In this case an uncle takes the initiative to realise the parents' socialisation goal. How this setup was agreed upon is not clear from the narrative. It is also not clear what the intended message of the story is. Perhaps this might seem a rather severe socialisation practice, although it proved effective.

A German example of socialising or disciplining the child is narrated by a participant who remembers: "because I supposedly caused 'trouble' I was asked to leave the car and walk home (in an unknown area). But my parents drove directly behind me. The whole thing lasted for a very short period of time and was supposed to scare me. It was my idea by the way (defiance)." Asked about her feelings, she writes, "I suppose it was a defiance reaction. I got out of the car immediately (because I was certain that they would not desert me). I did not have a bad feeling." The participant does not tell us about the situation that led to the escalation. However she implies that she as a child suggested or agreed to leave the car readily. While the situation could have had an effect of emotional abandonment for the child, in this case the child is very certain that nothing of the sort will happen. If the parents intended the request to leave the car as a disciplinary action it is not successful. It might have been able to calm the child, though, possibly acting as something similar to a time-out.

Another example of defiance can be found in an Iranian participant's first memory. "One day I received a boiled egg from my mother during a meal. I wanted to cut the egg myself but my mother did that. I was angry and started crying, ran away and told my mother that I would not eat anymore. I cried so hard that my mother got angry and shouted. To console me they brought me my toys and peeled almonds and walnuts. My sister and I started playing. That calmed me because I played that game for the first time." In this example the cause of the escalation, the chronology and how the situation was finally resolved are described. It starts with the narrator striving to do something independently that the mother does not approve of. The child then throws a tantrum, which angers the mother. Finally, the situation is resolved by giving the child something (else) to eat and playing a new game with her. The emotions involved in the situation from both the child's and the mother's side are mentioned. The narrative suggests the involvement of at least one additional person in the resolution of the conflict and it seems that the strategy involves mainly a distraction of the child from the conflict.

Both Iranian and German narrators remember defiance and somewhat harsh disciplinary measures. However, the German narrator portrays herself as being in control while the Iranian narrators seem less in control. However, contrary to the general pattern they were also younger at the time of the event.

Death

Several Iranian participants reported memories of the death / funeral of a member of the (extended) family. It was very difficult to find appropriate matches from the German sample. This could be due to differences in the family structures such that losses of more distant relatives are of greater importance in Iranian than in German families, and to cultural and religious differences. However it is probably also related to demographic characteristics. For instance, the life expectancy in 1980 was 57.7 in Iran but 72.5 in Germany. In 1990 under-five mortality was at 72 per 1000 live births in Iran and at 9 per 1000 live births in Germany. It can be assumed that because of these demographic parameters Iranian participants had a greater likelihood of being exposed to death than their German counterparts.

The deaths that are included in the participants' memories concern grandparents and a sibling. An Iranian participant remembers her brother's death when she was five. But the aspect that she wonders about in the narration is that she was playing and was not emotionally involved. She describes her feelings by saying: "completely without emotions, a light feeling, maybe complacency. I was involved in my game." This is in line with Iranian mourning ceremonies in which women get together and cry while the children play somewhere else. A German participant describes her memory of her grandfather who had always brought soap bubbles for her when he came to visit. He died when she was four and her narration includes the regret that he died so early and that this is the only memory she has of him. Both of the narratives are thus characterised by discussing an absence (of emotions or memories). Another absence is discussed in another Iranian participant's memory of her grandmother's death and funeral. In this case the absence of knowledge about death is mentioned. When asked about her feelings the participant writes: "...unclear. I did not know much about death but I knew that it is a bad event." Another interesting aspect of this memory is that although the narrator claims to "remember everything", the narrative itself is very brief and does not contain any details of the funeral for which her mother picked her up from school.

In summary, all the narratives about death are characterised by absences, mainly the absence of emotion that the narrators themselves remark upon, but also the absence of memories or knowledge about the topic at the time, even though death and loss appear as a topic.

Discussion and conclusion

As the samples for this study were very small, the results should be interpreted with some caution; they are exploratory, but can be suggestive for further research. Other factors certainly have affected the narratives besides the cultural ones considered here. Gender, personality factors and the subjects that the students were studying at university could undoubtless have influenced these memory narratives. The sample comprises university students who volunteered to narrate these memories and so they are no doubt highly selected compared to all Germans and Iranians. No claim is made that they are representative of their nation-states; we use the national terms for convenience. However, the fact that both samples are students makes possible *relative* national comparisons of similar populations in that context. We now turn to relating our results to the existing literature and trying to understand them in terms of cultural differences.

Interestingly, the narrators in both cultural communities produce similar patterns when asked to narrate the three different types of memories. Obviously a remembered event would be remembered more vividly than an event that one was only told about. However, it is interesting to note that the question on smells/feelings contained few emotions in both samples and thereby shared some characteristics with the narratives that participants produced when asked to narrate an event they do not remember.

Iranian and German students' narratives differ in respects that are in line with the literature. Iranian students remember later events than German students, a difference that has been found frequently when comparing Asian and Euro-American participants. They also generally mention more persons in their narratives than the German students, which probably reflects their greater orientation towards the social rather than the material world. This difference in orientation also becomes apparent in seemingly similar narratives as for example in the narratives about remembering thoughts, in which the Iranian participant both shares her thoughts with her brother and is concerned about her father's recognition. The German participants do not share their thoughts, but seem more often to recall situations in which there is social isolation. We also find examples of defiance and harsh discipline in both samples, but the German narrator portrays herself as being in control while the Iranian narrators do not. While this may be a cultural difference in which the agency of children in Germany is highlighted to a larger extent than in Iran, it could also be an effect of age. Contrary to the general pattern, the Iranian discipline/defiance events took place earlier in the children's lives which may have led to them actually being less in control. Also it is possible that German children show defiance until a later age compared to their Iranian counterparts.

Unexpectedly, there were no differences between German and Iranian participants in structural complexity, the treatment of emotions, or vocabulary concerning mental processes, volitions and needs. It may be important to consider the age of the children when the events took place. Particularly when others' emotions are concerned, it is important to keep in mind that the child may not have a full understanding that others also have opinions and emotions. The results also show a high variability of style between the students within each group, making differences in personal style of expression a relevant factor for understanding some of these results.

Iranian participants' narratives were longer than German participants'. This may be related to the rich Persian literary traditions that may have influenced the students' expressions. Some of the Iranian participants also seem to embrace the opportunity to reflect on their experiences, more so than their German counterparts seem to have done.

There are some interesting similarities in the German and Iranian participants' memories of missing their mothers and memories of death. In those cases in which missing the mother is a topic of the first memory, the narratives are comparatively emotional. The narrators remember crying, being jealous and feeling bitter. The fathers have a different role in the children's life when they are mentioned. They are more distant and cannot or do not satisfy the children's need for their mothers. It is interesting to see this similarity in societies that differ in so many respects, among them masculinity, as measured by Hofstede (1980). However, the age difference in the German and Iranian memories could point to a different developmental trajectory in which the Iranian children may show 'dependent' behaviour for longer. It would be interesting to see how changing gender roles change the children's perception of their parents.

Memories of death are narrated in a way that highlights absences, particularly the absence of emotions. It seems as though the adult narrator reflects on the grave nature of the topic and feels that as a child she or he did not really grasp the seriousness of the event. While they are not explicitly reproachful they do seem to find their thoughts and behaviours somewhat inappropriate in retrospect (e.g. playing nonchalantly when your own brother has died).

This chapter is a first exploratory attempt to see how cultural factors, along with framing effects, influence autobiographical narratives that are matched in their topics for different samples. Future research can address this question on a larger scale and include practices such as mourning ceremonies in a more systematic way. In this study, the results revealed some cultural differences but also showed that narratives are structured depending on the ways that questions are framed, and that there seem to be overarching similarities in the emergence of themes concerning children's separation from their mothers and their experience of death. We also found suggestive differences in how the children treat their thinking processes (Iranian participants including others, German participants being isolated) and feelings of being in control (German participants relatively more often producing narratives in which they exercise some control), which may be related to the participants' cultural background.

For future studies it would be particularly interesting to see whether there are more similarities, maybe also in style, driven by certain topics, and where the differences lie. Another aspect for the future could be to examine the developmental trajectories of topics and stylistic differences and how they relate to the narrators' cultural backgrounds.

Note
1 Shahrenaz Mortazavi has sadly passed away on August 17th, 2012.

References
Abbasi-Shavazi, M. J., Morgan, S. P., Hossein-Chavoshi, M., & McDonald, P. (2009). Family change and continuity in Iran: Birth control use before first pregnancy. *Journal of Marriage and Family, 71*, 1309-1324.

Abels, M. (2008). Kulturvergleichende Grundlagen frühkindlicher Selbstregulationsprozesse. [Culture-comparative foundations of self-regulation processes in infancy.] In J. Borke & A. Eickhorst (eds.). *Systemische Entwicklungsberatung in der frühen Kindheit* (pp. 44-59). Stuttgart: UTB.

Behzadi, K. G. (1994). Interpersonal conflict and emotions in an Iranian cultural practice: Qahr and ashti. *Culture, Medicine and Psychiatry, 18*, 312-359.

Bertram, H., & Spieß, C. K. (2010). Elterliches Wohlbefinden, öffentliche Unterstützung und die Zukunft der Kinder – der Ravensburger Elternsurvey. Kurzfassung der ersten Ergebnisse. [Parental well-being, public support and the future of the children – the Ravensburg parent survey. A short report of the first results.] www.ravensburger.de/imperia/md/content/2010/4.pdf.

Bronfenbrenner, U. (1979). *The ecology of human development: Experiments by nature and design.* Cambridge, MA: Harvard University Press.

Bruner, J. (1986). *Actual minds, possible worlds.* Cambridge, MA: Harvard University Press.

Chavoshian, A.-R. (1992). *Transitional objects: A cross-cultural study.* Dissertation retrieved from http://proquest.umi.com.

Greenfield, P. M., Maynard, A. E., & Childs, C. P. (2003). Historical change, cultural learning, and cognitive representation in Zinacantec Maya children. *Cognitive Development, 18*, 455-487.

Han, J. J., Leichtman, M. D., & Wang, Q. (1998). Autobiographical memory in Korean, Chinese and American children. *Developmental Psychology, 34*, 701-713.

Heitmeyer, W., & Olk, T. (1995). The role of individualization theory in adolescence socialization. In G. Neubauer & H. Hurrelmann (Eds.), *Individualization in childhood and adolescence* (pp. 15-35). Berlin: de Gruyter.

Hofstede, G. (1980). *Culture's Consequences – International Differences in Work Related Values*. Newbury Park, CA: Sage.

Hojat, M., Shapurian, R., Nayerahmadi, H., Farzaneh, M., Foroughi, D., Parsi, M., & Azizi, M. (1999). Premarital sexual, child rearing and family attitudes of Iranian men and women in the United States and in Iran. *Journal of Psychology: Interdisciplinary and Applied, 133,* 19-31.

Kağıtçıbaşı, C. (2005). Autonomy and relatedness in cultural context: Implications for self and family. *Journal of Cross-Cultural Psychology, 36,* 403-422.

Keller, H. (2007). *Cultures of infancy*. Mahwah, NJ: Lawrence Erlbaum Associates.

Keller, H., Zach, U., & Abels, M. (2005). The German family: Families in Germany. In J. L. Roopnarine & U. P. Gielen (Eds.), *Families in global perspective* (pp. 242-258). Boston, MA: Pearson.

Kitayama, S., & Markus, H. R. (1994) *Emotion and Culture: Empirical Studies of Mutual Influence*. American Psychological Association.

Lehmann, P., & Wirtz, C. (2004). Haushaltszusammensetzung in der EU – Alleinerziehende. [Household composition in the European Union – single parents.] *Statistik kurz gefasst, 2004*(5).

Markus, H. R., & Kitayama, S. (1991). Culture and the self: Implications for cognition, emotion, and motivation. *Psychological Review, 98,* 224-253.

Matsumoto, D. (2006). Culture and nonverbal behavior. In V. L. Manusov & M. L. Patterson (Eds.). *The Sage Handbook of Nonverbal Communication* (pp. 219-236). Thousand Oaks, CA: Sage.

McAdams, D. P. (2003). Identity and the life story. In R. Fivush & C. A. Haden (Eds.), *Autobiographical Memory and the Construction of a Narrative Self: Developmental and Cultural Perspectives,* (pp. 187- 208). Mahwah, NJ: Lawrence Erlbaum Associates.

Moghadam, S., Knudson-Martin, C., & Mahoney, A. R. (2009). Gendered power in cultural contexts: Part III: Couple relationships in Iran. *Family Process, 48*(1), 41-53.

Mullen, M. K. (1994). Earliest recollections of childhood: a demographic analysis. *Cognition, 52*, 55 - 79.

Nelson, K. (1993). The psychological and social origins of autobiographical memory. *Psychological Science, 4*, 7-14.

Nelson, K., & Fivush, R. (2004). The emergence of autobiographical memory: A social cultural developmental theory. *Psychological Review, 111*, 486-511.

Novin, S., Bannerjee, R., Dadkhah, A., & Rieffe, C. (2009). Self-reported use of emotional display rules in the Netherlands and Iran: Evidence for sociocultural influence. *Social Development, 18*, 397-411.

Ochs, E., & Schieffelin, B. B. (1984). Language acquisition and socialization: three developmental stories and their implications. In R. Shweder and R. A. LeVine (Eds.), *Culture theory: essays on mind, self and emotion*, 276–320. New York: Cambridge University Press.

Oveisi, S., Ardabili, H. E., Majdzadeh, R., Mohammadkhani, P., Rad, J. A., & Loo, J. (2010). Mothers' attitudes to corporal punishment of children in Qazvin-Iran. *Journal of Family Violence, 25*, 159-164.

Reese, E., Haden, C. A., & Fivush, R. (1993). Mother-child conversations about the past: Relationships of style and memory over time. *Cognitive Development, 8*, 403-430.

Rohner, R. P. (1999). Acceptance and rejection. In D. Levinson, J. Ponzetti, & P. Jorgensen (Eds.), *Encyclopedia of human emotions* (Vol. 1, pp. 6-14). New York: Macmillan.

Wang, Q. (2001). Culture effects on adults' earliest childhood recollection and self-description: Implications for the relation between memory and self. *Journal of Personality and Social Psychology, 81*, 220-233.

Wang, Q., Leichtman, M. D., & Davies, K. I. (2000). Sharing memories and telling stories: American and Chinese mothers and their 3-year-olds. *Memory, 8*, 159-178.

Watkins, D., Mortazavi, S., & Trofimova, I. (2000). Independent and interdependent conceptions of self: an investigation of age, gender and culture differences in importance and satisfaction ratings.

Cross Cultural Research: The Journal of Comparative Social Science, 34, 113-134.

Whiting, J. W. M. (1981). Environmental constraints on infant care practices. In R. L. Munroe & B. B. Whiting (Eds.), *Handbook of cross-cultural human development* (pp. 155-179). New York: Garland.

Willander, J., & Larsson, M. (2006). Smell your way back to childhood: Autobiographical odor memory. *Psychonomic Bulletin & Review, 13,* 240-244.

Willander, J., & Larsson, M. (2007). Olfaction and emotion: The case of autobiographical memory. *Memory & Cognition, 35,* 1659-1663.

Ole Michael Spaten

Making one-self 3

This chapter argues that the development of children's self-concept and self-making narratives arises from the interwoven factors of culture, family and peers. New research is presented, employing a mixed methods design and hence integrating quantitative and qualitative findings. The research shows that Danish boys and girls have a different self-conception than their American peers, for instance with respect to physical appearance. The multifactorial approach furthermore indicates that children's self-concept becomes increasingly differentiated through time.

Background of the field

The research presented here arises from a longitudinal study (Spaten, 2007) initiated in 1998 and extended through 2009. The motivation for this work is that, as observed by Hattie and Marsh (1996, p. 438), *"Too little is known about how self-esteem develops and there are few longitudinal studies of self-concept change"*. This chapter draws upon this data in order to survey and understand the multifaceted task of the making of one-self in culture.

The study is rooted in the research tradition established by Susan Harter, whose early extraordinary efforts (Harter, 1983, 1985) to establish and integrate theoretical and empirical literature made her one of the most prominent and influential scientists (Hart, 2000) in the field of self-development. Harter has focused her own empirical research in two main areas: the development and integration of self-representations through childhood and adolescence, and developmental writings on self-evaluation, particularly self-esteem (Bariaud, 2006). Most of her research is nevertheless based on deductive research paying little attention on qualitative and broader social and cultural perspectives (Hart, 2000). Bronfenbrenner (1985, 2000) argues that broader perspectives in theory and methodology can overcome the scientific limitations of this approach. Hence, as well as building on Harter's seminal studies, this research expands the reach of prior work by adopting the scientific perspective referred to as the ecology of human development (Bronfenbrenner, 2001). This study employs the bio-ecological model developed and refined by Bronfenbrenner (1995, 2006), in conjunction with a mixed methods design (cf. Spaten, 2010; see figure 1). Bronfenbrenner's model is used as a framework to understand and explain the rather complex relationships between children's activities, their narratives about these activities, and their cultural self-making, employing both quantitative and qualitative methodologies.

Bronfenbrenner further argued that the advantages of a chronosystem model can be achieved within the outline of a longitudinal design. Tracing children's development from year to year might shed light on changes and the varying impact of peers and family on children's self-concept in post-modern culture (Beck, 1992; Hasse, 2008).

How children actually make and conceptualise themselves in culture is a vast and long-standing research question. The directions of this research field have shaped the design of this study. From the Greeks throughout history, questions of self-concept (such as "Who am I?") have been raised by philosophers, scientists, and psychologists. A wide range of articles and book-chapters has likewise been devoted entirely to the study of self-concept issues, albeit to a lesser

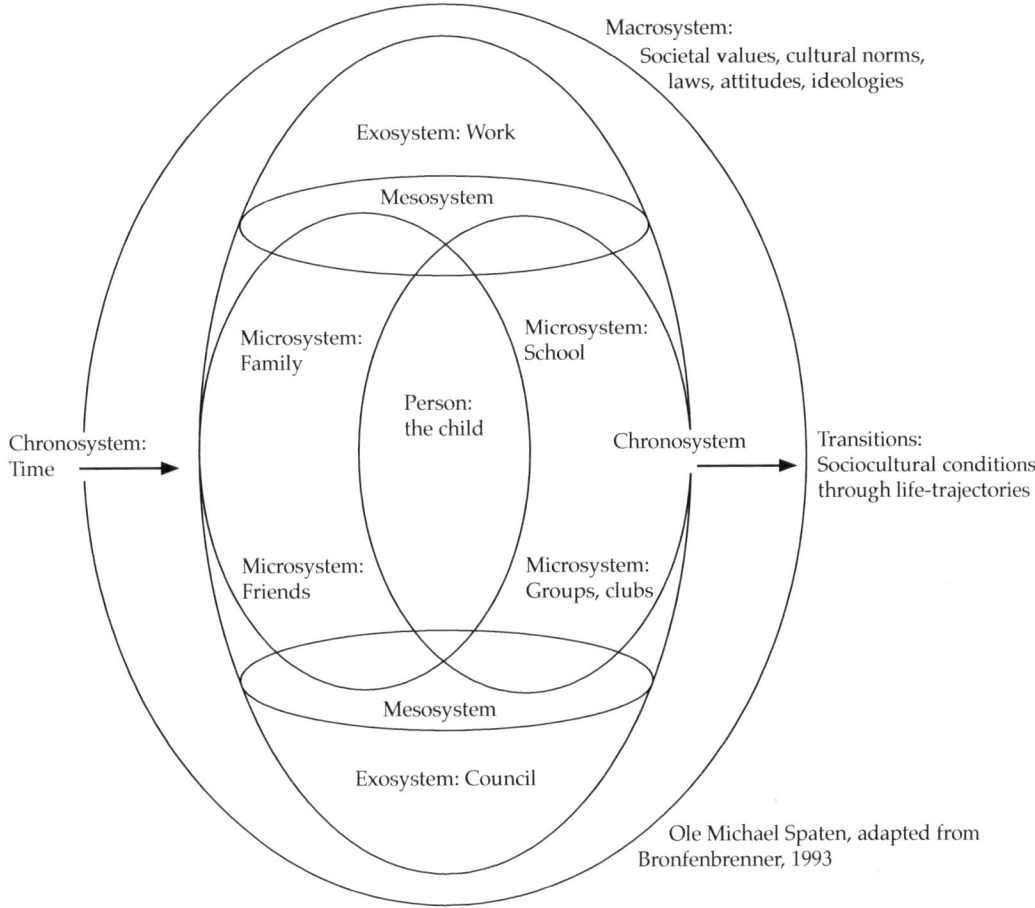

Figure 1. Bio-ecological model by Bronfenbrenner

degree self in culture. This field has been an increasingly important area of study for psychology since James (1890), Mead (1934) and Vygotsky (1934) – up to, more recently, Cole (1996), Bauman (2001), Hasse (2008) and Jensen de Lopez and Hansen (2011).

Precursory earlier scholars were talking about the 'I' and the 'Me' or personality: *"L. S. Vygotsky, to the limited extent he wrote about person-*

ality, was like Mead in his view of self as a complex emergent phenomenon, continually produced in and by persons in their interchanges with others and with the culturally transformed material world" (Holland & Lachicotte, 2007, p. 128).

But how can self-in-culture-in-mind be understood, along with how humans use cultural concepts to organise their social world and to construct themselves in meaningful ways (McAdams, 2001)? Internal dialogues and self-other dialogues have been proposed, going back to a view in which *"The self is developed through internalization of 'I'-'Me' relations"* (Valsiner & Van der Veer, 1988, p. 127). Both Vygotsky and Mead accentuated active internalisation and self-other dialogues and paid attention to the semiotics of behaviour. From a semiotic perspective, contextual variation co-determines person's opportunities for change and identity formation, where persons eventually develop an inner sense of public opinion and social assessment, which occurs as a reciprocal reaction to one's behaviour (Holland & Lachicotte, 2007).

What implications do the above research, and the decision to base this study upon the Bronfenbrenner developmental model, have for the research foci? First, according to Bronfenbrenner, proximal processes are central to children's self-making. These are everyday interactions between the developing person and symbols, objects and the most important persons in their everyday life. These parent-child or child-child interactions constitute the 'engines of development', driving and setting its course.

Proximal processes will not only be influenced by the personal characteristics of the persons participating in the processes, but also by contextual variation. Bronfenbrenner (1993) argued that to understand development the research design should contain a contrast between *"at least two macro systems most relevant to the developmental phenomenon under investigation"* (ibid., p. 39). Thus the research should either take a cross-cultural approach or compare groups distinguished by ethnicity, social class etc. In the current study, the sample consists of 174 children, half from low socio-economic status families and half from high socio-economic status families. Consequently the families' socio-economic status is employed as a contextual divider. Bronfenbrenner's theory can help us to explain and understand the connection between aspects of the context (e.g. culture or social class) or aspects of the individual (e.g. gender) and the research outcome (Tudge, Gray & Hogan, 1997). The main focus of this study is precisely upon the interrelatedness between person and context in the processes of human development. The intention of Bronfenbrenner's research is *"to create a picture of how multiple forces of development operates in a dynamic system"* (according to Wertsch, 2006, p. 151), and this study aims towards that end.

With this in mind, the rationale of this study was to shed light empirically on the emergent self and children's self-concept change (e.g. Hattie & Marsh, 1996), in order to understand more fully how children and adolescents undertake the making of one-self. It is assumed that children's self-concept and identity development should be understood within in its proper context. Hence, the study is driven by data from the "Copenhagen longitudinal research on Children's self-concept development" project collected from 1998-2009, (Spaten, 2001, 2007, 2012). The overall study follows the children from age 7 onwards; this chapter focuses on data gathered when the participants were 10, 14 and 17 years old. During the ten-year period of the overall study, the nature of interactions, significant others and contexts varies widely. Bronfenbrenner was intensely concerned about how the blueprint of society (macrosystem) and how relations (mesosystems) between different microsystems such as school, peer groups, and family actually work together as a buffer and as a mediator between cultural values and children's development through time (chronosystems), as depicted in figure 1 above. The present research aims to acknowledge the reciprocal connections between these different systems.

It is crucial to select carefully defined and delineated research questions for such a study. Theorists in the field of psychology have historically separated self and other, individual and culture, subject and object. These rather sharp distinctions make it difficult to understand connections and interactions (Schweder, 1990) and any departure from these dichotomies suggests that it is possible to study children's behaviour and self-construction without any regard to culture and sometimes with only one narrow theoretical focal lens. Understanding the reciprocal nature of self and culture, Markus & Kitayama (1991) introduced a now classical distinction between independent and interdependent self-construals. The main differences are in the role that is given to the 'other' while defining the self. In both construals others and the social context are important, *"but for the interdependent self, others are included within the boundaries of the self because relations with others in specific contexts are the defining features of the self"* (Markus & Kitayama, 1991, p. 245-246).

These assumptions and state-of-the-art research above have shaped the design and research question.

Method and design of this study

Research Question: This study aims to better explain and understand the interwoven nature of culture, family and peers, and the development of children's self-concept and narratives. It addresses the central question of how children actually make and conceptualise themselves in culture.

Overall Study: Data in this chapter was drawn from the "Copenhagen longitudinal research on Children's self-concept development" begun in 1998 and planned to continue until 2015. This research was undertaken in collaboration with eight school classes and high schools in Denmark. The overall study seeks to gain a deeper contextual understanding of children and adolescents' self-concept development. Some of the questions in this study concern how children's self-concept is related to gender, neighbourhood, culture and social class. The overall study (reported in Spaten, 2007) also investigated development of language and problem solving capacities and more clinical issues such as childhood depression.

Data gathering: Both interviews and questionnaires were used. The Mixed Methods (MM) research design, integrating by definition both quantitative and qualitative data collection and analysis, was employed on the basis that multiple methods can differentiate and support each other (Camic, Rhodes, & Yardley, 2003, p. 10; Rank, 1992, p. 297ff.; Creswell et al., 2007). More specifically, the study employs an MM design with a sequential, explanatory strategy, mainly because this type of MM maintains the specificity of quantitative and qualitative methodologies and the former was given priority.

Questionnaires: One of the instruments – every year – for data collection was the Self-Perception Profile for Children (SPPC) and later on the Self-Perception Profile for Adolescents (SPPA) (Harter, 1983, 1985). On a 36 item self-report scale the children answer questions concerning the following six sub-domains of self-perception: Scholastic Competence, Social Acceptance, Athletic Competence, Physical Appearance, Behavioral Conduct and Global Self-Worth. Each scale has six items formulated as bipolar statements like: "Some kids often forget what they learn" but "Other kids can remember things easily". The children has first to decide which kind of child he/she is like, and then to report whether the description is "sort of true" or "really true" of them. Each item is scored from 1-4, a high score reflecting a higher degree of perceived competence. Following Harter, ANOVA and Pearson's correlational analysis are used in the statistical analysis. Harter's self-report scales are used and validated around the world, and the Danish version has been shown to be psychologically sound (Spaten, submitted).

Interviews: Several series of interviews have also been conducted. The interviews were semi-structured, with open-ended questions about the children's lives and world. Example questions are "How would you describe yourself?", and "When that (x) happens, what do you do and who do you talk with?" The interviews were transcribed and analysed using interpretative phenomenological analysis (IPA) (Smith, 2010; Langdridge, 2007). A simple coding for transcription symbols was used: [(-) = pause, (-4) = pause 4 seconds, (…) voiced].

The focus of an IPA study is placed on what meaning the individual ascribes to a specific experience (Smith et al., 1999; Smith, 2003). In this study, results from IPA and quantitative findings are integrated. Quantitative findings and work on the five stages of IPA resulted in the emergence of three major themes: 1) Microsystems and self-making narratives, 2) Symbolic mediation and gender differences, and 3) Self-concept development as a journey.

The design of mixed methods and the model of the procedure for data collection throughout the longitudinal design are illustrated in figure 2.

CONCEPTUAL AND APPLIED APPROACHES

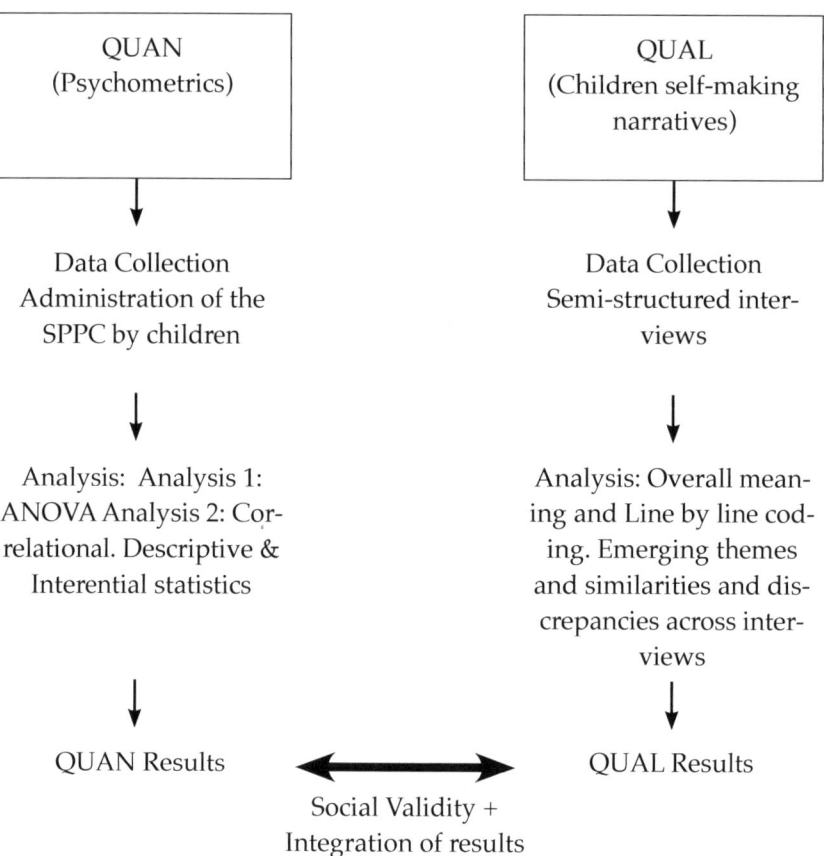

Figure 2. Mixed methods study design detailing study phases.

Participants: Since 1998, 174 children living in different parts of the Greater Copenhagen area have participated in the study. Half of the children in the study (N=88) live in the old blue-collar working-class areas in the inner city (inside the ramparts of the medieval city of Copenhagen). Today, mostly small apartments are found in this area, but during the last 20 years many of them has been renovated with indoor plumbing. The apartments are in blocks of 4-5 storeys high. Recall that the context divider for the sample is the parents' socioeconomic status. The other half of the children (N=86) live in the newer suburbs outside the inner city, in single family houses, typically in middle-class areas such as Vanlose and Soborg. The sample represents almost 10% of the children beginning in Copenhagen schools at the outset of the study.

Over the period of data gathering, the children completed different tests and self-rating scales; observations and four in-depth interviews were conducted. The children's ages during the four interview phases were 7-8, 10-11, 14-15 and 18-19 years old. From the pool of children representing different social class/SES and gender, four children were randomly chosen as a sample.

In this chapter the results from the SPPC/SPPA self-rating scales are reported, and data from interviews with four of the children are also used. Broad quotations with 'rich' context (Geertz, 1973) of the interviews with four children will be discussed below. Klaus (boy) and Nanna (girl) live in apartments in downtown Copenhagen while Andrea (girl) and Morten (boy) live in villas in the suburb approximately 3 km from downtown, thus different genders and backgrounds are represented in this subsample.

Exploring the data

As discussed above, this section explores the data from the four waves of interviews and adjoining questionnaires with reference to the following major themes.

1) Microsystems and self-making narratives,
2) Symbolic mediation and gender differences,
3) Self-concept development as a journey.

The first theme (Microsystems and self-making narratives) discusses primarily the reciprocal nature of microsystems like family and friends in relation to the children's and the adolescents' self-formation process. It also considers how they navigate different roles through time and place, and how this is related to self-making narratives. The second theme (Symbolic mediation and gender differences) deals with the use of clothing as an expression of one's identity and the gender differences found in this regard. Cultural differences regarding children's assessment of their physical appearances are also discussed. The last theme (Self Concept Development as a Journey) is centered upon children's increasing conceptual distinctiveness as they become older. These themes are discussed in more detail in the following subsections.

Microsystems and self-making narratives

Through their self-representation, the participants in this study display narratives in the making of one-self: how they become active agents in the process, and how they learn to compose their own *"novel patterns of personality, still within the frame that is provided for them by society"* (Valsiner & Van der Veer, 1988, p. 121). Within this theme, we see that microsystems such as peer-groups and parents become the frame of reference for self-making narratives in culture. Excerpts from interview transcripts display active internalisation, and self-other dialogues, where cultural values and norms affect the person and vice versa.

The 'role(s)' inhabited by the children and adolescents seem to be quite different between contexts (macrosystem) and through time (chronosystem). During childhood, active internalisation encompasses imitation which will ultimately form a productive imitation pattern, which means that the person becomes an active agent in the internalisation process (Vygotsky, 1978). When Morten was around ten years old he described how his early interest in aquariums was inspired by his father. Morten finds his own position during this mimetic enterprise adapting skills, frames, and roles. Imitations are refined in an active process of self-development. The theoretical conclusions above are grounded in the data, excerpts of which are given below.

"Who are you" was one of the open ended questions from the semi-structured interview guide. When Morten was interviewed in 2001 he hesitated for a while when the question was *"How have you become the person you are?"* The interview continued after the pause as follows:

> M: I don't know...
> I: What could have contributed to..., to the making of that person you are now?

> M: Because my dad he did many of the same things when he was a kid himself
> I: Okay, yes okay
> M: He was fishing a lot and he was making small aquariums himself, he showed me...
> I: Yes, yes okay, so that's some of the reasons, why you have become the person who you are
> M: I think so; it is a large part of it....

Father and son engaged in a common activity and it could be assumed as a mimetic enterprise in which cultured routes of fishing are shared and handed over from father to son.

Four years later Morten's main interest was still aquariums, but the interest had matured into fresh water aquariums which he explained were much more difficult to manage and required much more advanced knowledge. And notably here he told that he was not sure from where his interest in aquariums has emerged. Contrast the above transcript with the following, from the interview at 15 years.

> I: We were talking about your dad and mum, what... would you be Morten, if you had another mother and father?
> M2: It's hard to say... but it's funny because my parents have never had an aquarium, so from where these interests have grown, I don't know, but I don't think so. No, I wouldn't have been the same, because you experience... you are affected by your parents...
> I: Yes....

How can this and several other similar findings (see Spaten, 2007) be understood? Out of many possible alternatives, Morten is collecting his own images and is making the most meaningful self-narratives at his disposal. When Morten four years later no longer makes reference to his father, he is reviewing history from another position and performing a narrative reconstruction. As Sarbin (1986, p. 19) told us more than twenty years ago: *"human beings are authors of self-narratives and actors in self-narratives"*. These findings might suggest that Morten engaged in writing and rewriting their narratives to achieve a 'best fit' in relation to culture, family and peers alike. As Bruner (2002, p. 210) puts it, *"... there is no such thing as an intuitively obvious and essential self to know, one that just sits there to be portrayed in words. Rather, we constantly construct and reconstruct a self to meet the needs of the situation we encounter"*. At age 15, Morten may be in the midst of an agentic reconstruction of himself where uniqueness, separateness and independence in relation to his father have become of utmost importance. He acts like an entrepreneur while undertaking his rather special aquarium activities. He tells us that he is making good money, advising the ministry and continues to underline that "I am not like any other boys at my age".

While independence was an overall foundational theme for the majority of the boys they are of course not all alike in their interests: for instance, Klaus does not emphasise uniqueness so strongly and tells this story to himself and the audience: *"I: What kind of person are you? K: A boy, I love playing soccer ... I think it is fun!"* Briefly examining interview data, it becomes clear that active internalisation and self-other dialogues were embedded. Most of the boys engage in activities for which individual performance is a cornerstone, but in general the outlook is consistent with a view of human development as the *"internalization of external social experiences by individuals in the process of socialization"* (Valsiner & Van der Veer, 1988, p. 118). So the study recognises that narratives changes across microsystems, persons, and time. Klaus, speaking in 2009, describes the theme in the process of talking about relations between his self-understanding and various microsystems: school, teacher, family and peers.

> I: Ehhm, how do you think you've become the person you are today?
> K: My upbringing and my friends (yes). The school probably is... our teacher special (-4) my entire circle of friends and family (yes). (-4) Friends from different groups (...).
> I: What do you like about the different groups?

> K: (-) So... (-). I don't know... So, the fact is that you take different roles in different groups. (-) And in the group here, it is more the case that we joke with each other and make fun of everything. Uhhhm. The second is more serious. And we talk about things and stuff....

As the children grow into adolescence, changes in self-narratives seem to reflect a trajectory in the dominant self-concept, from being associated with family to being associated with peers (Spaten et al., 2010; Antalíková et al., 2011).

> I: Ehmm, if you are unsure about anything in everyday life (m), is there anyone you ask for advice?
> K: Yes, if I'm at home, I ask my parents (yes). And if I'm over here [at school], so I ask my friends (yes), or peers (yes).
> I: Is it dependent upon where you are, or does it depend upon what things you should ask about?
> K: Both and, therefore, ehmm, there are of course some things that I cannot ask my friends about [...] and I can ask my family about (m) and vice versa (yes)".

Klaus further adds to this by his description of how family in time loses its influence and friends become more central to him – an important developmental psychological perspective. *"I: What do you think has changed the most for you? K: Mostly the relationship to friends and girls and so. Like, what is okay? How much attention do you pay to things? The family is pushed more and more away and the friends enter the picture more and more"*. This pattern has also been found in other research (e.g. Antalíková et al., 2011) and is further supported by statistical analysis of children's and adolescents' self-report scales. The 174 participants were asked how long they spent every day on common activities such as talking or leisure time. The questions did not include time spent eating, drinking or watching television. For 10 year olds, the mean time spent with family was 53 minutes, against 48 minutes spent with peers. 16 year olds, by contrast, reported spending an average of 11 minutes with family and 82 minutes with peers. Although it is easy to grasp that time spent with parents is diminishing, there are still possibilities for an important co-creative meaning formation during the children's and adolescents' development.

The mesosystems – relations between microsystems, macrosystems and exosystems – are of importance in their reciprocal interaction. During analysis a hypothesis emerged that for several negotiations of self-making narratives, peer-group and parents might be embedded in what could be assumed as a working-class culture. This particularly arose during interviewing around associations between parenting and self-conception. Nanna (Low Socio-Economic Status (LSES)) was asked in the middle of the semi-structured interview:

> I: Mmm… you mentioned something about it before, but do you think that you would have become another person, if you have had other parents?
>
> N: Yes, my mother was a real troublemaker when she was a child, and my parents definitely wanted me to be different… so they have always brought me up to be very serious about doing schoolwork. I should work hard to be something… they warned me, if I wasn't serious I would not become anything, and I have never been that kind of girl who steals and knocks folk down and things like that… I think if I have had other parents I would have been brought up differently…
>
> I: Yeahh…
>
> N: …because if you see my peers in this class, I am the one best brought up, but OK, Rose, and Else and Annika are also well enough brought up… I guess we are the ones most eager to become something…".

This conversation above about 'becoming something' is typical of interviews with children from LSES families in this research but subtle or absent during the interviews with participants from HSES families. In the latter case, values and expectations about "being something" seem to be assumed, and not a matter of any controversy. Conversely, it is a point of departure and a rather constant formative debate in interviews with children and adolescents from LSES families.

The qualitative and quantitative findings in this section depict family relations as a central foundation for self-making narratives throughout childhood, although other microsystems such as school and club activities also play important roles. Peer groups are increasingly important in this respect as the children move into adolescence. At this stage, through the transition from the children's imitative encounters with their parents, a more independent and autonomous process of rewriting narratives emerges. The example with Morten and the aquarium could be understood as an active internalisation where a new self-narrative reconstruction appears as much more meaningful in relation to new specific circumstances. Furthermore, in this research, it seems important for children from low socio-economic status (LSES) family to achieve the goal of 'becoming something'.

Symbolic mediation and gender differences

The second major theme concerns symbolic mediation as a means of identity expression, and the gender variations found in this respect. Cultural and gender differences concerning physical appearance are discussed, as well as the limitations of the resulting conclusions.

The presence of symbolic messages mediated by clothes, brands etc. and the possibility of buying clothes was expressed throughout the study, primarily by girls. Gender, clothes, and culture seem to permeate conversations about everyday life interactions. Clothes, as a mediational device, emerged as a divider through analysis of the in-depth interviews.

Andrea (HSES) states very honestly (but with a somewhat low voice) that clothes from Føtex (a budget retailer) deliver clear status messages about who you are:

> I: Do you think you'll be accepted more easily according to the specific kind of clothes you wear?
> A2: Yes (low voiced)...

I: Yes?

A2: It is, eerhhhm... I mean ... personally clothes are the first thing I recognise, when I look at another person, because clothes, it shows something about who you are, and... even if you go around wearing clothes from... let's say Føtex, not because it's bad to do it, you can still be a nice person, but... I mean, you don't do it on purpose, or you do not think about it: Oh no, "now I judge this person", but you do it anyway".

Andrea directly expresses a sentiment that is often not said aloud. Girls are especially exposed to societal stereotypes about being slim and attractive and scholars have long argued that self-perception and judgemental values about others are influenced by culture and branded consumer goods (Jackson, 1992; Ussher, 1997). Moreover, it will not be possible for many LSES families or working-class parents to afford Andrea's preferences in brand and frequency for buying new pairs of trousers:

I: Can you say something about the clothes that you wear, or is it just sort of random?

A: Erhm, it is certainly not random. I have become... or I am... I'm a sucker for fashion. I'm a lot like... I can't wear a brand, that is not the right one, I feel a little like, I must have the right ones, and my parents are going... going crazy, because well... my pants... the real pants, the cheapest pair of jeans, I have, cost 190 US$, right, and it's like that... I need pants pretty often, because you grow, right, so it has to be the right ones, but otherwise my style of clothes... Right now it's very casual, I think, just, like... nice and easy, just whatever I feel like wearing.

I: What kind of brand is it at the moment?

A: Right now it is very much... Diesel and Levi's and Miss Sixty and Donna Karan, New York and Nørgaard and... (-3). What else do I wear, I don't know, things like that... (-10). Yeahh, I don't know... it is it I guess, very casual....

This could perhaps also be understood as an example of Andrea participating actively in ever shorter cycles of consumption (cf. Bauman, 1992), a feature of late modernity that is especially affordable for her and her peers with a certain economic background.

Self-making narratives about what kind of clothes the speakers wear can be treated as symbolic mediation between themselves, microsystems and the culture. The analyses revealed that these interviewees had a strong focus on clothes and seem to be very aware about the signals and (sometimes powerful) expressions that different kinds and styles of clothes are creating. Andrea says *"I must have the right [pants]... so it has to be the right ones, but otherwise my style of clothes... Right now it's very casual, I think, just, like... nice and easy, just whatever I feel like wearing"*. She seems to be negotiating with herself as to whether she is dominated by fashion or casual and relaxed. It is precisely this kind of self-other dialogue which forms a central part of the making of one's self, and through collaborations of narratives contributes to the children's identity. Various clothes function as semiotic mediational devices magnifying differences and group membership, which also sometimes applies for (middle class) boys in the study:

I: What kind of clothes do you wear?
M: (-) uhhh, I wear (-) fairly expensive clothes [...].
I: Why do you wear fairly expensive clothes?
M: I think it's because I'm very influenced by my friends. Uhhh and what they buy (-). Uhhm, I don't know.
I: Yes, do they sometimes wear the same clothes as you, your friends?
M: Oh, Yes.

Cole (1985, p. 155) argues that *"Children compare and classify through semiotic mediation in order to learn to manage their own emotions"*. They achieve a valuable sense of connection to peers when they choose what to wear; this also gives the adolescents a possibility of a direct and visible way to compare themselves with others. Through this mediational device they create a point of departure, a possible base for defining identity. Physical appearance is an important aspect of self-representation, e.g. Klaus says: *"I will not look like such a nerd"*. Through the quote, Klaus suggests that part of the way he creates his identity is through his choice of clothing, and this is based on comparing himself with others, and differentiating himself from the 'nerds'. The research found that physical appearance becomes more important with age, and it is apparent that there was a difference in cash spent by children from HSES compared to the children from LSES.

Beck (2000) argues that the concept of social class is no longer an issue for social research, but the findings of this study suggest that culture and social class continue to permeate words and actions, as also suggested by Reay (1998), both as stated explicitly during interviews and as more subtly observable. Other substantial gender differences were also found during qualitative analysis of these interviews. Girls were more concerned, worried and generally interested in clothes and peer relations (potentially linking up to the notion of interdependent selves). From the quantitative findings it was noted that girls rated themselves more critically in physical appearance than did the boys, although findings from North America have been more striking in this regard.

The results from this part of the study can be viewed in the context of prior research. Harter (1985), working in the USA, found that scores on her Self-Perception Profile for Children (SPPC) sub-scales tend to decrease with age for both boys and girls. Furthermore, Harter (1988) found systematic gender differences, with girls rating themselves lower than boys do in Bodily Competence, Global Self-Worth and especially Physical Appearance (see Figure 3). By contrast, in Chinese and African studies (Wu & Smith, 1997; Akande, 1999) only minor gender differences were observed.

A 5 x 2 mixed design ANOVA was conducted to investigate the effect of grade versus gender (grade: 3, 4, 5, 6, 7) x (gender: boy and girl) on scores on the self-perception sub-scale Physical Appearance. A significant effect by grade was found $F(4, 170)=4.85$, $p<.001$, but a relatively weak effect of gender (see Spaten, 2007 for full details).

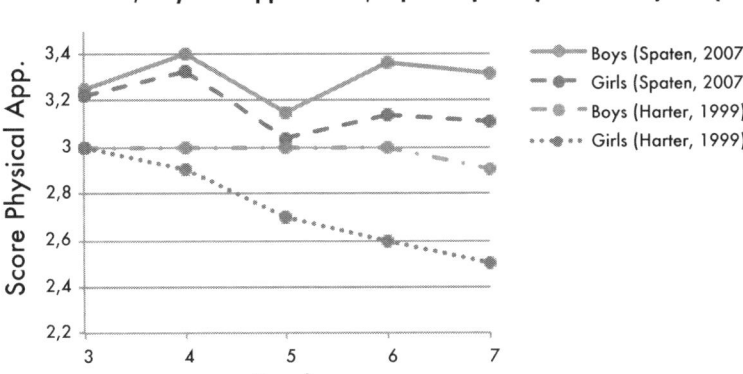

Figure 3. Self-Perception: Physical Appearance broken down by gender through time N=174

The most striking difference between the Danish study and Harter's results is the lack of a major difference between boys' and girls' perceptions of their physical appearance. Danish girls and boys rate themselves more similarly regarding physical appearance and the girls exhibit only a slight decline in their perceptions of their physical appearance. Do these results mirror social and cultural differences and expectations in relation to boys and girls? When comparing the findings from the USA and Denmark, the results must be understood in their historical, cultural context. The children and adolescents are constructed by the social practices of local communities, and although Harter (1985, 1999) refers to other findings (like Skaalvik et al., 1999 etc.), she does not attempt to argue that her results are universal.

These findings emphasise to us that it is crucial not to extrapolate across different cultures from studies of children's development. Applying this observation to gender, we note that the Danish culture to some extent values specific gender stereotypes, hence the study acknowledged gender differences in independent and interdependent self-orientation. Recall that children with an interdependent self-orientation are especially oriented to their social surroundings, while those with an independent self-orientation are more 'inner self' focused (Markus & Kitayama, 1991, 1998). It could be argued that Morten (middle-class boy) conceptualises himself through the model of independent self-construal, when he says:

> "and one can see how other friends are still tied to their parents, well, there I am both financially independent, and I live by myself (yes). In this way, then you cannot avoid ... But when / Sometimes I / among others have something to learn from their parents, well, I'll just sit and completely (yes) can decide for me, myself, I am on my own (yes)".

It appears that some of the observed class and gender differences might be captured by appeal to the notions of independent and interdependent self-orientation. Regarding symbolic mediation through clothing and brands, it is predominantly the girls who value this as essential to their self-perception. In close relation to these qualitative findings, it appears that the girls rated themselves somewhat more critically in relation to physical appearance than boys. However, given the relatively small differences along this dimension in the Danish sample, we take a cautious approach, aiming to draw local and contextualised conclusions rather than global and universal ones.

Self-concept development as a journey

This section of the chapter focuses on a more holistic approach to understanding children's and adolescents' self-concept development. We present, integrate and discuss the analysis of interviews and correlations between sub-scales on the Danish Self-Perception Profile for Children, in an attempt to elucidate the complex nature of the formative processes of the self-concept.

The correlations between the subscales (Scholastic Competence, Social Acceptance, Athletic Competence, Physical Appearance, Behavioral Conduct and Global Self-Worth) are presented in Table 1. For clarity, results from alternate years are used as a basis for this analysis. In summary, moderate to high correlations are documented at 3rd Grade, moderate correlations at 5th Grade and weak correlations at 7th Grade.

	Grade	Social Acceptance	Athletic Competence	Physical Appearance	Behavioural Conduct	Global Self-Worth
Scholastic Competence	3	.46	.55	.31	.44	.44
	5	.34	.28	.27	.44	.39
	7	.07	.11	.13	.34	.25
Social Acceptance	3		.50	.44	.43	.53
	5		.46	.42	.29	.66
	7		.32	.31	.09	.32
Athletic Competence	3			.31	.30	.36
	5			.35	.17	.31
	7			.44	.09	.24
Physical Appearance	3				.35	.72
	5				.26	.67
	7				.03	.62
Behavioural Conduct	3					.56
	5					.46
	7					.34

Table 1. Correlations between subscales in 3rd Grade, 5th Grade and 7th Grade. N=174

The correlations are generally of the same order of magnitude as in Harter's (1985) research, and the trend towards reduced correlations with age is replicated. Harter (1999) posited that as children grow older their self-conception becomes more and more independently conceived, specific and differentiated. When the children are younger they do more general, global evaluation, and when they are older they tend to evaluate themselves differently across different sub-scales. For instance, a typical early childhood self-concept statement might be "I am good at schoolwork, I really like going to school". In seventh grade, it would be more typical to state "I am good at mathematics, and have many friends, but I perform poorly and dislike doing sports" (additional details of this correlational analysis can be found in Spaten, 2007).

In the following discussion, these findings are related to qualitative interviews, and self-concept development is synthesised into a model of self-construction validated through the longitudinal study (Spaten, 2007).

Period	Self-concept	Examples
Childhood (2-6 years)	Observable, concrete characteristics.	I've got blue eyes. I am a boy.
	Specific interests, activities.	I play soccer.
Late childhood (7-11 years)	General interests.	I love animals..., I love playing soccer.
	Social comparison.	
	Interpersonal qualities.	I know more than anyone about aquariums.
		I look smarter than ..., I don't tease ....
Adolescence (12-19 years)	Concepts.	I am a lively person.
	Hidden, abstract psychological qualities.	I am like an angel, but can be like a devil sometimes...

Table 2. Self-concept development

On the basis of these findings, it seems plausible that self-concept development moves from more concrete descriptions in early childhood to proper concepts incorporating more abstract qualities towards adolescence, as illustrated in table 2. We can understand children's and adolescents' self-concept development as a journey through different self-construals, while the flexible notion of self provides a sense of continuity. For instance, at age 6, Klaus gave the self-description *"I play soccer"*, and at 11 he continues to use quite concrete descriptions, although he adds a subjective quality to the message: *"I love playing soccer"*. When Klaus talks about soccer at fifteen he describes himself as the bullfighter in the game, appealing to vivid imagery in the description of his strengths. The development of different self-concepts is not to be understood as a matter of passing stages, but as transitioning through periods during which certain conceptual approaches dominate.

It is proposed that such conceptual thinking becomes increasingly refined during late childhood. The children perform more social comparisons, and evaluate themselves more specifically and in a more domain-specific manner as they grow towards adolescence. For instance, Nanna at 11 states: *"I am smarter than most girls doing math, but I don't like athletics at all"*. The results obtained earlier point in the same direction: the older children construct much more multifaceted and abstract narratives about themselves. Klaus at 19 says: *"...when I meet people I do not know, I can be quite shy, but in reality I am very funny and extrovert, when I have had the opportunity to meet people"*. According to Mead (1925, p. 262) it is only possible to become self-conscious in a social context: *"... this development has taken place only in a social group, for selves exist only in relation to others' selves"*. During this self-reflexive interaction Klaus conducts self-other dialogues, meeting people at different times, and labels himself with psychological qualities like 'shy' and 'funny'. These self-constructions are linked to culture in historically specific time and to significant others. Nevertheless, some kind of sameness which is part of the core meaning of identity is also argued e.g. by Nanna:

> I: The things you are talking about characterising you – would they be the same or would they change?
> N: I think ... even when I will be in ninth grade I will still be a very lively person
> I: yes
> N: I don't think I will be alone. I have been very lively since kindergarten...
> I: yes
> N: ehh
> I: mmm [-] it will still characterise you...? [-3] So, you think the things will still be the same when you are seventeen...?
> N: yes, the three things will remain the same
> I: yes
> N: I am very lively, a good humoured person and I am an angel...
> I: mmm
> N: but I will add, I can be like a devil sometimes...

The above findings indicate the complex nature of self-making, during this period of self-concept development. Cohering with Harter (1999), the study indicates that the children's self-concept becomes more and more multifaceted: as the children become older, they differentiate to a greater extent between multiple dimensions of the self-concept according to context and situations.

In summary, the theme of 'Self-concept development as a journey' was approached by integrating interviews and correlational analysis. Self-concept development was documented as a constructive, formative journey through different self-construals, from a more global, concrete self-concept to a much more flexible, independent and specific conceived self-concept. These findings are suggestive for further research concerning how children actually make and conceptualise themselves in culture.

General discussion and conclusions

Recalling how Morten as a ten year old boy described how his early interest in aquariums was inspired by his father; it could be argued that Morten finds his own position by adapting skills, roles, and within a mimetic enterprise. Imitation is, in a subtle way, changing into an active process of self-formation. When Morten gets older he declares that his father has never had an aquarium! Morten furthermore expresses that he does not know where his interest stems from. This remarkable change in his narrative story illuminates that roles and self-concepts are relative and changeable: available narratives aim to substantiate the current edition of self-concept aligned to new circumstances and contexts. Bruner (1991) argues that the acceptance of narratives does not depend on its proper reference to reality: rather, a narrative has a relative meaning and has reference in relation to the life world of the individual. It is thus irrelevant for Morten's narrative understanding of his situation, whether he would have been the same person regardless of what parents he might have had. His self-making narratives are assumed to be acts of meaning, and to be meaningful in relation to the current situation and context in which he is embedded.

Vygotsky and Mead emphasised the role of active internalisation – the children's internal dialogues and self-other dialogues – but contextual variation co-determines the openings for these self-making narratives and identity formation. Through active participation in proximal processes, children develop an inner sense of social assessment, and this could be understood as a reciprocal reaction to one's behaviour (Holland & Lachicotte, 2007). Self-making narratives are thus to be understood as flexible according to situational and personal factors. Identity consists precisely of the narratives constructed by interactions between the person, his peers, his cultural context and the community at the current historical moment, at which there is also a constant and continued adaptation to new situations (McAdams, 2001).

Experimental findings have further suggested that boys and girls conceive themselves differently – the gender differences, emphasised through qualitative data, and could be seen as evidence that self-making narratives proceed along gendered routes (Bjerrum-Nielsen, 2003; Rudberg & Nielsen, 2011). Gender differences could partly be understood in terms of interdependent versus independent self-stories, on which scale Morten is – by and large – presenting an independent model of self (Markus & Kitayama, 1998), being rather self-focused and very assertive in his approach towards life, which is characteristically male. Although this general gender difference (independence versus interdependence) is found in classical research (ibid.), the findings from this study also illustrate its limitations. For instance, Klaus is oriented towards playing soccer (a social activity) and has a more modest approach. So it seems that a complex, multidimensional and situated perspective on self-construals is warranted (Santamaria et al., 2010). Both Nanna and Andrea talk extensively about the importance and range of peer and family relations, but also with variations associated with personal and situational factors (ibid.).

The empirical research suggests that the children construct their identity through social interaction (Mead, 1934), and that they reconstruct their narratives (Bruner, 2003; Sarbin, 1986) along the way with agentic engagement. The 'self' could therefore meaningfully be understood as a dynamic functional framework in its double nature: as a product of interaction and as a reflexive centre, a subject of activity in relation to the social-cultural context, controlling and interpreting behaviours and experiences.

Additionally the research acknowledges that self-making narratives frequently include family and peer relations and interactions as a major mediator between cultural values, norms and the developing person, although as time passes the findings suggest a trajectory of dominant self-making narratives, with associations shifting from family to peers (Antalíková et al., 2011). This seems to be in line with earlier research presented by Bronfenbrenner (2001) and Elder (1995).

The overarching research question of this study was to explore how children actually make and conceptualise themselves in culture. The question is embedded in the research field's agenda of gaining a contextual understanding of children's identity and self-concept development. It is approached here from the perspective of the ecology of human development, drawing particularly on the work of Bronfenbrenner and Harter.

The "Copenhagen longitudinal research on children's self-concept development" has gathered data from 174 children for more than ten years. Analysis of interviews and questionnaires revealed three major themes: 1) microsystems and self-making narratives, 2) symbolic mediation and gender differences and 3) self-concept development as a journey. The findings in these areas can briefly be recapitulated as follows.

1) Self-making narratives are embedded in culture and the microsystems the children's live by. The construction of self-making narratives is meaningful in relation to the current situation and context in which the children are embedded. It is apparent that self-making narratives change for all participants in this study, mediated by culture and chronosystem influences. They seem to be negotiating with themselves how they are influenced by parents, peers, fashion etc. These kinds of self-other dialogue form a central part of the making of one's self. As the children grow into adolescence, their changes in self-narratives reflect a trajectory of different microsystem involvement in general, from family- to peer-orientation.

2) Gender differences are found in this study. Symbolic messages mediated by clothes, brands etc. are particularly relevant to girls. Al-

though the girls rated themselves more critically on physical appearance than the boys did, the disparity is relatively small compared to that documented in the USA by Harter. Both studies can thus be argued to produce locally- and culturally-specific results. At a macro level, it appears Danish culture maintains and values (to some extent) specific gender differences in self-making narratives, independent and interdependent self-orientation. For instance, clothes function as a semiotic mediational device magnifying differences and group belonging. So gender, clothes, socio-economic background and culture seem to permeate everyday interactions.

3) The results indicate that children's self-concept development might be understood as a constructive, formative journey of active internalisation through different self-construals according to diverse microsystems. The self-concept is shown to change from a more global and concrete one in early childhood to a more flexible, independent and specific one towards adolescence. Going beyond the early concrete descriptions of self, other and the world, the children perform more social comparisons as they get older, and also evaluate themselves quite specifically, with the use of distinct concepts differentiated between sub-domains. In addition, the research acknowledges that self-making narratives regularly include family and peer relations and interactions as a major mediator between cultural values, norms and the developing person.

Apart from the findings concerning three 'master' themes, the results of this chapter touch upon numerous established research trends in the literature, such as interactional construction (Mead, 1934), reconstruction of children's self-concept (Sarbin, 1986), and self-making narratives (Bruner, 2003). The design mixed rich quotations (cf. Geertz, 1973) from the study with findings from several surveys (Harter, 1999; and replications). Part of the study used a phenomenological interpretation (Smith & Osborn, 2003) of the data and part of the study used descriptive and inferential statistics pointing to culturally specific self-concept development.

The findings also emphasise that culture and family can be used as dynamic frameworks for understanding specific identity constructions. As time goes by, family remains important in this respect, while friends become more and more important. The present study adopted a narrow focus on single dimensions, e.g. microsystems, but future research is recommended to include the relations between processes of person-context-behaviour. Finally, this research emphasises that the mesosystems and macrosystems of culture and context are important to our understanding of children's meaning-making and active identity-formation (Bruner, 2003; Cole, 1996; Valsiner, 2000), and of particular patterns in their development as independent and interdependent selves (Markus & Kitayama, 1998; Wang, 2004). The research both expands our understanding and illustrates some limitations of the classic notion of independent selves. Children and adolescents engage actively as selves influencing and being influenced by the culture they inhabit: *"In the end, while mind creates culture, culture creates mind"* (Bruner, 1996, p. 165). Role and identity shifts occur frequently during children's identity-formation processes, mainly as a result of movement between groups and socio-cultural settings (Bronfenbrenner, 2005).

This chapter has illustrated how some developmental changes in individual functioning could be understood as mirrored by changes in social functioning and vice versa. Building on the work of the aforementioned scholars in this research field, it seems plausible to conclude that the children and adolescents in this study create their identity embedded in the social and cultural settings they inhabit – their self-making is socially, culturally, historically and institutionally situated. The present chapter hopes to add to the extant literature in the research field by broadening the scope of qualitative studies and contributing to debates regarding some well-established findings.

Limitations of this research concern the self-concept, the interviews, the scales, and the framework. Among scholars in the research field of self-concept development, some define the self-concept similarly to Harter as mainly a result of self-other interactions while some acknowledge a more stable and continuous core-self. Different definitions and a historical lack of a common conceptual understanding among researchers in this field makes the boundaries blurred, demarcations unclear and dialogue challenging. Further research should try to empirically argue how the concept might best be understood.

As regards the interviews, caution should be exercised in attempting to generalise the findings of this study. I have discussed data drawn from interviews with four children and adolescents and subjected these to interpretational phenomenological analysis. A different sample or analytical strategy might have offered different insights.

As mixed methods approach is rare in this research field, and thus the present study suffers from a lack of access to established analytical precedents, particularly with respect to the quantitative analysis. Further consideration of this approach regarding significance, the influence of intervening variables and confounds, and effect sizes are on the agenda for future research.

The combination of Bronfenbrenner's bio-ecological framework, the sociocultural approach and Harter's self-development model could constitute a valuable foundation for theory development, as it includes a wide range of interactions and relations between different systems, levels, and time. The present study could have contributed more to understanding the developing person by addressing psychological changes around and within the individual. Focus could, for instance, be placed on siblings, as they might exert a long-standing influence on self-concept development alongside parents and peers (the foci of this study). Future research should examine more parts of the extended microsystem and the relations between life conditions, identity change and stability. An even more wide-ranging theory of the development of the self should embrace cognitive and sociocultural variables of proximal processes in which children and adolescents actively construct knowledge of themselves, participate in problem-solving or work together with others. In closing this chapter, it is appropriate to remark that much more cross-cultural and longitudinal research is needed to fully understand children's and adolescents' making of one-self in culture.

References

Akande, A. (1999). South African children's conception of self. *Early Child Development and Care, 152*, 55-76.

Antalíková, R., Hansen, T. G. B., Gulbrandsen, K. A., De La Mata, M., & Santamaría, A. (2011). Adolescents' meaningful memories reflect a trajectory of self-development from family over school to friends. *Nordic Psychology, 63,* 4-24.

Bariaud, F. (2006). Le self-perception profile for adolescents (S.P.P.A.) de S. Harter: Un questionnaire multidimensionnel d'évaluation de soi. [Self-perception profile for adolescents (S.P.P.A.) by S. Harter.] *Orientation Scolaire et Professionnelle, 35,* 282-295.

Bauman, Z. (1992). *Intimations of post modernity.* London: Routledge.

Bauman, Z. (2001). *Identity in the globalising world. Social Anthropology, 9,* 121-129.

Beck, U. (1992). *Risk society. Towards a new modernity.* London: Sage.

Beck, U. (2000). Zombie categories. In J. Rutherford (Ed.), *The Art of Life: On Living, Love and Death* (pp. 35-51). London: Lawrence and Wishart.

Bjerrum Nielsen, H. (2003). *One of the boys? Doing Gender in Scouting.* Geneva: World Organization of the Scout Movement.

Bronfenbrenner, U. (1977). Toward an experimental ecology of human development. *American Psychologist, 32,* 357-414.

Bronfenbrenner, U. (1979). *The ecology of human development.* Cambridge, MA: Harvard University Press.

Bronfenbrenner, U. (1986). Ecology of the family as a context for human development: Research perspectives. *Developmental Psychology, 22,* 723-742.

Bronfenbrenner, U. (1993). The ecology of cognitive development. In R. H. Wozniak & K. W. Fischer (Eds.), *Development in context: Acting and thinking in specific environments* (pp. 3-44). Hillsdale, NJ: Erlbaum.

Bronfenbrenner, U. (2000). [Personal communication]

Bronfenbrenner, U. (2005). *Making human beings human: Bioecological perspectives on human development.* Thousand Oaks, CA: Sage.

Bronfenbrenner, U., & Morris, P., A. (2006). The bioecological model of human development. In R. M. Lerner & W. Damon (Eds.), *Handbook of child psychology* (Vol. 1, pp. 793-826). Hoboken, NJ: John Wiley & Sons.

Bruner, J. (1991). The narrative construction of reality. *Critical Inquiry, 18,* 1-21.

Bruner, J. (1996). A narrative model of self constructionism. *Psyke og Logos, 17,* 154-170.

Bruner, J. (1996). *The Culture of Education.* Cambridge, MA: Harvard University Press.

Bruner, J. (2003). Self-making narratives. In R. Fivush & C. A. Haden (Eds.), *Autobiographical memory and the construction of a narrative self* (pp. 209-225). Mahwah, NJ: Lawrence Erlbaum.

Camic, P. M., Rhodes, J. E., & Yardley, L. (Eds.). (2003). *Qualitative Research in Psychology. Expanding Perspectives in Methodology and Design.* Washington, DC: APA.

Cole, M. (1985). The zone of proximal development: Where culture and cognition create each other. In J. Wertsch (Ed.), *Culture, communication, and cognition* (pp. 146-161). New York: Cambridge University Press.

Cole, M. (1996). *Cultural psychology: A once and future discipline.* Cambridge, MA: Harvard University Press.

Creswell, J. W., & Piano Clark, V. L. (2007). *Designing and conducting mixed methods research.* Thousand Oaks, CA: Sage.

Elder, G. H. (1962). Structural variations in the child rearing relationship. *Sociometry, 25,* 241-262.

Geertz, C. (1973). Thick description: Toward an interpretive theory of culture. In *The interpretation of cultures:* Selected essays (pp. 3-30). New York: Basic Books.

Hart, D. (2000). The maturing of research on the self. *PsycCRITIQUES, 45,* 645-648.

Harter, S. (1983). Developmental perspectives on the self-system. In P. H. Mussen & E. M. Hetherington (Eds.), *Handbook of child psychology: Socialization, personality and social development* (Vol. 4, pp. 275-386). New York: Wiley.

Harter, S. (1985). *The self-perception profile for children: Revision of the perceived competence scale for children. Manual.* Denver, CO: University of Denver.

Harter, S. (1985b). Competence as a dimension of self-evaluation: Towards a comprehensive model of self-worth. In R. Leahy (Ed.), *The development of the self* (pp. 55-122). New York: Academic Press.

Harter, S. (1988). *Manual for the Self-Perception Profile for Adolescents.* Denver, CO: University of Denver.

Harter, S. (1999). *The Construction of the Self. A Developmental Perspective.* New York: The Guildford Press.

Hasse, C. (2008). *Kulturpsykologi. Kulturens rolle [Cultural psychology: the role of culture].* Copenhagen: Frydenlund Akademisk.

Hattie, J. A., & Marsh, H. W. (1996). Future directions in self-concept research. In B. A. Bracken (Ed.), *Handbook of self-concept* (pp. 421-462). New York: Wiley.

Holland, D., & Lachicotte, W. (2007). Vygotsky, Mead, and the new sociocultural studies of identity. In H. Daniels, M. Cole & J. V. Wertsch (Eds.), *The Cambridge Companion to Vygotsky* (pp. 101-135). New York: Cambridge University Press.

Jackson, A. P. (1992). Implications of an Afrocentric worldview in reducing stress for African American women. *Journal of Counseling & Development, 71,* 184-190.

James, W. (1963 [1890]). *Principles of Psychology.* New York: Fawcett.

Jensen de López, K., & Hansen, T. G. B. (Eds.). (2011). *Development of Self in Culture* (Vol. 1). Aalborg: Aalborg University Press.

Langdridge, D. (2007). *Phenomenological psychology: Theory, research and methods.* London: Pearson Education.

Markus, H. R., & Wurf, E. (1987). The dynamic self-concept: A social psychological perspective. *Annual Review of Psychology, 38,* 299-337.

Markus, H., & Kitayama, S. (1991). Culture and the self: Implications for cognition, emotion, and motivation. *Psychological Review, 98,* 224–253.

Markus, H. R., & Kitayama, S. (1998). The cultural psychology of personality. *Journal of Cross-Cultural Psychology, 29,* 63-87.

McAdams, D. P. (2001). The psychology of life stories. *Review of General Psychology, 5,* 100-122.

Mead, G. H. (1972 [1934]). *Mind, self and society.* Chicago: University of Chicago Press.

Rank, M. R. (1992). The blending of qualitative and quantitative methods in understanding childbearing among welfare recipients. In J. F. Gilgun, K. Daly & G. Handel (Eds.), *Qualitative Methods in Family Research.* Newbury Park, CA: Sage Publications.

Reay, D. (1998). Rethinking social class: Qualitative perspectives on class and gender. *Sociology, 32,* 259-275.

Rogoff, B., Gauvain, M., & Ellis, S. (1984). Development viewed in its cultural context. In M. Barrister & M. Lamb (Eds.). *Developmental Psychology: An advanced textbook.* Hillsdale, NJ: Erlbaum.

Rudberg, M., & Nielsen, H. B. (2011). Gender in three generations: Narrative constructions and psychological identifications. In K. de López & T. G. B. Hansen (Eds.), *Development of self in culture. Self in culture in mind* (Vol. 1, pp. 169-195). Aalborg: Aalborg University Press.

Santamaría, A., de la Mata, M. L., Hansen, T. G. B., & Ruiz, L. (2010). Cultural self-construals of Mexican, Spanish, and Danish college students: Beyond independent and interdependent self. *Journal of Cross-Cultural Psychology, 41,* 471-477.

Sarbin, T. R. (1986). The narrative as a root metaphor for psychology. In T. R. Sarbin (Ed.), *Narrative Psychology: The storied nature of human conduct* (pp. 3-21). Westport, CT: Praeger Publishers/Greenwood Publishing Group.

Schaffer, H. R. (1996). *Social Development.* Oxford: Blackwell.

Shapka, J. D., & Keating, D. P. (2005). Structure and change in self-concept during adolescence. *Canadian Journal of Behavioural Science, 37,* 83-96.

Shevlin, M., Adamson, G., & Collins, K. (2003). The Self-Perception Profile for Children (SPPC): a multiple-indicator multiple-wave analysis using LISREL. *Personality and Individual Differences, 35,* 1993-2005.

Skaalvik, E. M., & Valas, H. (1999). Relations among achievement, self-concept and motivation in mathematics and language arts: A longitudinal study. *Journal of Experimental Education, 67*, 135-149.

Smith, J. A. (Ed.) (2003). *Qualitative Psychology: A practical guide to research methods.* Thousand Oaks, CA: Sage Publications.

Smith, J. A., Jarman, M., & Osborn, M. (1999). Doing interpretative phenomenological analysis. In M. Murray & K. Chamberlain (Eds.), *Qualitative Health Psychology: Theories and methods.* London: Sage.

Smith, J. A., & Osborn, M. (2003). Interpretative phenomenological analysis. In J. A. Smith (Ed.), *Qualitative psychology: A practical guide to research methods* (pp. 51-80). Thousand Oaks, CA: Sage publications.

Spaten, O. M. (2001). *Impact of neighborhood, ethnic, and gender differences on self-esteem among children in Copenhagen.* Invited paper presentation at ATEA Conference: STANDARDS, TESTS, QUALITY: Multiple Choice for the New Millennium, Weber State University, Salt Lake City, UT.

Spaten, O. M. (2007). *Børns identitet og selvopfattelsesudvikling – en længdesnitsundersøgelse med forskellige børnegrupper i Danmark [Childrens' Identity and Self-Concept Development – a Danish Longitudinal Study].* Aalborg: CHREB Press.

Spaten, O. M. (submitted). The Danish Self-Perception Profile for Children: Psychometric properties and validation. *Nordic Psychology,* (16 pages)

Spaten, O. M., Christiansen, N., Rahbek, J., Rahbek, L. E. B., Dahl-Jensen, S., & Ovesen, M. L. (2010). Unges selvopfattelse, køn og forældrestil [Adolescents' Self-Conception, Gender and Parental Support] *Psyke og Logos, 31,* 333-362.

Tudge, J. R. H., Gray, J., & Hogan, D. M. (1997). Ecological perspectives in human development: A comparison of Gibson and Bronfenbrenner. In J. Tudge, M. Shanahan & J. Valsiner (Eds.), *Comparisons in Human Development: Understanding time and context* (pp. 72-105). New York: Cambridge University Press.

Ussher, J. M. (1997). *Fantasies of Femininity: Reframing the Boundaries of Sex.* London: Penguin.

Valsiner, J. (2000). *Culture and Human Development.* London: Sage Publications.

Vygotsky, L. S. (1934 [1971]). *Tænkning og sprog [Thinking and Speech].* Kbh.: Hans Reitzels forlag.

Vygotsky, L. S. (1978). *Mind in Society.* Cambridge, MA: Harvard University Press.

Vygotsky, L. S. (1997 [1934]). *The collected works of L. S. Vygotsky* (Vol. 5). New York: Plenum Press.

Wang, Q. (2004). The emergence of cultural self-construct: Autobiographical memory and self-description in European-American and Chinese children. *Developmental Psychology, 40,* 3-15.

Wertsch, J. (2005). Essay review of 'Making human beings human: Bioecological perspectives on human development' by U. Bronfenbrenner. *British Journal of Developmental Psychology, 23,* 143-151.

Wu, Y.-J., & Smith, D. E. (1997). Self-esteem of Taiwanese children. *Child Study Journal, 27,* 1-19.

Pilar Sanjuán

Self-serving bias and psychological health
A cultural approach

Introduction

Authors from different theoretical perspectives have argued that there is a positive bias in human cognition, and now there is some evidence to support this proposal. This bias leads to reality being ignored, selectively interpreted or distorted by people seeking a positive image of themselves. This self-enhancement motive is defined as the tendency to see oneself in a more positive way (Baumeister, 1998; Taylor & Brown, 1988). Different phenomena can be viewed as forms of self-enhancement. Thus, people recall information about their successes better than their failures and they rate themselves as above average on positive personality traits and abilities and rate themselves more favourably than they rate their peers based on identical behavioural evidence (Sedikides, Horton & Gregg, 2007). One of these phenomena is labelled 'self-serving attributional bias' (SSAB), which is the tendency to explain situations that happen in life in a way that is more favourable to the person. Thus, SSAB would be displayed when people explain positive situations as arising from causes that are *internal* (coming from the individual), *stable* (continuing in the future), and *global* (applying to lots of different life areas), and negative situations as arising from causes that are *external* (coming from someone or something else), *unstable* (not likely to be repeated in the future), and *specific* to that particular situation (Mezulis, Abramson, Hyde & Hankin, 2004).

At present there is some controversy about the universal nature of the self-enhancement motive. Some researchers consider that the different forms of self-enhancement, including SSAB, are the expression of an universal human motive, with the goal of protection or enhancement of self-esteem (Campbell & Sedikides, 1999; Sedikides, Gaertner & Toguchi, 2003; Sedikides, Gaertner & Vevea, 2005, 2007), while others argue that the tendency to enhance or maintain a positive self-view is not a universal motive, and that its occurrence and extension depend on cultural aspects (Hamamura & Heine, 2008; Heine, Kitayama & Hamanura, 2007; Heine, Lehman, Markus & Kitayama, 1999; Kitayama, Takagi & Matsumoto, 1995; Markus & Kitayama, 1991).

Cultural psychologists emphasise the mutual constitution of culture and personality (Cross & Markus, 1999; Fiske, Kitayama, Markus & Nisbett, 1998; Kitayama & Markus, 1999). That is, they consider that cultural practices and meanings on the one hand, and psychological processes of the individuals in that culture on the other, are mutually constitutive. These psychologists believe that this mutual constitutive relationship is formed through development. The knowledge we have at the moment of birth is much less than we need in order to survive, and therefore humans need the social world, to which we are very receptive, in order to develop (Carpendale & Lewis, 2011). Human relationships are essential to survival, reproduction and well-being, so the human mind is developed through interaction with the social world (Fiske et al., 1998; Heine, 2001). In cultural psychology we consider that humans have to adapt to the culture into which they are born. We see culture as a set of practices and meanings which have been shaped by different and successive generations, who have not only created and maintained them but also have been changing them over time. People actively seek to behave adaptively, in accordance with the cultural context in which they exist. When people act according to the way that predominates in that context, they also secure their status as a legitimate member of the community and feel good as a result.

According to the concept of mutual constitution of culture and the person (Cross & Markus, 1999, Fiske et al., 1998; Kitayama & Markus, 1999), different cultures foster different constructions of the self. The self refers to how people see themselves, how they evaluate and how they explain their behaviour. How the self is construed in turn influences, and even determines, the individual experience, i.e. how to think, feel and act. Self construal includes self-relevant schemes which are used to evaluate, organise, and regulate experiences and actions. Therefore, different ways to construe the self lead to different constitutions of cognition, affect and motivation.

Through the interaction between the individual and the environment, the self is constructed. Thus, the self that emerges in individualistic cultures differs substantially from that which arises in collectivist ones. In this way, an independent self is characteristic of individualistic cultures, while an interdependent self is more common in collectivist societies (Church, 2000; Markus & Kitayama, 1991)

Individualistic people perceive themselves to have internal attributes which make them distinctive, unique and different from others. They also consider that these characteristics are stable and unchanging over time and across situations. Therefore, an important motivation of individualistic people will be to perceive the self as positively as possible, since on the one hand, they feel that they cannot change, and on the other, the culture values independent and competent people. The self-perceptions of individualistic people tend to be biased toward a positive view of self, and thus they view themselves in a manner consistent with their culture (Heine & Hamamura, 2007; Heine et al., 1999; Markus & Kitayama, 1991). By contrast, in collectivist cultures, people define themselves by roles and occupations, which they perceive to be changeable, and therefore their fundamental motivation is to improve their self, so as to maintain harmony with the meaningful persons in their lives and demonstrate adherence to norms, which are the best predictors of wellbeing (Church, 2000; Cross & Markus, 1999; Fiske et al., 2008; Markus & Kitayama, Markus & Nisbett, 1998; Markus & Kitayama, 1991; Kitayama & Markus, 1999; Heine, 2001; Heine et al., 1999; Heine & Hamamura, 2007; Triandis & Suh, 2002).

In this sense, and with respect to SSAB, research has shown that this bias is only found in societies where self-esteem is the best predictor of well-being – that is, in individualistic cultures like the United States, Canada or Western Europe (Heine, 2005; Heine & Hamamura, 2007; Mezulis, et al., 2004) – while this bias is reversed, absent or strongly attenuated in samples from Asian societies like Japan (Heine et al., 1999; Kitayama, et al., 1995; Mezulis et al., 2004), China (Anderson, 1999) or India (Pal, 2007).

Several studies, conducted with samples from Western cultures, have found that SSAB is inversely associated with psychological distress (Sweeney, Anderson & Bailey, 1986) and psychopathologies such as depression (Alloy, Just & Panzarella, 1997; Mezulis et al., 2004; Morris, 2007), anxiety (Fresco, Alloy & Reilly-Harrington, 2006; Mezulis et al., 2004) or schizophrenia (Fraguas et al., 2008; Moore et al., 2006; Sanjuán, Fraguas, Magallares & Merchán-Naranjo, 2009). As mentioned above, most studies of different forms of self-enhancement, including SSAB, have been conducted in White, Western participants, predominantly from the United States, but significantly less research has been conducted outside of North America. Most cross-cultural research has studied Asian samples, predominantly Japan or China, but individuals from Southern Europe (e.g. Greece, Italy or Spain) or Latin America have rarely been studied. However, knowledge about whether people self-enhance and whether this bias reaches a similar magnitude across cultures is important for any theory that aspires to understand why individuals are motivated to view themselves positively. Moreover, the controversy about the universality of the self-enhancement motive, and all its manifestations, can only be resolved when the different cultures which have not been studied so far are also considered.

Therefore, the main purpose of the current study was to examine the self-enhancement motive in a sample from Spain. Specifically, we studied SSAB by examining individuals' explanatory styles for positive and negative situations.

Traditionally, Spain has been considered a collectivist culture. However, over the past decades, there have been different cultural and economic changes in Spain, and the current characteristics of Spanish society do not match those of collectivist cultures (Triandis, 2000, 2001). Specifically, the economy is no longer based on agriculture, work distribution is not interdependent, and exposure to the mass media of other individualistic societies is very high. Additionally, Spanish society fundamentally values competent and successful people. These observations were supported by a recent study (Kuppens, Realo & Diener, 2008) which assessed the individualism-collectivism cultural dimension in different countries, since the score on this measure indicated that Spain is an individualistic culture.

According to the arguments above, we expected that a current sample of Spanish people would display SSAB. The first step was to explore SSAB as a function of gender and age. Since men and women differ in their level of self-esteem from adolescence (Robins & Trzesniewski, 2005), and since SSAB is motivated by a desire to enhance or maintain self-esteem, gender differences in SSAB would be expected. In this respect, it has been shown that females display a lower SSAB than males in adulthood (Mezulis et al., 2004).

Our second objective was to study the relationship between SSAB and well-being, measured by symptoms of depression and anxiety, and negative and positive affect. As in the studies mentioned above, we hence expected that in this Spanish sample SSAB would be directly related to positive affect, and inversely related to negative affect and depression and anxiety symptoms.

Method
Participants
777 adult individuals [235 males and 542 females, with mean age=35.2 years (Standard Deviation=9.7), and range from 17 to 55] participated in the study. Participants were recruited from different workplaces in various urban areas of Spain. They were eligible if they had no past or current history of psychological disorders. On average, the participants had completed 13 years of education. 70 (9.0%) had finished elementary school, 402 (51.8%) had finished high school, and 305 (39.2%) were holders of a university degree.

Measures and procedure

All the subjects (n=777) who agreed to participate in the study were asked to complete the *Attributional Style Questionnaire* (ASQ; Peterson et al., 1982; Spanish version: Sanjuán & Magallares, 2006) and the *Positive and Negative Schedule* (PANAS; Watson, Clark & Tellegen, 1988; Spanish version: Sandin et al., 1999). 220 of these participants also completed the *Beck Depression Inventory* (BDI; Beck, Rush, Shaw & Emery, 1979; Spanish version: Sanz & Vázquez, 1998) and the *State-Trait Anxiety Inventory* (STAI; Spielberger, Gorsuch & Lushene, 1970; Spanish version: Spielberger, Gorsuch & Lushene, 1982). Another subgroup of 219 of those participants also completed the *Symptom Checklist* (SCL-90-R; Derogatis 1975; Spanish version: González de Rivera et al., 1989).

The ASQ is a self-report instrument containing twelve hypothetical events, six negative and six positive. For each situation, subjects decide what they believe would be the major cause of the event and they indicate on three seven-point scales the extent to which they would attribute these events to internal, stable, and global causes. A rating of "1" on the each of these scales indicates respectively an attribution that is external (totally due to other people or circumstances), unstable (the cause will never again be present), and specific (the cause influences just this particular situation), while at the other extreme "7" reflects an attribution that is internal (totally due to the subject), stable (the cause will always be present), and global (the cause influences all situations in the subject's life).

Two composite scores, for positive and negative situations, were calculated, which respectively correspond to attributional style for positive (ASP) and negative situations (ASN). These scores were computed by averaging the items for positive and negative situations respectively.

The Spanish version of ASQ, like the original version (Peterson et al., 1982; Reivich, 1995; Reivich & Gillham, 2003; Sweeney et al., 1986), has proved to be both a valid and a reliable instrument. Studies have revealed good internal consistency, ranging from 0.73 to 0.82 for ASP (mean=0.78) and from 0.64 to 0.78 for ASN (mean=0.74) (Sanjuán & Magallares, 2006, 2007, 2008, 2009; Sanjuán, Pérez, Rueda & Ruiz, 2008;

Sanjuán et al., 2009). In addition, test-retest coefficients were 0.67 for ASP and 0.72 for ASN (Sanjuán & Magallares, 2006).

The concurrent validity of the Spanish version of ASQ has been supported since ASN has been directly associated with depressive symptoms and negative affect, and inversely associated with positive affect, while the opposite pattern of results was found when ASP was considered (Sanjuán & Magallares, 2007; Sanjuán et al., 2008). Predictive validity has also been tested in a longitudinal study which found that ASN could predict depressive symptoms seven weeks after the completion of the questionnaire (Sanjuán & Magallares, 2009). Likewise, the Spanish version of ASQ has also shown factorial validity, since it has been found that causal explanations reported in ASQ correspond to the three attributional dimensions proposed (Sanjuán & Magallares, 2008).

The alpha coefficients of the current sample for ASP and ASN were high, 0.78 and 0.76 respectively.

A self-serving attributional score was calculated by subtracting attributions for negative outcomes from attributions for positive outcomes. This score provides an index of the direction or valence (negative or positive) of bias as well as its magnitude. A positive score reflects a SSAB (stronger attributions for positive than for negative outcomes), a negative score reflects a self-derogating bias (weaker attributions for positive than for negative outcomes) and a score of zero reflects even-handedness.

The PANAS is a 20-item measure that evaluates 2 dimensions: positive affect (10 items) and negative affect (10 items). The response scale was a 5-point Likert-type. Respondents were asked to report how they usually felt. Higher scores on the two sets of itmes reflect greater reporting of positive and negative affect, respectively. In our study the alpha coefficient was 0.88 for the positive affect subscale and 0.9 for the negative affect subscale.

The BDI is a 21-item self-report instrument that broadly assesses the symptoms of depression including the affective, cognitive, behavioural, somatic, and motivational components. For each item, respondents chose the alternative which best matched how they felt over the past 2 weeks. Higher scores reflect greater reporting of depressive symptoms. In the present sample the alpha coefficient was 0.81.

The SCL-90-R is a 90-item self-report symptom inventory designed to reflect patterns of current psychological symptoms. Each item is rated on a 7-point scale, from 0 = *not at all* to 6 = *extremely*. The measure yields nine primary symptom dimensions: Somatization, Obsessive–Compulsive, Interpersonal Sensitivity, Depression, Anxiety, Hostility, Phobic Anxiety, Paranoid Ideation, and Psychoticism. In the present study, we only used the 13 items which measure depressive symptoms. Higher scores reflect greater report of depressive symptoms. The alpha coefficient for the present study was 0.91.

The STAI consists of two 20-item scales: the state and trait anxiety scales. The trait anxiety (STAI-T) scale was used in the current study and considers long-term manifestations of anxiety. Items are rated on a 4-point Likert scale (from "almost never" to "almost always"). Higher scores reflect greater report of anxiety symptoms. In our study the STAI produced an alpha coefficient of 0.83.

Results
Extent of SSAB as a function of age and gender

In order to assess possible differences on SSAB as a function of gender and age, we performed an analysis of variance with two between-subject factors: gender, with two levels [male vs. female], and age range, with four levels [(17-24)-(25-35)-(36-45)-(46-55)]. Partial etas squared (η^2_p) were also calculated as indices of effect size.

We divided the sample into four age ranges, since the adult period covers a wide range of ages. This would make it possible to determine whether any differences appear across the entire course of adulthood, or whether changes only occurred in specific age ranges.

The mean and standard deviation of SSAB by group according to gender and age can be seen in Table 1. All groups showed positive scores, demonstrating the presence of SSAB. Neither a main effect nor a significant interaction were found [gender: F=1.75, df=1,776, p>0.2, η^2_p=0.002; age range: F=0.78, df=3,774, p>0.5, η^2_p=0.003; gender X age

Table 1 Means (M) and Standard Deviations (SD) for Self-Serving Attributional Bias as a function of gender and age

	Male		Female		Total	
Age 18-24	n=26		n=100		n=126	
	M	SD	M	SD	M	SD
	0.98	1.17	1.05	0.84	1.03	0.91
Age 25-35	Male		Female		Total	
	n=95		n=172		n=267	
	M	SD	M	SD	M	SD
	1.01	0.83	1.04	0.84	1.03	0.83
Age 36-45	Male		Female		Total	
	n=74		n=167		n=241	
	M	SD	M	SD	M	SD
	1.08	0.83	1.16	0.93	1.13	0.90
Age 46-55	Male		Female		Total	
	n=40		n=103		n=143	
	M	SD	M	SD	M	SD
	1.03	0.83	1.26	0.80	1.19	0.89
TOTAL	Male		Female		Total	
	n=235		n=542		n=777	
	M	SD	M	SD	M	SD
	1.03	0.87	1.12	0.86	1.09	0.86

range: $F=0.34$, $df=3,774$, $p>0.7$ $\eta^2_p=0.001$], indicating that SSAB magnitude did not differ with age or gender.

In order to compare our results with those obtained in other samples, the SSAB effect size was also computed using d, which is defined as the mean internal, stable, and global attribution for positive situations minus the mean for negative situations, divided by the mean standard deviation, as in Mezulis et al. (2004). The d value, calculated for the total sample, since the intensity of SSAB did not differ by gender or age, was 1.63. This magnitude is similar to the mean effect sizes for SSAB found in samples of healthy individualistic people like North Americans (Mezulis et al., 2004).

Relationships between SSAB and well-being

Table 2 shows the means and standard deviations for all well-being measures, and correlations between these measures and SSAB.

Table 2 Means (M), and Standard Deviations (SD) on well-being variables, and Correlations (r) between well-being variables and Self-Serving Attributional Bias

	M	SD	r
Negative affect$_a$	18	6.3	-0.25**
Positive affect$_a$	33.19	6.18	0.3**
Depressive Symptoms-DSCL$_b$	19	13.88	-0.32**
Depressive Symptoms-BDI$_c$	5.45	5.71	-0.31**
Anxious symptoms-STAI$_c$	18.79	9.94	-0.25**

a= data based on n=777; b= data based on n=219; c= data based on n=220
BDI = Beck Depression Inventory; DSCL = Depressive Symptom Checklist; STAI= State-Trait Anxiety Inventory
** $p<0.001$

As can be seen, SSAB showed a direct relationship with positive affect, while it was inversely linked with negative affect. Similarly, this bias was negatively correlated with anxiety symptoms and the two measures of depressive symptoms. These results indicate that, the more bias displayed, the fewer anxiety and depressive symptoms as well as negative emotions are reported. In the same way, the more bias, the more positive emotions reported.

Discussion

The main goals of the present study were to analyse both the degree of SSAB and its relationships with well-being measures in a Spanish sample. The results have shown that Spanish people display SSAB, and that its degree is similar to those individuals from other individualistic cultures, as had been hypothesised.

According to previous findings, it was expected that gender differences would appear in all or some of the age ranges into which we divided the period of adulthood in this sample. However, there were no significant differences in the magnitude of SSAB as a function of gender within any of the analysed age groups. Since it has been shown that SSAB is a psychological strategy for protecting or enhancing one's self-esteem (Campbell & Sedikides, 1999), it could be suggested that the lack of difference between men and women in SSAB indicates that there were no differences in their levels of self-esteem. In the current study, since the participants' level of self-esteem was not assessed, we can only make assumptions about this. However, some known facts seem to support this idea. Specifically, we know that there were no differences between men and women in either negative affect or depressive symptoms (all $Fs<0.9$, $p>0.4$ and $\eta^2_p<0.0001$). Since poor self-esteem and depressive symptoms are directly related (Fontain & Jones, 1997; Roberts & Monroe, 1994, 1999), it could be assumed that, just as there were no differences in depressive symptoms, there were no differences in the level of self-esteem between men and women. In any case, it would be necessary to corroborate these findings with other Spanish samples, in which the participants' level of self-esteem was known.

Regarding the relationship between SSAB and well-being, these findings show that SSAB is inversely related to depression and anxiety symptoms, and negative affect, as has already been reported elsewhere (Alloy et al., 1997; Mezulis et al., 2004; Morris, 2007; Sweeney et al., 1986). On the other hand, they show that SSAB is directly related to positive affect. It could be said that SSAB serves to protect the individual against emotional distress. As other researchers have suggested, self-serving appraisals may be an automatic strategy that many people tend to use to maintain psychological homeostasis when coping with difficult and stressful situations.

Although well-being is achieved by the combined influence of different factors, the results obtained in this study reinforce those obtained in a previous review, which concluded that the traits that focus on making attributions in a healthy fashion may be among the most important personality traits which influence well-being (DeNeve & Cooper, 1998).

In fact, the studies mentioned above, which have associated SSAB and well-being, have exclusively focused on negative aspects of well-being, such as depressive symptoms. However, well-being is not the absence of mental illness or negative symptoms. In this study, a direct relation between SSAB and positive affect is shown, but it is necessary that future studies can confirm this direct relation within other cultures and across different populations. They also should include different positive measures of subjective and psychological well-being such as life satisfaction or effective psychological functioning. Within this line of research, in a recent study we found that SSAB was positively related to life satisfaction and a positive affect balance in two samples of Spanish and Danish women (Sanjuán & Jensen de López, 2013). Moreover, in another study with Spanish participants, which included both men and women, we also found positive associations between SSAB and different measures of effective psychological functioning (such as self-acceptance, autonomy, purpose in life, positive relations with others, etc.) (Sanjuán, Magallares & Gordillo, 2011).

Further research is needed to deepen the understanding of the relationship between SSAB and well-being. It could be suggested that the nature of this relationship depends on the magnitude of self-enhancement displayed. When self-enhancement biases are not too extreme they could be associated with adaptation. However, excessive self-enhancement biases could be associated with different experiences that produce long-term emotional distress. Thus, for example, since modesty is generally valued (although there are differences depending on the cultural context), people with an inflated self-view could be socially rejected. In the same way, people who excessively self-enhance are prone to feelings of invulnerability that can lead to the realisation of risk behaviours. Moreover, people with excessive self-enhancement could be prone to aggression when their feelings of self-worth are threatened.

It is also necessary for future studies to explore the different manifestations of self-enhancement bias in Spanish samples, using not only self-reports, which can be distorted, but also objective criteria. There is some evidence showing that when well-being is assessed by alternative measures to self-reports, its relationship with self-enhancement persists (Colvin & Griffo, 2008). However, it is necessary to corroborate these results.

Longitudinal studies that provide insights into how SSAB interacts with different stressful experiences are needed. This would be a way to know whether SSAB is a relevant factor in promoting psychological well-being and preventing emotional distress.

Finally, research in this area will have to pay attention to the study of the specific mechanisms through which culture influences the development of self and, in particular, of how people explain their behaviour.

References

Alloy, L. B., Just, N., & Panzarella, C. (1997). Attributional style, daily life events, and hopelessness depression: Subtype validation by prospective variability and specificity of symptoms. *Cognitive Therapy and Research, 21,* 321-344.

Anderson, C. A. (1999). Attributional style, depression, and loneliness: A cross-cultural comparison of American and Chinese students. *Personality and Social Psychology Bulletin, 25,* 482-499.

Baumeister, R. F. (1998). The self. In D. T. Gilbert, S. T. Fiske & G. Lindzey (Eds.), *The handbook of social psychology* (pp. 680-740). New York: McGraw-Hill.

Beck, A. T., Rush, A. J., Shaw, B. F., & Emery, G. (1979). *Cognitive therapy of depression.* New York: Guilford Press.

Campbell, W. K., & Sedikides, C. (1999). Self-threat magnifies the self-serving bias: A meta-analytic integration. *Review of General Psychology, 3,* 23-43.

Carpendale, J. I. M., & Lewis, C. (2011). Self constructed in culture. In K. Jensen de López & T. G. B. Hansen (Eds.), *Development of self in culture* (pp. 25-40). Aalborg: Aalborg University Press.

Church, A. T. (2000). Culture and personality: Toward an integrated cultural trait psychology. *Journal of Personality, 68*, 651-703.

Colvin, C. R., & Griffo, R. (2008). On the psychological costs of self-enhancement. In E. C. Chang (Ed.) *Self-criticism and self-enhancement: Theory, research, and clinical implications* (pp. 123-140). Washington DC: APA.

Cross, S. E., & Markus, H. R. (1999). The cultural constitution of personality. In L. A. Pervin & O. P. John (Eds.), *Handbook of personality: Theory and research* (pp. 378-396). New York: Guilford.

DeNeve, K. M., & Cooper, H. (1998). The happy personality: A meta-analysis of 137 personality traits and subjective well-being. *Psychological Bulletin, 124*, 197-229.

Derogatis, L. R. (1977). *Symptom Checklist (SCL-90-R), administration, scoring and procedures manual for the revised version.* Baltimore: Johns Hopkins University.

Fiske, A. P., Kitayama, S., Markus, H. R., & Nisbett, R. E. (1998). The cultural matrix of social psychology. In D. T. Gilbert, S. T. Fiske & G. Lindzey (Eds.), *The handbook of social psychology* (pp. 915-981). Boston: McGraw-Hill.

Fraguas, D., Mena, A., Franco, C., Martín-Blas, M. M., Nugent, K., & Rodriguez-Solano, J. J. (2008). Attributional style, symptomatology and awareness of illness in schizophrenia. *Psychiatry Research, 158*, 316-323.

Fontaine, K. R., & Jones, L. C. (1997). Self-esteem, optimism, and postpartum depression. *Journal of Clinical Psychology, 53*, 59-63.

Fresco, D. M., Alloy, L. B., & Reilly-Harrington, N. (2006). Association of attributional style for negative and positive events and the occurrence of life events with depression and anxiety. *Journal of Social and Clinical Psychology, 25*, 1140-1159.

González de Rivera, J. L., Derogatis, L. R., de las Cuevas, C., Gracia Marco, R., Rodríguez Pulido, F., Henry Benítez, M., & Monterrey, A. L. (1989). *The Spanish version of the SCL-90-R. Normative data in the general population.* Towson: Clinical Psychometric Research.

Hamamura, T., & Heine, S. J. (2008). The role of self-criticism in self-improvement and face maintenance among Japanese. In E. C. Chang (Ed.), *Self-criticism and self-enhancement: Theory, research, and clinical implications* (pp. 105-122). Washington: APA.

Heine, S. J. (2001). Self as cultural product: An examination of East Asian and North American selves. *Journal of Personality, 69*, 881-906.

Heine, S. J. (2005). Where is the evidence for pancultural self-enhancement? A reply to Sedikides, Gaertner, and Toguchi (2003). *Journal of Personality and Social Psychology, 89*, 531-538.

Heine, S. J., & Hamamura, T. (2007). In search of East Asian self-enhancement. *Personality and Social Psychology Review, 11*, 4-27.

Heine, S. J., Kitayama, S., & Hamamura, T. (2007). Which studies test whether self-enhancement is pancultural? Reply to Sedikides, Gaertner, and Vevea, 2007. *Asian Journal of Social Psychology, 10,* 198-200.

Heine, S. J., Lehman, D. R., Markus, H. R., & Kitayama, S. (1999). Is there a universal need for positive self-regard? *Psychological Review, 106,* 766-794.

Heine, S. J., Kitayama, S., Lehman, D. R., Takata, T., Ide, E., Leung, C., & Matsumoto, H. (2001). Divergent consequences of success and failure in Japan and North America: An investigation of self-improving motivations and malleable selves. *Journal of Personality and Social Psychology, 81,* 599-615.

Kitayama, S., & Markus, H. R. (1999). Yin and Yang of the Japanese self: The cultural psychology of personality coherence. In D. Cervone & Y. Shoda (Eds.), *The coherence of personality. Social cognitive bases of consistency, variability, and organization* (pp. 242-302). New York: Guilford Press.

Kitayama, S., Takagi, H., & Matsumoto, H. (1995). Causal attribution of success and failure: Cultural psychology of the Japanese self. *Japanese Psychological Review, 38,* 247-280.

Kuppens, P., Realo, A., & Diener, E. (2008). The role of positive and negative emotions in life satisfaction judgment across nations. *Journal of Personality and Social Psychology, 95,* 66-75.

Markus, H. R., & Kitayama, S. (1991). Culture and the self: Implications for cognition, emotion, and motivation. *Psychological Review, 98,* 224-253.

Mezulis, A. H., Abramson, L. Y., Hyde, J. S., & Hankin, B. L. (2004). Is there a universal positivity bias in attributions? A meta-analytic review of individual, developmental, and cultural differences in the self-serving attributional bias. *Psychological Bulletin, 130,* 711-747.

Moore, R., Blackwood, N., Corcoran, R., Rowse, G., Kinderman, P., Bentall, R., & Howard, R. (2006). Misunderstanding the intentions of others: an exploratory study of the cognitive etiology of persecutory delusions in very late-onset schizophrenia-like psychosis. *American Journal of Geriatric Psychiatry, 14,* 410-418.

Morris, S. (2007). Attributional biases in subclinical depression: A schema-based account. *Clinical Psychology and Psychotherapy, 14,* 32-47.

Pal, G. C. (2007). Is there a universal self-serving attribution bias? *Psychological Studies, 52,* 85-89.

Peterson, C. M., Semmel, A., von Baeyer, C., Abramson, L. Y., Metalsky, G. I., & Seligman, M. E. P. (1982). The Attributional Style Questionnaire. *Cognitive Therapy and Research, 6,* 287-300.

Reivich, K. (1995). The measurement of explanatory style. In G. M. Buchanan & M. E. P. Seligman (Eds.), *Explanatory style* (pp. 21-47). Hillsdale, NJ: Erlbaum.

Reivich, K., & Gillham, J. (2003). Learned optimism: The measurement of explanatory style. In S. Lopez & C. Snyder (Eds.), *Positive psychological assessment* (pp. 57-74). Washington: APA.

Roberts, J. E., & Monroe, S. M. (1994). A multidimensional model of self-esteem in depression. *Clinical Psychology Review, 14*, 161-181.

Roberts, J. E., & Monroe, S. M. (1999). Vulnerable self-esteem and social processes in depression: Toward an interpersonal model of self-esteem regulation. In T. Joiner & J. Coyne (Eds.), *The interactional nature of depression: Advances in interpersonal approaches* (pp. 149-187). Washington: APA.

Robins, R. W., & Trzesniewski, K. H. (2005). Self-esteem development across the lifespan. *Current Directions in Psychological Science, 14*, 158-162.

Sandin, B., Chorot, P., Lostao, L., Joiner, T. E., Santed, M. A., & Valiente, R. M. (1999). Escalas PANAS de afecto positivo y negativo: Validación factorial y convergencia transcultural [Positive and Negative Affect Scales (PANAS): Factorial validity and cross-cultural convergence]. *Psicothema, 11*, 37-51.

Sanjuán, P. (2007). Estilos explicativos, bienestar psicológico y salud [Explanatory styles, psychological well-being and health]. *Ansiedad y Estrés, 13*, 203-214.

Sanjuán, P., Fraguas, D., Magallares, A., & Merchán-Naranjo, J. (2009). Depressive symptomatology and attributional style in patients with schizophrenia. *Clinical Schizophrenia and Related Psychoses, 3*, 31-38.

Sanjuán, P., & Jensen de López, K. M. (2013). Relationships between self-serving attributional bias and subjective well-being among Danish and Spanish women. In H. H. Knoop & A. Delle Fave (Eds.), *Well-Being and Cultures: Perspectives from Positive Psychology* (pp. 183-194). Dordrecht: Springer.

Sanjuán, P., & Magallares, A. (2006). La relación entre optimismo disposicional y estilo atribucional y su poder predictive en un studio longitudinal [The relationship between dispositional optimism and attributional style and its predictive power in a longitudinal study]. *Revista de Psicología General y Aplicada, 59*, 71-89.

Sanjuán, P., & Magallares, A. (2007). Estilos explicativos y estrategias de afrontamiento [Explanatory styles and coping strategies]. *Clínica y Salud, 18*, 83-98.

Sanjuán, P., & Magallares, A. (2008). *Reliability and factorial validity of Attributional Style Questionnaire in a Spanish sample*. Paper presented at the III European Congress of Methodology of the European Association of Methodology. Oviedo, Spain.

Sanjuán, P., & Magallares, A. (2009). A longitudinal study of the negative explanatory style and attributions of uncontrollability as predictors of depressive symptoms. *Personality and Individual Differences, 46,* 714-718.

Sanjuán, P., Magallares, A., & Gordillo, R. (2011). Self-serving attributional bias and hedonic and eudaimonic aspects of well-being. In I. Brdar (Ed.), *The human pursuit of well-being: A cross cultural approach,* (pp. 15-26). London: Springer.

Sanjuán, P., Pérez García, A. M., Ruiz, M. A., & Rueda, B. (2008) Interactive effects of attributional styles for positive and negative events on psychological distress. *Personality and Individual Differences, 45,* 187-190.

Sanz, J., & Vázquez, C. (1998). Fiabilidad, validez y datos normativos del Inventario para la depresión de Beck [Reliability, validity, and normative data of Beck Depression Inventory]. *Psicothema, 10,* 303-318.

Sedikides, C., Gaertner, L., & Toguchi, Y. (2003). Pancultural self-enhancement. *Journal of Personality and Social Psychology, 84,* 60-79.

Sedikides, C., Gaertner, L., & Vevea, J. L. (2005). Pancultural self-enhancement reloaded: A meta-analytic reply to Heine (2005). *Journal of Personality and Social Psychology, 89,* 539-551.

Sedikides, C., Gaertner, L., & Vevea, J. L. (2007). Evaluating the evidence for pancultural self-enhancement. *Asian Journal of Social Psychology, 10,* 201-203.

Sedikides, C., Horton, R. S., & Gregg, A. P. (2007). The way's the limit: Curtailing self-enhancement with explanatory introspection. *Journal of Personality, 75,* 783-824.

Spielberger, C. D., Gorsuch, R. L., & Lushene, R. E. (1970). *STAI: Manual for the State-Trait Anxiety Inventory*. Palo Alto, CA: Consulting Psychologist Press.

Spielberger, C. D., Gorsuch, R. L., & Lushene, R. E. (1982). *State-Trait Anxiety Inventory*. Madrid: TEA.

Sweeney, P. D., Anderson, K., & Bailey, S. (1986). Attributional style in depression: A meta-analytic review. *Journal of Personality and Social Psychology, 50,* 974-991.

Taylor, S. E., & Brown, J. (1988). Illusions and well-being: A social psychological perspective on mental health. *Psychological Bulletin, 103,* 193-210.

Triandis, H. C. (2000). Culture and conflict. *International Journal of Psychology, 35,* 145-152.

Triandis, H. C. (2001). Individualism-Collectivism and personality. *Journal of Personality, 69,* 907-924.

Triandis, H. C., & Suh, E. M. (2002). Cultural influences on personality. *Annual Review of Psychology, 53,* 133-160.

Watson, D., Clark, L.A., & Tellegen, A. (1988). Development and validation of brief measures of positive and negative affect. The PANAS scales. *Journal of Personality and Social Psychology, 54,* 1063-1070.

Kristine Jensen de López

Weddings, funerals and other important activities
Playing the Zapotec way

5

Introduction

Traditional approaches to children's play regard pretend play as serious business. Following this view, the activity of play is often seen as the main source of cognitive or social development resulting in, to echo Vygotsky *"a pedantic intellectualization of play"* (Vygotsky, 1978, p. 92). In recent criticisms of this traditional Western and somewhat ethnocentric approach to understanding the function of play, several limitations have been pointed out within the so-called "outcome approach" to development (Winterhoff, 1997). One main preoccupation has been that outcome approaches tend to posit that certain supposedly well-defined aspects of play, e.g. socio-dramatic or symbolic play, are healthy for children, and consequentially that their presence in early development has a profound positive effect on a child's desired development. However, what follows from this positively defined purpose of play is that the absence, or the low frequency, of these specific and supposedly well-defined play activities is consequently expected to have either no effect or, in the worst case, a negative effect on the child's development.

The consequence of the numerous studies that have focused on such outcome ideology is that one unavoidably ends up with a rigid definition of play as an outcome rather than a process, within which the notion of ecological validity comes into question. A second limitation is that very few studies have focused on variability across cultures or even among individual children.

Historically, developmental views on the function of playfulness in childhood have been influenced either by Freud's psychoanalytic approach with its focus on instincts or by the Piagetian approach, which sees play as a mere cognitive challenge. In Freud's psychoanalytic interpretation of play, he formulated play as a displacement of instinctual activity and argued that one can work through internal tensions and conflicts by playing them out in a therapeutic situation (Bruner, Jolly & Sylva, 1985). Piaget, on the other hand, enlaced his approach within the epistemological premises of realism and rationalism. In his view, play is simply the cognitive assimilation of the child's experience with its preconstructed personal schema of the world, and serves as a preparation for later accommodation (ibid., p. 20). To quote Piaget's own words on the role of symbolic play:

> "…..the child's make believe play, as opposed to simple motor games, is based on familiar schemas ritualized in prior games, but instead of using them in presence of the objects, the child assimilates to them new objectives unrelated to them, and used with *no other purpose than that of allowing the subject to mime or evoke the schemas in question*"
> (Piaget, 1951/1985, p. 558-559, italics by the author).

Thus for Piaget symbolic play had as its sole aim the satisfaction of the ego, i.e. the individual truth as opposed to the collective and interpersonal truth. More recent theories of play are critical of Piaget's theorising and point out several limitations in only paying attention to lower-level and content-influenced categories of play, with limited possibilities of fostering new directions in thought (Sutton-Smith, 1983). These limits are clearly mirrored in the methodology behind Piaget's theory: first, in that he only studies play as an infantile state, and second, in that he restricts his observations to the actions of the young child engaging in purely solitary play. More recently, a similar critique has been raised by social-cultural psychologists, such as Gaskins (1999), who points out that the dichotomy between fantasy as expressed in the play of children contra rationality as expressed in the work of adults has become a methodological straitjacket for the measures applied in most cross-cultural studies of children's play, where the main *a priori* categories of comparison are symbolic play, socio-dramatic play, and complexity of peer interaction (measured by the number of participants involved). Gaskins suggests that if we take an alternative view of children's play as situated within a type of engagement in the real world, where the distinction between play and work is seen as less clear-cut than in the traditional view, play can be seen as a socially and culturally motivated practice in which the child actively engages. This view takes into account sociological construction, where play is seen as contributing to cognition as this emerges within a social interpersonal context. It is consistent with Vygotsky's social/historical view, a theory which, in opposition to that of Piaget, views play as a unique form of activity with several purposes. In Vygotsky's social/historical approach play is said to reflect the needs of the child, which cannot be realised immediately, e.g. the desire to engage in activities performed by the significant others surrounding the child. And often the interval between the child's motive and its realisation is extremely short (Vygotsky, 1933/1985, p. 538). Also within Vygotsky's view, play *is* essentially wish fulfilment. However, these wishes are not isolated individual wishes, but more generalised desires (Werstch, 1985, p. 5).

To illustrate the notion of the child using play to fulfil a desire, let us suppose a child comes to imagine himself riding a horse, but given the circumstances is not able to do so. In this situation the child's engagement in the sensorimotor activity of running across the yard at a horse-like galloping pace might allow him to fulfil this desire imaginably. Rather than contributing to the child's cognitive abilities, this imaginary and illusory world of symbolic play might serve the child by resolving the tension of the unrealisable desires (Vygotsky, 1978, p. 93). Vygotsky further stressed the unique importance of play at reality and its contribution to the child's metacognitive development and that in fact reality and play often coincide. Play at reality hence can be seen as just as serious as symbolic play. In the classic example put forward by Sully (1904 in Russian, but cited in Vygotsky, 1978, pp. 94-95), two sisters are described as playing the game of being sisters. Now, what function might playing what one already IS in real life have for the child? Should we categorise such play activity as primitive or less mature than, for example, acts of symbolic play? Can this type of play have any meaning at all? In this case of playing at being sisters the child is trying to be what she thinks a sister should be like. So she steps out from the real world and into the play world where she explicitly is able to reflect on the general cultural rule of what it means or feels like to be a sister, as opposed to, for example, just a friend or a stranger, and with this she is forced to experience and acquire the rules underlying kinship. One of the most important facts concerning playing at reality is that it offers the possibility of a situated and embodied internalisation and externalisation of the conventional rules and canonical modes within a specific culture. This process of inculturation may in fact be seen as complementary to the process Vygotsky described in which *"what passes unnoticed by the child in real life becomes a rule of behavior in play"* (Vygotsky, 1978, p. 95).

However the rules of behaviour or the 'sameness' of everything, to use Vygotsky's term, constitute part of the child's conceptualisation and simultaneously include notions of cultural conceptualisations at a more concrete level than is the case in the learning of kinship relationships illustrated by the 'sisters playing sisters', activity. In the same way that kinship relationships and epistemological notions are at first unnoticed by the child and only become metacognitively available through play at reality, canonical and cultural values can also become internalised by the child during play at reality. Play activity and play at reality hence becomes the zone of proximal development (Vygotsky, 1978), in which the child's basic level of action and morality will be formed. To quote Vygotsky, *"As in the focus of a magnifying glass, play contains all developmental tendencies in a condensed form and is itself a major source of development"* (ibid, p. 102).

Vygotsky also stressed that children are able to project themselves into the adult activities of their culture and rehearse their future roles and values during play activities. In this way play can be seen as being in advance of development, and in this manner children begin to acquire the motivation, skills, and attitudes necessary for their social participation (Vygotsky, 1978, p. 129). This notion can be extended to include the notion of play as the zone of proximal development *in relation to the child's culturally specific awareness* and its development of self construal. Despite setting the stage for what later became the socio-cultural theory, Vygotsky did not however fully account for the role of cultural differences in children's play activities, and how these may shape the developmental trajectory of the child. I address this issue in the following section.

Culture as an unexamined independent variable

An additional limitation of traditional approaches to play activity is seen in the methodological error within Western approaches where culture is treated as an "unexamined independent variable" or as "packaged variables" whereas in fact these need to be "unwrapped" in order to be scientifically meaningful (Farver, 1999). This calls for the study of cultural effects to make a closer examination of the contexts, processes and experiences that may be associated with different types of play activity. A proposal as to how to "unpackage" culture in development has been set out by Farver in the so-called activity setting approach which has the purpose of identifying how broad cultural factors become translated into specific contexts that influence children's daily activities and the relevant skills and behaviours they learn (ibid.).

What follows from the lack of focus on culture as an important variable is the assumption that social class differences are directly manifested in socio-dramatic play: for instance, that economically disadvantaged children compared to middle-income children engage in less frequent and lower-quality socio-dramatic play (McLoyd, 1982). This assumption has been challenged by a group of contemporary scholars (Farver, Kim & Lee, 1995, Farver & Shin, 1997; Göncü, Tuermer, Jain, & Johnson, 1999, Gaskins, 1993; Mcloyd, 1982) who argue that this interpretation is misleading and may in part be influenced by methodological procedures, confounding variables (e.g. the setting) and situated variables.

Cross-cultural studies of children's play activities

As a consequence of the abovementioned problems, recent cross-cultural studies now take into account some of the methodological criticism posited by McLoyd, and comparative studies of children's social interaction and play behaviours have documented considerable variation in children's social play across different cultures. For example, Farver and colleagues' comparison of Korean- and Anglo-American preschoolers both living in the southwest United States (Farver et al., 1995, Farver & Shin, 1997) identified differences between the two groups of children's social behaviours, pretend play activities, social competence, and cognitive functioning. They explain the differences as partially due to the differences in the children's environmental and socialisation practices (Farver et al., 1995, Farver & Shin, 1997). Also, when comparing European- and Korean-American preschoolers' social pretend play, Farver and Lee (in Farver, 1999) found that during free play European-American children engaged in more social pretend play than Korean-American children did. Competing with these results, however, a later study showed that when the two groups of children were compared in an experimental toy-play condition, where the children were provided with an equal quantity of toys, time and space in which to play, the difference in the frequency of their social pretend play disappeared. This suggests that the play environment and the actual activity setting are important factors influencing children's play activity.

Adding to the list of confounding variables is the notion of extended households, which challenges the prevailing notion that mothers are the "better" facilitators of children's early pretend play (as posed for example by Bornstein & Tamis-LeMonda, 1995) and the assumption that siblings provide "less than optimal educational environments" for young children's social and cognitive development. Farver points out that although scaffolding or the social support provided by a more skilled partner, the so-called *what* aspect, may be essential to the development of children's pretend play, the question of *who* does the scaffolding, as well as *how*, *when*, and *why* it gets done, may be culture-specific and highly dependent on the environmental context (Farver, 1999). In summary, contemporary researchers have shown that the factors influencing preschoolers' play are time and space to play, access to objects, adult behaviour and attitudes toward play, and the availability of play partners (Gaskins, 1999, Göncü et al., 1999; Haight, 1999).

In a plea to ground generalisations about development in adequate data, Gaskins (1999) introduced a dual-faceted approach to studying children's engagement in their environment. Her approach is on the one hand inspired by Russian scholars (Vygotsky's sociocultural theory, Leont'ev's (1978) activity theory) and more recent anthropological theorists (Lave, 1988; Rogoff, Mistry, Göncü, & Mosier, 1991), who focus on the individual as situated in a social practice, and on the other hand by the broader view launched in Bronfenbrenner's (1979) ecological model of several contextual layers that influence the development process of the child. Through detailed case study observations of Mayan Meso-American children's spontaneous engagement in their world, Gaskins proposed three basic cultural principles to explain what motivated the specific engagements of the children, which made it possible to interpret the Mayan children's behaviour in a culturally meaningful way. The three principles are as follows (Gaskins, 1999, pp. 32-38):

> *Primacy of adult work*...."life in the compound as experienced by children is structured around adult work activities..... it is not structured around the children's interest or desires, nor around adult goals for children".
>
> *Importance of parental beliefs*...."cultural understandings about the nature of the world and about the nature of children significantly shape children's experiences".
>
> *Independence of child motivation*...."general respect for individuals, many of a young child's activities are determined by the child's own interests and motivations, as well as by her own understandings of cultural expectations and restraints. Little self-directed behavior is socially manipulated.... and the child has little expectation that she will have much influence on the activities of others".

The main promise of Gaskins' alternative view for both theoretical and methodological advances can be seen in the way it converts the mainstream view of development and socialisation as a static phenomena into a dynamic dual research agenda, in which the unit is the child-in-activity-in-context integrated with the study of the cultural belief systems and institutions as these appear in the everyday contexts of children's behaviour. Despite the crucial advance offered by Gaskins' proposed methodology, we should be careful not to throw out the child with the bathwater. In order to avoid this, I argue it is additionally necessary to maintain focus on the psychological or functional aspects that a given play activity may have for a particular child, and hence to focus on the developmental processes changing with the child's play activity within the particular culture. With this in mind, the primary purpose of this chapter is to illustrate the role of culture in children's engagement in spontaneous play activities and its relevance for self construal within the framework of Gaskins. A second purpose is to compare the results from Gaskins' case study with case studies carried out in a different Meso-American community. This will make it possible to compare play across Mayan communities from a micro-perspective as opposed to that of mainstream cross-cultural psychology, which mainly compares Western culture with non-Western culture. The focuses of the present case studies are play at reality, symbolic play, socio-dramatic play and the role of the space and setting for play activities.

Methodology of the study

The approach adopted in this study of play activity by Zapotec children is inspired by a multi-level and ecological model (Bronfenbrenner, 1979) and aims to analyse micro-processes. This approach is merged with Gaskins' socio-cultural child-in-activity-in-context approach. The method consists of a set of case studies, which each serve the purpose of illustrating different types of spontaneous play activities emerging in the specific Mesoamerican community. The episodes were selected for their richness and illustrative capacity, and their descriptions vary in their level of detail. The data was collected during the period 1999-2001 as part of a different study. The analysis proceeds at two levels, the first of which considers the ethnographic context and includes parental values, behaviours and attitudes concerning children's play activity. The second level concerns the cultural time, ecological space and practices available for and influencing the children when carrying out play activities, and in particular the children involved in the specific play activity. The overall aim of this chapter is to illustrate a theoretical and methodological approach to the understanding of children's activities in their world, based on the ecological and socio-cultural approach, which places the notion of embodied and situated cultural practices (Sinha, 1999) in the foreground of what has traditionally been defined in developmental psychology as play activity. In integrating this approach with the theory of Göncü and Becker (1992), I wish to show the importance of play at reality as an activity motivated by the child's desire to work through real-world experiences, as well as a desire to become part of the particular culture in order to promote the child's construal of self. I also explain from a more functional view the child's purposes in engaging in the specific socio-dramatic play activities.

These aspects are then illuminated by ethnographic observations and examination of the spontaneous and constructed play activities of Zapotec children aged 2 to 6 years growing up in a small rural Mexican indigenous community. The observations of the children's play activities were drawn from a mixture of video recordings, which had the purpose of documenting the children's communicative development, and extensive fieldwork observations during prolonged stays in the village. All play activities consisted of the children's natural engagements in their home environments[1].

The ethnographic context of the Zapotec society: parental values, behaviours and attitudes

The particular Zapotec community under study is situated in the breaches of the southern Mexican state of Oaxaca. All the families are subsistence farmers, raising primarily corn and beans for their own family's consumption. Both men and women participate in the cultivation of the fields. All families raise livestock for farming and consumption. Within the last two decades, a common practice for the younger men has been to seek waged employment as illegal immigrants in restaurants in southern California. Women produce pottery, which is used as cookware and to a small extent sold at markets in Oaxaca City. Although men have had primary responsibility for working in the fields, due to the increased number of men working in the United States, women are often responsible for cultivating the fields either on their own, with reciprocal help from relatives in the village, or by buying labour from neighbouring villages.

The responsibility for taking care of the livestock is shared by both the men and the women, while children above the age of 5 are in charge of pasturing the animals in the afternoon. It is primarily the boys who carry out this work, while the girls stay in the compound assisting the mothers with the household chores. This involves tasks such as preparing corn for grinding and making tortillas for the family, an activity which takes place every other day and lasts for several hours, collecting firewood from the forest, and washing clothes by hand. After the main meal has been prepared and served at noontime, the women mostly engage in the making of pottery. Parallel to these activities, the women are responsible for care-taking and supervision of the younger children, an activity in which they are assisted by the older children. The typical multi-generation Zapotec household consists of grandparents, aunts/uncles, parents and children, while the size of the compound is determined by the number of married sons. Although each family in principle has its own household and sleeping house, most often the main activities of cooking, eating and childcare take place in a shared community with families alternating the cooking responsibilities or engaging in it as a shared activity. The spatial setting for this is most often determined by considerations of which space and material setting is most convenient, but often the latest daughter in-law is expected to be in charge. Due to the many complex activities constantly taking place within this type of compound, the preschool child is born into a constant flow of cultural practices and household routines being carried out before the child's very eyes (for a detailed description of an infant's typical engagement in a similar Mesoamerican agrarian household see Gaskins 1999).

Zapotec children's engagement in an agrarian society differs from that of Western middle-class children in at least two important ways. Firstly, the Western provision of children with scaled-down versions of adult articles, specially designed to constrain and guide the infant's activity, is very infrequent in the Zapotec culture. This means that children's activities from the very beginning are nested within the adult and "real" world and its objects, which also emphasises the notions of responsibility and seriousness involved in object manipulation and play. Children at the age of five years are left to use objects which are strictly forbidden to Western children, e.g. handling sharp knives, lighting fires with matches or stirring a large clay pot of boiling beans over an open fire. And secondly, there is a crucial difference at the dyadic and interactive level. Although mothers are in close proximity to their children while being engaged in their daily chores, little interaction is seen between them (compared to the traditional developmental literature accounts). However, contrary to Gaskins' (1999) ethnographic study suggesting Mayan adults' discouragement of their children from engaging in play, Zapotec adults do in fact encourage children to engage in play activity. In fact, the conventional utterances "gutdzit" (play) or "gudziting" (play with it) are among the most frequent words in early child-directed speech. However, the purpose of uttering these imperatives is not that of promoting educational benefits, as would be presumed in industrialised societies, but that of getting the children out of the way so that the adults can get on with their daily chores. In this sense, children's play activities are conceived as more parallel in value to the adult's chores, and as a kind of apprenticeship towards self-motivated and self-organised activity. Zapotec children are never heard expressing utterances such as "I'm bored" or "I don't know what to play at". Furthermore, on the infrequent occasions where mothers, aunts, adult cousins or siblings do interact with children in toy-play contexts, the adult's role is not that of facilitating the child's pretend play, as in the prevailing view of the role of Western mothers. These seldom occurring adult-child play activities are characterised by simple social play, parallel play and reciprocal/complementary play (e.g. throwing a ball for the child to fetch, or stacking items for the child to knock down), but never suggesting pretend play (see Farver et al. (1995) for definitions of these play categories). And consequently the performance part of the play activity, which frequently is expressed in Western cultures as the "mommy, look at me" phenomenon, is not part of Zapotec children's behaviours, which again reflects Zapotec mothers' ideology towards play activity. The emotional independence expected of children above three years also plays a role (see Jensen de López, 2003 and Jensen de López, 2006 for a detailed description of Zapotec child-care). Children's play activities also tend to be more spontaneously organised during the course of daily tasks.

Play at reality and the socio-cultural canonicity of objects

Few studies have addressed the role of cultural objects in children's play activities and its importance for children's identity with culture meanings. In the following I illustrate how cultural artifacts set the stage for Zapotec children's spontaneous play. When Zapotec young children engage in play at reality, their play often demonstrates specific cultural traditions and rituals, sometimes with twists of symbolic play. On one occasion, which took place during the prolonged Zapotec 'wedding session', two sisters repeatedly and frequently were observed acting out different gender specific themes from the Zapotec wedding ceremony. These included for example the act of dancing in small semi-circles, while tossing sweets and fruits to the wedding guests (in this play activity they pretended the researcher was a guest) from a colourful traditional gourd. Often these traditional examples of playing at reality are closely situated in "real space", as for example was observed when the same two sisters repeatedly ran into the street in order to perform a traditional dance, which they previously had observed being performed in the exact same space during the wedding procession. Another occasion illustrating the children's play at reality was a group of children engaging in a pretend burial ceremony. Shortly before this observation a funeral had taken place in the village, and it is customary in the Mesoamaerican culture that adults are always accompanied by their children when they attend large community activities, such as weddings and funerals. Similarly to the case of weddings, funerals include a procession through the village, and also involve several community rituals in the graveyard. One of the central and important themes of a Zapotec burial consists of cleansing one's hands above the grave. In the particular pretend play burial the six year-old boy, who was the oldest child and only male child in the compound, repeatedly carried out acts of cleansing the hands of the younger girls in the compound, including those of a two-year-old who clearly had no idea of the cultural purpose of this embodied activity. Despite this, she found the joint activity of splashing around with water entertaining and obediently followed the actions of the older children. Although younger children do not participate actively in this particular and clearly embodied act when they attend real burials, they apparently find it important to practice in play.

Another frequently observed activity commonly played out by girls from the age of two years consists of tying small objects onto their backs with a traditional shawl similar to the one that women use to carry babies, young children and firewood. From the age of two, girls also often engage in the act of forming pieces of flat round corn dough for baking tortillas. When carried out in parallel with an adult preparing the "real" large-scale tortillas, the children are often given their own piece of dough so they can form miniature tortillas on their own. When the act is initiated spontaneously, however, the children integrate whatever natural materials happen to be available around them, typically leaves from a banana palm. These activities could be understood as similar to the well-observed activities of Western children pushing play dolls' prams or making mud pies in a sandpit. And they certainly carry similar universal functions in this case. However, the content of these activities is different in meaningful and clearly culture dependent ways. These observations support the view posed by Göncü at al., (1999) and inspired by Leont'ev's (1978) activity theory, suggesting that play themes will vary from one community to another, and placing emphasis of play as a unit in life in which children try to be like adults in their community. This view also follows Bruner's plea to understand play as the means of transformation of cultural knowledge from one generation to another (Bruner, 1990).

The following observation of a two-year-old girl's early play at reality illustrates that the symbolic mediation of cultural practices in children's play also can be seen in the child's object manipulation, and this supports the hypothesis concerning material objects embodying intentional behaviour and cultural-cognitive schemas (Sinha &

Jensen de López, 2000). The particular family from which this example was taken follows a somewhat less typical Zapotec tradition in that they provide their two daughters with scaled down cooking utensils, possibly influenced by the men's prolonged stay in the United States. From the age of two years both daughters of the family spontaneously engaged in Zapotec cooking rituals; however, in this particular case, the act of pretence consisted of foaming hot chocolate with a specific Zapotec artifact. An important ingredient of Zapotec chocolate, which carries a similar role as does coffee in Western societies, is fried ground almonds, which makes it possible to whip up a nice foamy topping on the chocolate, which then is used to dip the accompanying dry bread in. In order to produce this special foamy topping, one needs to use a specially hand-made wooden whisk. This culturally specific tool is of the following shape: round and thin at the handle end, and with two separate wooden rings balancing above a round carved thicker end, which is inserted into the pot of hot chocolate. The operation of the whisk demands a very specific complex motoric technique, rolling the whisk handle briskly between one's palms, while at the same time ensuring that the wooden rings balance perfectly. Now, this particular affordance of the wooden whisk, although socio-culturally constructed to meet the needs of the Zapotec chocolate drinkers, is clearly not an inherent and perceptually invariant property of the object itself, as confirmed in a natural experience with my Danish graduate students. Despite this opaque function, these Zapotec toddlers are fluently aware of the preferred affordance of the cultural tool and find it important to integrate in their spontaneous play. This ability to infer the object's affordance cannot be accounted for by appeal to the perceptual invariances of the object, as a traditional reading of Gibson's theory of direct perception would posit. The only explanation of how young Zapotec toddlers, unlike Danish university students, are knowledgeable about this particular artifact is through the cultural mediation of the canonical or preferred affordance of the object, probably interwoven with the universal property of humans as highly imitative creatures in their cultural learning.

Vygotsky stresses the paradox of object play as the notion that:

"things have an inherent motivating force in respect to a very young child's action and determine the child's behavior, but also that through play the child begins to act independent of what he sees, although this freedom of action is not acquired in a flash, but goes through a long process of development" (Vygotsky, 1978, p. 96 and 1933/1985).

However, Vygotsky does not explain in what way culture may play a role in children's play. During this process of cognitive development, proceeding from the concrete to the abstract through the emergence of symbolic play needs to be seen as the culturally specific practice of the child. The activity is clearly constructed in a particular setting and with a particular set of conventional practices operating as the psychologically inherent motivating forces of the object. Thus pretend play activities may be seen as directing children to survival in the real world in a second order manner, which reflects the child's needs to learn the adult's perception of what is culturally valuable (Göncü & Becker, 1992). This contributes to the emergence of self construal. In the following section I illustrate, contra Vygotsky's claim that children younger than 3 years are not able to engage in symbolic play activity, the important influence of culturally specific meanings in the formation of Zapotec children's pretend play activities.

The role of conventional cultural practices in imitative activities

As posited by cultural learning theory (Tomasello, Kruger, Ratner, 1993, Tomasello, 1999), children beyond the age of 4 years are best characterised as small 'imitative machines'. True imitative learning, as opposed to emulation and mimicry, involves the infant reproducing an adult's novel behaviour in both its form and appropriate function, requiring an understanding of what the adult is perceiving and intending (Tomasello et al., 1993, pp. 106-108).

Similar to Vygotsky's theory of cultural development, the theory of cultural learning does not take into account the way in which the specific socio-cultural knowledge of the child may influence the extent to which the child is able to engage in true imitation learning. In order to capture such individual and cultural differences, cultural learning theory needs to be extended beyond the level of immediate inter-subjectivity, to include the influence of the child's prior history of activity settings and his implicit cultural cognitive schemas. In this sense, the child's novel activity and object use is viewed as dependent on both the child's perspective taking abilities in the broad sense, as well as on the subjective and cultural conventional meaningfulness of the object in within the child's existing cultural frame. Mismatches sometimes occur, which can account for example for the following response of a Zapotec 2;5 year old boy when invited to imitate the use of a novel Western item in his play activity.

The observed situation emerged during a routine video recording as part of a longitudinal study of the Zapotec boy. For the video recording I presented the child and his older siblings with a Fisher Price scaled down multi-level garage for him to play with. At first he was quite reluctant to engage with the toy, so his teenage sister and joint caretaker, who obviously had some knowledge of the functionality of the toy, immediately began to 'drive' model cars up and down the ramps, while inviting him to engage in the activity. And in encouraging him to imitate her action she expressed the following in Zapotec:

bzuub ra cuchi ré dxii chul
Put the little cars here, ok sweety

Bxuuin ra cochi loy ganu
Make the cars drive through it, you see

The response of the infant, although now becoming more enthusiastic about the novel object and the game, showed a clear reluctance to imitate or externalise the highly unfamiliar, also but cultural meaningless, activity of driving cars along the ramps of the novel object as modelled to him forcefully by his caregiver. Instead he suddenly stood up and started to search around for some more familiar toys, namely plastic bulls. He then re-approached the novel object which he now understood could be used in a meaningful way and spontaneously initiated the well-known and culturally conventional activity of rounding up the livestock and gathering them in their corral, consisting of the Fisher Price garage. The exclusively Western garage, which had carefully been constructed to scaffold children in learning the "rules" of parking cars in large cities, had been transformed into a corral by a Zapotec two-year-old, a perfect constraining structure for dangerous farm animals. Having succeedded in fitting toy bulls that were much too large into the middle levels of the garage, the child proudly gestured towards his completed handiwork, while exclaiming to his older sister and brother:

> *Rop ra gúun nuu lay*
> Both bulls are inside now
>
> *Láani guraly nuu ra gúun*
> The bulls are inside the corral
>
> *Te ganu?*
> Did you see that?
>
> *A tubim ré*
> Oh here's another animal (as he searched for more toy farm animals)
>
> *A tubim ré*
> Oh here's another animal

The older brother who also participated in the game immediately joined in with the toddler's choice of perspective in interpreting the function of the novel item, while prompting the child:

> *Tebe cún gúun ngaz?*
> Tebe, where's the black bull?

In response to which the child then uttered:

> *Ay nuu láani re*
> It's right in here

> *Ay nuu láani guraly*
> Now it's inside the corral

The game abruptly changed direction and content and both older siblings immediately agreed with the theme selected by the toddler and went on to engage collaboratively with him.

This short observation serves to illustrate three general aspects of children's play activities in this Zapotec community and the model of interaction. First, it is the older siblings, and not the mother, although present, who provide the modelling of object/toy use for the younger child. Second, despite the older children's verbal and nonverbal encouragement of the toddler to engage in the Western canonical or preferred affordance of the object, the child – due to the fact that the object was decontextualised from the Zapotec culture familiar to him – did not agree merely to mimic this strange affordance which was being modelled to him by a significant other. Instead he preferred to engage with the garage in the Zapotec way, thus proposing a non-canonical function. The child's response may on the one hand be seen as a failure to fully integrate the end (the car driving activity) of the adult's action into the themes of his pretend play, and a choice instead to use the novel object integrated in an identifiable way. Thirdly, an additional aspect of interest present in this particular observation is the fact that, when the child deviated from producing the model illustrated to him by the two caregivers, they did not in any way attempt to modify or correct his "choice" of affordance towards the object by employing any approach of the kind "no, now look once again, this is how you are supposed to use the garage", but instead simply followed the theme proposed by the toddler. Now although this behaviour at first sight might be taken to indicate that the caregivers were not committed to getting the child to engage appropriately with the canonicalised affordance of the object, it can also be explained with reference to one of the sociological principles of agrarian societies posited by Gaskins (1999). The particular principle is termed the *principle of independence of child motivation*, and is in part defined as "... *many of a young child's activities are determined by the child's own interests and motivations, as well as by her own understandings of cultural expectations and restraints*" (ibid., p.

36). This principle can perhaps be seen as less restraining than the Western principle of "I will show you how to do it properly".

Gaskins' principle also applies to engagement in social activities, where the child is considered to be independent and to make its own decisions as to how to act on a moment-by-moment basis. This in turn accounts for the fact that neither Mayan nor Zapotec children engage in imitative behaviour to gain favour from their mothers, as in the Western "look at me, mommy" phenomenon. Because the child's culturally mediated engagement in symbolic play is constrained by the novel and culturally meaningless object, in order for the child to make sense of the object he must interpret the interpersonal and imitative modelling presented to him by his caregivers and adapt it to his well-known cultural frame of reference, namely the activity of herding animals, an culture activity that is meaningful for himself. In this sense the all-powerful magic of inter-subjective social interaction nested within the infant's heavy reliance on the significant others is overridden by the child's own situatedness in terms of his embodied cultural knowledge of meaningful actions. Hence, we should perhaps in fact reanalyse our traditional understanding of the triadic setting to include instead the notion of the adult, the object, and the child's *specific cultural practices* rather than simply the child independent of context. This example also supports the notion that objects can be construed differently by different people, and that any person (or young child) can apprehend meanings that are person-dependent, rather than object-specified, as is the view of Hobson (in Williams & Costall, 2000). This is not to downplay the notion of meaning as a negotiative process between the child and his elders, but to illustrate that the perspective of the child in early development is influenced by the child's prior embodied experiences in a cultural sphere, as well as in interaction with its more experienced elders. We should thus expect play activities to unfold in different ways depending on the specific cultural settings and values of the child and its society.

Socio-dramatic play

Now, turning to yet another type of play activity which is well-documented to play an important role in the development of Western children, let us consider the function of children's socio-dramatic or make-believe play, which has been argued to be a major means through which children extend their cognitive skills and learn about important activities and skills in their cultures. In Gaskins' case studies of Yucatec Mayan children, she set out to address the issue of whether socio-dramatic play is frequent in the daily activities of non-Western children, but also to investigate the daily engagements of the children, when compared to what is documented for children from Western societies. She carried out spot observations of 3 Mayan children at the ages of 20 months, 3½ years, and 5½ years during their daily activities, and she identified four very different main categories that characterised these children's engagement, namely: *maintenance* (eating, sleeping, being taken care of), *social orientation* (making requests or observations of ongoing household activities), *play* and *work*. Interestingly, the most common activity for all three children was that of (self-)maintenance, accounting for 46% of the youngest child's activities and 34% of the oldest child's activities. During the remaining time observed, the children were primarily engaged in social orientation or in work. Gaskins' detailed analysis revealed that the Mayan children engage in less symbolic play compared to children from technological societies.

Given that Zapotec is a Mesoamerican society similar to the society that Gaskins observed, I applied the methodology of Gaskins in order to make comparisons of the two communities. The data consisted of randomly collected video recordings of a group of four Zapotec boys, while they engaged in free spontaneous activity for a total of 80 minutes. For the analyses I divided the full sequence into 16 intervals of five minutes. A total of 13 people, including myself and my two-year-old son, who engaged in the play activities of the boys, were present somewhere in the compound as the play activity took place. I then applied Gaskins' four categories of activity in order to analyse the presence of symbolic play and the frequency of the different types of activity identified in Gaskins' study in several ways. The results of this small study differed substantially from the results of the Gaskins study. One main difference is that play (either socio-dramatic, symbolic or both) occurred during as many as 11

(69%) of the 16 intervals (although the youngest boy did not participate in the last play sequence). Self-maintenance and social orientation activity, primarily eating or sitting and talking with the adults, accounted for 5 (31%) of the intervals (the middle ones). However, even during the self-maintenance/social orientation activities some play activity was often still going on. When comparing the modes of play that took place in the play activity of the rural Zapotec children with those of the rural Mayan children, the following cultural differences appeared. First, there was relatively more play of all types among the Zapotec children, and often socio-dramatic play even for the youngest participant of just 2 years old. Despite this cultural variation in terms of the frequency of socio-dramatic play, the result suggests the universality of socio-dramatic and symbolic play, specifically because it was primarily seen as a self-motivated activity by the children themselves.

The main activities occurring during the observation were different types of ball play between all the boys. Parallel to the ball playing activity, there were additionally a series of socio-dramatic and symbolic play activities taking place within the same setting of time and space. These activities shared the similarity that they were never planned, negotiated or organised in advanced by the boys, but appeared more or less spontaneously as emerging activities, which came to be incorporated into the ongoing activity of the children. Often the function of the socio-dramatic or the symbolic play was to exclude one of the participants from the ball activity by either distracting or "punishing" the child, in order to maintain the main ball playing activity.

The first scene of symbolic play occurred at the start of the observation, and had the purpose of distracting the youngest boy (Isma) from interrupting the ball playing game. Isma's role in the game consisted of him constantly fighting to get the ball from the other boys, while whining and throwing a tantrum every time the older ones then snatched it away from him again. On one of these occasions, Isma caught the ball, but would not hand it over to the other boys. In order to avoid a new tantrum from Isma, while recovering the ball, the older boys distracted Isma from the game by creating a symbolic play activity, consisting of sitting on stacked firewood, pretending it to be a horse. While fully engaged in the pretend activity, the older boys then attempted to persuade Isma to join them in the pretend horse-riding activity, prompting him with "do you want to ride the horse". Once they had accomplished the task of getting Isma engaged and out of their way, the older boys quickly returned to the ball game, although some of the boys continued to engage in the horse riding activity on and off to ensure that Isma would stay put. Eventually the firewood became transformed into the imaginary motion of a jumping horse by wiggling the log from side to side.

A second theme of socio-dramatic play that occurred similarly served the function of distracting one of the participants in the ball game because he was no longer obeying the rules of the game, but this time it also carried the function of sanctioning the participant. This event occurred thirty minutes into the observation and in the context where the oldest boy (Aaron) had arranged a game where all the boys were to sit in a circle and throw the ball back and forth to each other. The younger boy (Beto), however, proceeded to disrupt the game by not following the implicit rules, and after several verbal attempts to get Beto to conform to the rules, Aaron and Beto engaged in a corporal pulling-and-pushing activity, which gradually moved them away from the ball game area. Suddenly the two boys had moved themselves over to a large wooden table stored away at the far side of the cooking hut and away from the ball-playing area. The observation of the table immediately caused both boys to perceive it as a possible artifact for socio-dramatic play. Aaron suddenly switched from the tumbling game into a dramatic play sequence exclaiming:

>   *Betit, gulúun te láani lizllibi*
>   Beto, get inside this (the table), it can be a jail

as he shoved Beto, who cooperatively squatted down underneath the table in the imaginary jail. While carrying out this action, Aaron, who had not forgotten the act of punishment, spotted a large shovel lying on the ground beside the table and immediately fastened it between the two legs of the table pretending that it was a padlock, while exclaiming:

> *Anruan, te cuan candad*
> Now I will lock it, I will put a padlock on it

Beto voluntarily switched into the imaginary role of a gangster in the imaginary prison, picked up a stick and pointed it to Aaron, while exclaiming from beneath the table

> *Aguity family*
> Now the family is dead

and continued to shout in ungrammatical Spanish, exclaiming:

> *Las manos está arriba*
> The hands is up

After completing his mission of capturing Beto, Aaron then returned to join the ball game with the other boys. Soon after this the ball was accidentally thrown into a small area of bushes, surrounded by a two-metre chicken wire fence. Isma, being the only one small enough to crawl under the fence, was persuaded by the older boys to crawl into the bush area to retrieve the ball. With this new situation of the gangster held in the jail created by the table, the boys then started to construct a new pretend jail situation arranged around Isma being captured by the chicken wire fence. Parallel to this activity, Beto suddenly escaped from the first jail and approached the group of boys, while again shouting in Spanish "las manos está arriba" (the hands is up) while grasping a stick and exclaiming in Zapotec:

> *Gac xpistoli*
> this will be my little pistol

and

> *Gac xpalit*
> this will be my bullet

Due to the boys' engagement in trying to regain the ball from within the fence, and because the functionality of the imaginary jail was not initially meant as an invitation to engage in reciprocal socio-dramatic activity, none of the other boys paid any attention to Beto's socio-dramatic game, which consequentially faded away.

Although these detailed examples of the sporadic ongoing socio-dramatic and symbolic play activities of these Zapotec children at first sight may resemble the activities undertaken by Western children, they differ both in the content of the themes, and even more importantly in the pragmatics motivating their very emergence. First, the themes of the socio-dramatic play are mixtures of real life experiences (riding horses and putting people in jail) with fictive notions of gangsters and pistols, integrated with Spanish code-switching, suggesting that the gangster and pistol themes are probably reconstructions from some Spanish-language television movie. Secondly, the pragmatics of the boys' socio-dramatic and symbolic play activities are always self-motivated by the children's own interest and immediate motivation and serve a specific function in relation to the main play activity. They are, so to speak, nested within the core activity of the ball game. This supports Gaskins' principle of the *Independence of Child Motivation* within the framework of agrarian children's behaviour, as described in an earlier section. However, the playing out of socio-dramatic and symbolic play also involves additional important cultural and pragmatic functions. What is common for all sequences of the socio-dramatic and the symbolic play activities is that the initiation of these activities did not consist of a planned and negotiated division of roles between the participants (e.g. "now you are the gangster and I will be the enemy"), but rather stemmed from the children's desire to distract the attention of a specific protagonist, in order to avoid that child interrupting the flow of the main activity, namely the ball game. In Western societies, such a disruption would commonly be met by an utterance such as "we not will play with you, if you don't stop that then…" or in the child tattling to a parent. However, in line with Gaskins' principle of respect, which could actually be integrated with the principle of independence, and with the expectation that older children serve as caregivers for younger children while adults are engaged in daily chores, these Zapotec children do not expect adults to interfere in resolving problems between children, but are instead able to cope with the problems by integrating them as parts of the ongoing play activity. The older children are aware that the only non-violent way of distracting a young "intruder" from spoiling the game is by creating a spontaneous symbolic or socio-dramatic play situation, which they can "trick" the "intruder" into engaging in with the goal of gaining play space for themselves[2]. The role adopted by the older child in order to maintain his own play activity, while at the same time obeying the implicit cultural demands placed upon him for being responsible for younger siblings, involves a high level of inter-subjectivity and meta-cognitive skills to coordinate and maintain what seems to be a strategy of "keeping everybody happy".

To summarise, children's symbolic and socio-dramatic play, although universal, cannot be fully understood as biologically constrained, nor as a result of the child striving towards a higher level of meta-representation *per se*, as such play has been interpreted within a Piagetian rationalistic account. Although the emergence of meta-representation may correlate with one of the several by-products of children's socio-dramatic/symbolic play, it cannot be seen as the only underlying motivating factor, leading children eagerly to engage in this specific activity. Socio-dramatic play as undertaken by Zapotec children is best accounted for as nested within the development of socio-cultural consciousness operating at different ecological levels.

The pragmatics of socio-dramatic play and the role of space and setting

Although the Mayan agrarian society, as described in the Gaskins study, shares several similarities with the Zapotec agrarian society, the parental beliefs concerning the role of play activity differ, resulting in significant differences in the quantitative as well as the qualitative structuring of activity behaviour in the two groups of children. This difference can be understood in terms of the third of Gaskins' principles, the principle of *Importance of Parental Beliefs*, which is defined as "*cultural understandings about the nature of the world and about the nature of children, which both significantly shape children's experiences*" (Gaskins, 1999, p. 34). The implications of this third principle are clear in the above observations which suggest that Zapotec children engage in play activity more frequently than is the case for Yucatan Mayan children. While the Mayan parents barely tolerate play behaviour and certainly do not encourage children to engage in play, the Zapotec parents hold the opposite beliefs, and encourage the children both verbally and non-verbally to engage in play behaviour. In both agrarian societies, however, parents do not see an educational advantage to play behaviour, which may explain why they do not engage in tutoring the children in how to play. When Zapotec adults engage in play with children the activity holds the character of parallel play rather than complementary and reciprocal play. Compared to the standard Western measure of play activities, based on the outcome approach I presented in the beginning of the chapter, Zapotec children may engage in less symbolic and socio-dramatic play, but on the other hand they seem to engage in plenty of play at reality. Importantly the particular themes expressed in Zapotec children's play at reality closely reflect the social settings and specific social ceremonies of this specific Zapotec community and may consequently serve as mechanisms of self construal.

In Winterhoff's (1997) view regarding ecological influence on children's behaviour activities, he extends the German word "spielraum", which conveys the notion of *free movement* within *prescribed limits,* to account for the prescribed cultural limits influencing the specific developmental path of the child. In doing so he cites Winegar's (1989) notion of prescribed limits as promotions (socio-cultural messages), which are based on socio-culturally and historically constructed preferences and beliefs about the developmental needs of children and the appropriate life goals of members of the particular culture. With this he suggests that the social activities and social relationships of children are selectively promoted by the adult caregivers in the children's social group (Winegar, 1989, cited in Winterhoff, 1997). Socio-cultural promotions are made concrete by the organisation and structuring of social settings for children and are constructively reproduced by children in their social activity as interpretive reproductions. This can for example be seen in the manipulation of the hot-chocolate whisk or in the Spanish code-switching executed by the pretend gangster.

Furthermore, the physical activity settings promoted in agrarian cultures, when compared to those of technocratic cultures, do not seem highly prescribed or structured. The geographic bounds of the compound allow the children to play in more open and varied settings, which are not directly constrained by the adults, and allow interaction with a wide age range of companions. Such a socio-culturally promoted subsystem of settings may, as suggested by Winterhoff (1997), be considered as generally enhancing the development of reciprocal social relationships. But such reciprocal social relationships should also be viewed as mediated through symbolic or socio-dramatic play, as demonstrated in this study, with these specific play activities serving the psychological function of structuring the lowly prescribed physical activity setting of the children.

Thus, although play at reality can be viewed as the onset of the child's internalisation of social and cultural awareness, and his desire to function within the culture, the specific institutionalised cultural rules and traditions expressed through symbolic/socio-dramatic play, despite its relatively low frequency, should also be viewed as serving the purpose of constraining the physical activity setting of selected participants within a complex peer interaction.

Discussion

It is often argued that the play of kindergarten children stresses the role of negotiation, planning and preparation as its central factors, and in fact these aspects often become the play act *per se*. However, neither Zapotec nor other Mesoamerican children are explicitly taught to negotiate, nor to question the decisions of elders (Quintanilla & Jensen de López, 2011). The pragmatics of Zapotec child socio-dramatic play carries with it a different purpose, leaving out the aspects of negotiation, preparation and planning. In some cases the function of socio-dramatic play is that of distracting an intruder or a younger sibling. Although these would be viewed as lower-level negotiations they do not appear to unfold in such a way. This also suggests a different developmental sequence than that theorised by Göncü (1993), who focuses on the role of meta-communication and communication in pretend play. However, for both developmental sequences, the notion of inter-subjectivity can be said to play an important role in the success of socio-dramatic play. Additionally, the child's use of cultural artifacts in his playing out of reality is an equally important mediator for the child in becoming a participant in the specific cultural setting.

Turning to the cultural differences between the Mayan and Zapotec Mesoamerican children's frequency of play activity, we can assume this to reflect the non-heterogeneity of sociocultural systems, considering psychological development as deterministically indeterministic. However, despite differences in culture and ecology across communities, comparative research such as is presented here can generate possible general principles about human development. With Farver (1999), this study suggests that social pretend play is a universal facet of early childhood, but however that culture strongly influences the frequency, the expression, and the social contexts in which children's play occurs. The focus on the pragmatics motivating symbolic play, the cultural awareness concerning the culturally specific institutionalised rules and practices within the community, and socialised thinking about cultural traditions are all aspects that need to be considered in the further understanding of children's play activities. Comprehensive theories of development should hence deal with both similarities and differences across different ecologies and cultures.

Notes

1 Like children's parallel engagement in daily chores from birth, Zapotec children also participate in all social events from birth, although for some events they may engage more peripherally than for others.
2 It should be noted that corporal punishment of younger children is not tolerated in this Zapotec society.

Author's Note

An earlier version of this chapter was presented at a symposium on play at the Jean Piaget Society, June 5-7, 2003, Chicago.

References

Bornstein, M. H. & Tamis-LeMonda, C. S. (1995). Parent-child symbolic play: Three theories in search of an effect. *Developmental Review,* 15, 382-400.

Bronfenbrenner, U. (1979). *The ecology of human development.* Cambridge, MA: Harvard University Press.

Bruner, J. S., Jolly, A., & Sylva, K. (1985). *Play: its role in development and evolution.* Harmondsworth: Pelican Books.

Bruner, J. S. (1990). *Acts of meaning.* Cambridge, MA: Harvard University Press.

Farver, J. A. M., Kim, Y. K., & Lee, Y. (1995). Cultural differences in Korean- and Anglo-American preschoolers' social interaction and play behaviors. *Child Development,* 66, 1088-1099.

Farver, J. A. M., & Shin, Y. L. (1997). Social pretend play in Korean- and Anglo-Amerian preschoolers. *Child Development,* 68, 544-556.

Farver, J. A. M. (1999). Activity settings analysis: A model for examining the role of culture in development. In A. Göncü (Ed.), *Children's Engagement in the World: sociocultural perspectives* (pp. 99-127). Cambridge: Cambridge University Press.

Gaskins, S. (1999). Children's daily lives in a Mayan village: A case study of culturally constructed roles and activities. In A. Göncü (Ed.), *Children's engagement in the world: sociocultural perspectives* (pp. 25-61). Cambridge: Cambridge University Press.

Göncü, A., Tuermer, U., Jain, J., & Johnson, D. (1999). Children's play as cultural activity. In A. Göncü (Ed.), *Children's engagement in the world: sociocultural perspectives* (pp. 148-172). Cambridge: Cambridge University Press.

Göncü, A. (1993). Development of intersubjectivity in social pretend play. *Human Development,* 36, 185-198.

Göncü, A., & Becker, J. (1992). Some contributions of a Vygotskian approach to early education. *International Journal of Cognitive Education & Mediated Learning,* 2, 147-153.

Haight, W. L. (1999). The pragmatics of caregiver-child pretending at home: Understanding culturally specific socialization practices. In A. Göncü (Ed.), *Children's Engagement in the World: sociocultural perspectives* (pp. 128-147). Cambridge: Cambridge University Press.

Jensen de López, K. (2003). *Baskets and Body-Parts: A Cross-Cultural and Cross-Linguistic Investigation of Children's Development of Spatial Cognition and Language.* Unpublished doctoral thesis. Aarhus University, Denmark.

Jensen de López, K. (2006). Culture, language and canonicality: Differences in the use of containers between Zapotec (Mexican indigenous) and Danish children. In A.

Costall, A & O. Dreier. (Eds.). *Doing Things with Things: The Design and Use of Everyday Objects*. (pp. 87-109). London: Ashgate.

Lave, J. (1988). *Cognition in practice: Mind, mathematics and culture in everyday life*. New York: Cambridge University Press.

Leont'ev, A. N. (1978). *Activity, consciousness and personality*. Englewood Cliffs, NJ: Prentice-Hall.

McLoyd, V. C. (1982). Social class differences in sociodramatic play: A critical review. *Developmental Review, 2*, 1-31.

Piaget, J. (1951/1985). Symbolic play. Reprinted in J. S. Bruner, A. Jolly & K. Sylva (1985), *Play: its role in development and evolution* (pp. 555-569). Harmondsworth: Pelican Books.

Quintanilla, L., & Jensen de López, K. (2011). Perceiving self through envy: A multiculture comparison of preschool children. In K. Jensen de López & T. Hansen (Eds.) *Development of self in culture* (pp. 65-87). Aalborg: Aalborg University.

Rogoff, B., Mistry, J., Göncü, A., & Mosier, C. (1991). Cultural variation in the role relations of toddlers and their families. In M. H. Bornstein (Ed.), *Cultural approaches to parenting* (pp. 173-183). Hillsdale, NJ: Lawrence Erlbaum Associates.

Sinha, C. (1999). Situated selves: learning to be a learner. In J. Bliss, B. Säljö & P. Light (Eds.), *Learning Sites: Social and Technological Resources for Learning* (pp. 32-48). Oxford: Pergamon.

Sinha, C., & Jensen de López, K. (2000). Language, culture and the embodiment of spatial cognition. *Cognitive Linguistics, 11*, 17-41.

Sutton-Smith, B. (1983). Piaget, play and cognition revisited. In W. F. Overton (Ed.) *The relationship between social and cognitive development* (pp. 229-250). New York: Erlbaum.

Tomasello, M. (1999). *The cultural origins of human cognition*. Cambridge, MA: Harvard University Press.

Tomasello, M., Kruger, A. C., & Ratner, H. H. (1993). Cultural learning. *Behavioral and Brain Sciences, 16*, 495-552.

Vygotsky, L. S. (1933/1985). Play and its role in the mental development of the child. Reprinted in J. S. Bruner, A. Jolly & K. Sylva (1985), *Play: its role in development and evolution* (pp 461-463). Harmondsworth: Pelican Books.

Vygotsky, L. S. (1978). *Mind in society: The development of higher psychological processes*. Cambridge, MA: Harvard University Press.

Wertsch, J. V. (1985). *Vygotsky and the social formation of mind*. Cambridge, MA: Harvard University Press.

Williams, E., & Costall, A. (2000). Taking things more seriously: psychological theories of autism and the material-social divide. In P. M. Graves-Brown (Ed.), *Matter, materiality and modern culture* (pp. 97-111). London: Routledge.

Winterhoff, P. A. (1997). Sociocultural promotions constraining children's social activity: Comparisons and variability in the development of friendships. In J. Tudge, M. J. Shanahan & J. Valsiner (Eds.), *Comparisons in human development: understanding time and context* (pp. 222-251). Cambridge: Cambridge University Press.

Andrew G. Ryder
Lauren M. Ban
Jessica Dere

Culture, self, and symptom
Perspectives from cultural psychology

6

The interdisciplinary study of culture and mental health has made considerable advances over the past quarter of the century (López & Guarnaccia, 2000), much of it driven by a mutual exchange between transcultural psychiatry and medical anthropology. This ongoing collaboration has highlighted the central position of culture in the shaping, labelling, interpretation, and impact of emotional distress at both individual and social levels. Psychology, by contrast, has been relatively absent from this project. We believe that cultural psychology has the potential to make a unique and substantive contribution, not least through its central tenet that culture and self are mutually constituted – they 'make each other up', in Shweder's well-known formulation – with implications for cognitive, emotional, and motivational processes. There is an unfortunate tendency, however, for cultural and clinical psychology to be pursued in isolation from one another, so that cultural psychologists can end up with a limited view of psychopathology when they choose to study it, and clinical psychologists often have the same constraints regarding culture (Ritsher, Ryder, Karasz & Castille, 2002). This chapter aims to demonstrate that cultural psychology, informed by clinical psychology, can make a valuable contribution to our understanding of the ways in which the mutual constitution of culture and self shapes psychopathology.

While there is broad agreement that human behaviour is determined by factors spanning a range of organisational levels – from the neurochemical to the socio-cultural – there is a pull to so-called 'lower' levels of organisation because variables at these levels are relatively easier to control. This bias has an impact on the study of psychopathology and, as Marsella (1985) notes, on clinical practice as well:

> "When a clinician is dealing with a patient the biological and psychological variables often appear more suspect than the more indirect cultural variables in which they are embedded, fostered, and nurtured. It is easier to speak of anxiety as mediated by biochemical processes or psychological stressors than to talk of the cultural foundations of the problem." (p. 284).

If scientists, clinicians and their patients, and the general public all see the world through a shared cultural lens, the idiosyncrasies of a given context may start to take on a universal tint. Consequently, research may remain focused on a narrow range of topics, and the quality of clinical care may be less than optimal for individuals from ethnic minority groups (Sue, 1992). At the very least, attention to culture can help to lessen the extent to which we develop a science of human behaviour based primarily on people in Western Europe and North America. At its best, a cultural approach can provide a powerful critique of simple reductionism, orient researchers to complexity while providing ways to begin to deal with it, and contribute to a more nuanced understanding of psychological phenomena.

The first part of this chapter will build the argument that culture and self are mutually constituted, that this deep interconnection has implications for emotion, and that these implications in turn can be extended to psychopathological symptoms. This central premise will then be supported, in the second part of this chapter, by five specific claims. These claims will be explored largely through discussion of a single example, namely the reputed tendency for Han Chinese patients to emphasise somatic symptoms of depression relative to North American patients of European origin.

The interrelation of culture, self, and symptoms
Culture
A review of the social science literature over at least the past century gives the impression that there are as many definitions of culture as there are theorists of culture. Kroeber and Kluckhohn (1952) famously identified several hundred definitions, and many more have been advanced since then. Indeed, anthropology, the discipline that has paid the most sustained attention to culture, went through a period relatively recently where the very notion that culture even exists was contested. If anything, psychology went in the other direction, either ignoring culture entirely in its quest for universals or treating culture as a nuisance variable that had to be explained away in order to get at these universals.

In the absence of a well-articulated conception of culture, even high quality cultural psychology research can end up being interpreted in problematic ways. The literature is full of contrasts between types of people: individualists vs. collectivists; independents vs. interdependents; analytic thinkers vs. holistic thinkers (Markus & Hamedani, 2006). In addition to gliding over the nuances of the original studies, this tendency encourages at least two problematic habits of thought. First, there is the slippage from culture back into categories with which most psychologists are comfortable – internal attributes or traits located within the person. Second, there is the assumption that these types of people are easily defined and map well onto seemingly clear categories of national origin, ethnic group, citizenship, residency, and so on. The consequence is stereotyping through blanket claims, so that Japanese people are interdependent, American people are individualistic, and Chinese people attend more to context, for example.

In an effort to anchor cultural psychology findings in definitions that provide space for the interplay of 'culture' and 'psychology', there has been a return to Kroeber and Kluckhohn's (1952) conclusions following their review of more than half a century ago (e.g., Adams & Markus, 2004; Markus & Hamedani, 2006; Shweder, 2003):

> "Culture consists of explicit and implicit patterns of historically derived and selected ideas and their embodiment in institutions, practices, and artifacts; cultural patterns may, on one hand, be considered as products of action, and on the other as conditioning elements of further action." (summarised by Adams & Markus, 2004, p. 341).

Here, to the extent that specific groups are studied at all, it is because they exemplify particular cultural patterns. The cultural psychologist's goal is therefore to study the implications of these patterns within and across cultural contexts. There is also an increasing appreciation in cultural psychology of the ways in which culture is dynamic rather than static. Cultural ideas (or values, practices, symbols, institutions, etc.) are created, accumulated, changed, and transmitted (D'Andrade, 1995), in processes that take place both within and across generations (Moscovici, 1984). As well, these ideas *"have multiple meanings that are constantly in flux, negotiated, manipulated, and arbitrated for a variety of reasons by all individuals who participate in a cultural community"* (Kitayama, Duffy, & Uchida, 2006, p. 138).

Self

As with culture, work on the self has a long tradition in the social science literature, again leading to a range of definitions. Unlike culture, mainstream psychology has provided numerous contributions to our understanding of the self. Attitudes, beliefs, intentions, norms, roles, and values are all aspects of self. Personal relevance has implications for the ways in which people sample, process, and assess information; self-relevant information is sampled more frequently, sampled more quickly, and assessed more positively when the current self-structure is supported (Triandis, 1989). Markus and Wurf (1987) argue that the unifying premise for most of this vast literature is that the self mediates and regulates ongoing behaviour, rather than merely being a reflection of it. The self is therefore viewed as active, forceful and capable of change, with cognitive, emotional, and motivational consequences.

Within the symbolic interactionist tradition in sociology, Gecas (1982) argues that there is an important distinction to be made between the self and the self-concept. Self is the reflexive process that emerges from the dialectic between subject and object, the 'I' that does the observing and the 'me' that is observed. The self-concept is the product of this dialectic, the concept that the self has of his- or herself as a physical, social, spiritual, or moral being. This distinction between subject and object, with an acknowledgement of how tightly intwined they are, will be important when we describe the self as both the subjective experiencer of suffering and the object of scrutiny by self and others in an effort to evaluate this suffering. First, however, we will turn to the idea that this dialectical self is – itself – in a dialectical relation with the socio-cultural environment, with implications for the structure of the self-concept in different cultural contexts.

Culture and self

That the self is conceptualised differently in different cultural contexts is a recurring theme in psychological anthropology and has also become a central concern of cultural psychology. Both disciplines have found various ways of characterising the dominant concept of self in 'Western' cultural contexts as individualistic, as well as materialistic and rationalistic (Geertz, 1975; Hofstede, 1980; Kirmayer, 2007; Markus & Kitayama, 1991; Morris & Peng, 1994; Triandis, 1989). Most often, some form of collectivism serves as the foil; indeed, this alternative view of self is sometimes stretched to encompass everyone in the world who lives outside of North America or Western Europe. The danger here is that a single dichotomy limits the field to particular questions in particular parts of the world, oversimplifying and then overgeneralising cultural variation. To its credit nonetheless, the distinction between individualism and collectivism (or independent and interdependent self-concepts), especially in comparisons between North American and East Asian cultural contexts, has spawned a rich literature demonstrating that fundamental psychological processes are shaped in important ways by culture.

In keeping with the dominant discourse in Western Europe and North America, psychology and psychiatry assume a single, independent, model of the self wherein the individual is a separate and autonomous entity comprising distinct attributes which in turn cause behaviour (Markus & Kitayama, 1991). A major goal of the independent self is assumed to be the maintenance of this independence, accompanied by the exploration and expression of a unique personality composed of stable attributes (Johnson, 1985; Miller, 1988). In both social and clinical psychology, the healthy self is defined as one that maintains its integrity and boundaries across many and varied social contexts, differentiates itself from significant others as it matures, and successfully defends itself from others (Greenwald, 1980; Markus, 1977; Markus & Kitayama, 1994; Tesser & Campbell, 1983).

As discussed previously, while there are several different views of self that can be contrasted with independence, the interdependent view has received the most sustained theoretical and empirical attention. Indeed, societies in many parts of the world place a much greater emphasis on the interconnectedness of selves with one another. The major task of the interdependent self is not differentiation, but instead involves maintaining good relationships, fulfilling the obligations of one's role in a particular in-group, and accounting for the thoughts, emotions, and behaviours of other people (Markus & Kitayama, 1994). This view of self, in general terms, has been said to characterise so many of the world's peoples that it may in fact be the independent self that is relatively unusual, atypical, and exotic.

If there is a core claim of cultural psychology, it is not simply that there are cross-cultural differences in the self-concept but that culture and self 'make each other up' (Shweder, 1991). As part of the socialisation process in a given community, children develop a psychological system of regulating thoughts, feelings, and actions in a way that is deeply shaped by the surrounding socio-cultural environment (Kitayama, Mesquita & Karasawa, 2006).

> "People exist everywhere in social networks, in groups, in communities, and in relationships. They are chronically sensitive and attuned to the thoughts, feelings, and ac-

tions of others. Their actions (i.e., their ways of being an agent in the world, their identities, their selves) require, reflect, foster, and institutionalise these socio-cultural affordances and influences. Thus, as people actively construct their worlds, they are made up of, or "constituted by," relations with other people and by the ideas, practices, products, and institutions that are prevalent in their social contexts (i.e., environments, fields, situations, settings, worlds). The people whose thoughts, feelings, and actions are included in this circuit of mutual constitution include the individuals' contemporaries, the individual him or herself, and many others who have gone before and left their respective worlds replete with representations, products, and systems reflecting prior thoughts, feelings, and actions." (Markus & Hamedani, 2006, p. 4; emphasis in original)

We cannot understand selves unless we understand them in cultural context; we cannot understand culture unless we understand the participating selves. We therefore must find ways of engaging with the psychological and the cultural without reducing one to the other (Shweder, 1995).

If these claims are valid, we would expect to find that the cultural shaping of human psychology should go beyond the social world to impact on what many psychologists would consider to be basic cognitive and perceptual processes. Over the past two decades, Nisbett and his colleagues have generated a body of research findings demonstrating exactly that. This literature has shown that people from East Asian cultural contexts tend to view the world holistically, focusing on interactions among many disparate elements. People from 'Western' cultural contexts, by contrast, tend to perceive the world analytically, focusing on discrete elements separated from their background. Cultural differences in line with this distinction have now been found across a wide variety of domains including attention (Chua, Boland, & Nisbett, 2005; Hedden, Park, Nisbett, Jing, & Jiao, 2002; Ji, Peng, & Nisbett, 2000; Masuda & Nisbett, 2001), attribution (Choi & Nisbett, 1998; Morris &

Peng, 1994), categorisation (Choi, Nisbett, & Smith, 1997; Ji. Nisbett & Su, 2001; Norenzayan, Smith, Kim & Nisbett, 2002), memory (Masuda & Nisbett, 2001), logical reasoning (Norenzayan et al., 2002) and tolerance for contradiction (Peng & Nisbett, 1999).

While most of this paper will be dedicated to exploring the implications of these differing views of self for psychopathological symptoms, we wish to acknowledge other potentially important ways in which culture shapes the self-concept. Along with idiocentric (i.e., independent) and sociocentric (i.e., interdependent) concepts of self, Kirmayer (2007) discusses the ecocentric self. Indigenous people in many cultural contexts have long recognised that human beings are interconnected with the natural world (Kirmayer, Brass, & Tait, 2000; Waller, 2001). In this view of self, people and land are engaged in a relationship that is inter-personal, with the person in constant ongoing transaction with the physical environment (Gone, 2008; Kirmayer, Fletcher, & Watt, 2009; Wilson, 2003). Research with indigenous people has also suggested a distinction between essentialist and narrative selves, two different ways of establishing the continuity of the self over time and in spite of change. Chandler, Lalonde, Sokol and Hallett (2003) argue that most people raised in 'Western' cultural contexts maintain self-continuity through a sense that there is an underlying essence of the self that knits together its various manifestations through time (essentialist), whereas many people raised in indigenous cultural contexts achieve the same end through telling stories about the changing self (narrative). These findings have striking real-world implications, in that they have been linked to intra- and intercultural variation in suicide rates (Chandler & Lalonde, 1998).

Kirmayer (2007) has also posited the cosmocentric view of self, involving a personal connection to a divine or spiritual order in the universe. For example, in Yoruba thought, the self is seen as the union of body, mind, and 'inner head'; the latter is seen as a deity, and is the source of the individual person's unique qualities and ultimate destiny (Adeofe, 2004). Understanding a personality therefore requires attention to ongoing relationships with deities (Kirmayer, 2007). The cosmocentric view has a parallel in Shweder's work on moral orientation. Like Kirmayer, Shweder acknowledges concepts analogous to individualism and collectivism, which he terms ethics of autonomy and community, but adds an ethic of divinity. More than just conventionality with supernatural overtones, the ethic of divinity is concerned with issues of sacred order, sin, purity, and pollution aimed at promoting spiritual refinement and avoiding spiritual degradation (Miller, 2006; Shweder, Much, Mahapatra & Park, 1997).

Culture-self and emotion

The mutual constitution of culture and self is vital to understanding the cultural psychology literature on emotions. Although cross-cultural emotion research has isolated some coarsely defined general emotions with recognisable accompanying facial expressions (Ekman & Friesen, 1986), anthropologists have been quick to point out that these emotions have little meaning when isolated from their context (e.g. Geertz, 1973; Lutz, 1988). In this view, emotions are *"…partly physical responses that are at the same time aspects of moral or ideological attitudes; emotions are both feelings and cognitive constructions, linking person, action, and sociological milieu"* (Levy, 1983, p. 128). The same basic physical emotion might have, across cultural groups: features with differing salience; different contexts in which it is expected, allowed, or stigmatised; different metaphors of description; different associated behaviours; different levels of intensity; and so on (Jenkins, Kleinman & Good, 1991). To focus only on the universal characteristics of emotion, in the anthropological view, is to elevate the crude and the obvious at the expense of nuances that may be critical to the emotional experience of people within a given cultural context.

Within cultural psychology, independent and interdependent self-construals have informed a substantial amount of recent culture and emotion research. Fundamental to this work is the idea that the independent self-concept promotes emotional expression as a means of validating and promoting one's autonomy and individuality; in contrast, the interdependent self-concept promotes the control of emotional expression, in the interest of maintaining social harmony and avoiding the disruption of interpersonal relations (see Markus & Kitayama, 1991; Heine, Lehman, Markus, & Kitayama, 1999). In line with theoretical expectations, this growing body of research reveals recurring patterns of variation across cultural contexts. While this work is currently limited by the tendency of cultural psychologists to focus on contrasting North American and East Asian samples, it suits our purposes in that we will use a similar distinction to illustrate how culture and self shape psychopathological symptoms.

There is evidence that cultural variation in emotions is observable early in development. For example, young East Asian children display less emotional expresivity as compared with their Euro-American peers, and they spontaneously refer to fewer emotions during both autobiographical memories and self-descriptions (Camras et al., 1998; Camras, Oster, Campos & Bakeman, 2003; Camras, Chen, Bakeman, Norris & Cain, 2006). Similarly, these children make more references to social interactions, make more neutral as opposed to positive self-evaluations, and are more likely to discuss others' emotions than their own (Wang, 2001, 2004). When asked to discuss emotional situations with their child, American mothers tend to demonstrate an 'emotion-explaining' style, with a focus on causal explanations of emotional reactions. Such a style fits with an independent self-construal, where *"talking about emotions is regarded as a direct expression of the self and an affirmation of the importance of the individual"* (Wang, 2001, p. 696). In contrast, Chinese mothers tend to demonstrate an 'emotion-criticising style', whereby recollections of emotional situations are presented as opportunities to reinforce proper social behaviour, emotional restraint, and a sense of social connectedness (Wang, 2001). Furthermore, American and Chinese children's comments regarding emotional experiences parallel those of their mothers (Wang, 2001; Wang & Fivush, 2005).

A number of differences that parallel developmental findings have been found within the adult literature, which is substantially larger. Recent studies have found cultural differences among Euro-American and East Asian samples in the perception and judgment of emotional expressions, including the use of specific facial cues (Cohen & Gunz, 2002; Matsumoto, Kasri & Kooken, 1999; Yuki, Maddux & Masuda, 2007; Wang, 2003), endorsement of emotional display rules (Matsumoto, Takeuchi, Andayani, Kouznetsova & Krupp, 1998; Matsumoto, Yoo, Hirayama & Petrova, 2005), and expressive behaviour (Tsai, Chentsova-Dutton, Freire-Bebeau & Przymus, 2002; Tsai, Levenson &

McCoy, 2006), all of which fit with theoretical predictions. For example, Euro-Americans are more frequently biased towards perceiving in others' faces the emotion they themselves are experiencing, while East Asians more frequently perceive the complementary emotion to the one they are experiencing, in line with a focus on interpersonal relations (Cohen & Gunz, 2002). Furthermore, Euro-Americans place a greater emphasis on the expression of positive emotions as compared to East Asians, an emphasis negatively correlated with collectivist values across both groups (Tsai et al., 2006).

Research regarding the interplay between cultural views of the self and emotional experiences are equally pertinent. For example, compared to Euro-Americans, East Asians or Asian-Americans report: lower levels of emotional intensity and more neutral, rather than positive, affect in retrospective reports of emotional experience (Eid & Diener, 2001; Mesquita & Karasawa, 2002); stronger feelings of pride in reaction to affiliated others' achievements; stronger feelings of guilt in reaction to a close other's social transgression (Stipek, 1998); and higher valuation of low- rather than high-arousal positive affect (Tsai et al., 2006). In a series of comparisons with Japanese samples, interdependent concerns among Americans had a weaker association with positive emotions (Mesquita & Karasawa, 2002). Indeed, frequency of general positive feelings in Americans has a closer association with interpersonally disengaged positive emotions (Kitayama, Markus & Kurokawa, 2000; Kitayama, Mesquita & Karasawa, 2006).

A recurring theme throughout this literature is the particular value that Euro-Americans place on the expression and experience of positive emotions. Euro-Americans have been found to report more frequent positive moods in retrospective reports (Oishi, 2002), display significantly more social (non-Duchenne) smiles when reliving happy episodes (Tsai et al., 2006), and generally report a more pleasant emotional life (Mesquita & Karasawa, 2002), compared with East Asians. This emphasis may be viewed as a means of maintaining and reinforcing the autonomous self, and may be related to the need for maintaining a positive self-image that has been highlighted as an aspect of the independent self.

For the interdependent self, by contrast, social harmony and the maintenance of social obligations are critical. Such cultural variation in the importance placed on positive emotions, particularly happiness, is likely to hold implications for the interpretation and experience of negative emotions, such as sadness. It is understandable that experiences of emotional distress, sadness, or depression would hold different consequences in a cultural context where maintaining a positive mood state is culturally valued and tied to conceptions of the self, as compared to a context in which 'happiness' is not a central cultural theme.

Culture-self and symptoms

Mainstream clinical psychology and psychiatry still tend to exemplify Geertz's (2000) characterisation of the behavioural sciences more generally, in which, *"culture is icing, biology, cake...difference is shallow, likeness, deep"* (p. 53). In the case of psychopathological symptoms, we have the parallel view that objectively observable disease is what really matters and subjectively experienced illness merely colours the experience for the sufferer. Moreover, these diseases represent fixed categories linked to specific neurobiological dysfunctions that are waiting to be revealed through an accurate accounting of symptoms. Kleinman (1980) defines disease as *"a malfunctioning of biological and/or psychological processes, while the term illness refers to the psychosocial experience and meaning of perceived disease"* (p. 72; emphasis in original). The disease model of psychopathology has recently come to dominate much of mainstream psychiatry and clinical psychology, and research from this perspective has resulted in important advancements in our understanding of the neurobiological and neurochemical underpinnings of mental illness.

The tendency of the disease model to essentialise psychiatric diagnoses ignores that there has been a gradual but pervasive shift in thinking over the past few decades away from the idea that psychiatric categories are 'real latent kinds' represented by sets of necessary defining features (Acton, 1998). Far from being a minority critical view, this shift was reflected in the move from DSM-II to DSM-III and continuing with DSM-IV. There has been a growing appreciation that diagnoses are better thought of as Roschian categories (Lilienfeld & Mariono, 1992) or theory-based constructs (Kim & Ahn, 2002), in which category members share a certain proportion of features and membership is graded so that certain instances are more representative of the category than others (Markman & Ross, 2003; Medin, 1989).

Moreover, whereas the classical approach to categories draws a sharp distinction between concepts and theories, so that the concept identifies the domain that subsequent theories try to explain, the theory-based approach posits that categorisation is inextricably linked to explanation (Medin, 1989). In keeping with this notion, Kirmayer (1995) claims that concepts of mental disorder cannot be distinguished from beliefs about etiology and symptoms. Of course, the implications of these beliefs play out in specific socio-cultural milieus rather than some abstract 'life-in-general'. As theories differ across cultural contexts, "*Culture influences the experience and expression of distress from its inception*" (Kirmayer, 1989, p. 327). In light of the evidence that the mutual constitution of culture and self has implications for cognitive, emotional, and other psychological processes, it is not surprising that we find a similar relation for dysfunctions in these processes (Jenkins, 1994). The subjective and value-laden experience of illness is not only important to the sufferer but has its own causal arrow pointing back to biology, creating another dialectical relation between the objective and the subjective.

The premise that culture is deeply implicated in psychopathology is the guiding principle of cultural psychiatry, leading to a considerable body of research covering a wide range of mental health problems. Our aim in this chapter is more modest in that we will primarily take a cultural psychology perspective and apply it to a single collection of symptoms, namely those that cluster into the clinical syndrome of depression. Conveniently for our purposes, much of the cultural literature on depression has been carried out in regions of the world that have also been the focus for many cultural psychologists. Moreover, many modern psychological models of depression emphasise that depression is in many ways a problem of and for the self, which is viewed by the depressed person in a pervasively negative manner (Beck, Rush, Shaw & Emery, 1979). So, given what we know about the cultural psychology of self and emotion, we anticipate that a proper understanding of depressive symptoms will require that they be contextualised within a cultural frame.

When attempting to reach an acceptable definition of depression, the first challenge is determining the level at which it is best discussed. Depression can be thought of as a mood state, a constellation of symptoms, or a disease category with specific inclusion and exclusion criteria (Kendall, Hollon, Beck, Hammen & Ingram, 1987). Depressed mood, which would seem to be central to any definition of depression, is only one of many symptoms involved in a Major Depressive Episode (MDE) and is not even necessary for diagnosis, as defined in the current edition of the Diagnostic and Statistical Manual of Mental Disorders (DSM-IV-TR; APA, 2000). Measures of depression contain a range of psychological and physical symptoms, only a few of which relate directly to depressed mood (Bagby, Ryder, Schuller & Marshall, 2004). An MDE, meanwhile, can be observed in individuals undergoing a non-pathological bereavement process, as part of a general medical condition such as thyroid dysfunction, as part of a broader psychopathological condition such as Bipolar Disorder, or as a stand-alone category, Major Depressive Disorder (MDD).

Recent efforts to create an international research database on depression have demonstrated that DSM-defined MDD can be identified throughout the world. However, these efforts have also revealed considerable variation in prevalence rates across cultural contexts. A large international study conducted by the World Health Organization (WHO) showed that 11.7% of those sampled had a current depressive disorder (Lecrubier, 1998). The Cross-National Study, conducted by the Cross-National Collaborative Group (Weissman et al., 1996), studied ten nations in the late 1980s and early 1990s, and found a fairly narrow 1-year prevalence for MDD of 2% to 6% but a much wider range in lifetime prevalence estimates, from 1.5% to 19%. Depression was associated with suicide attempts, substance use problems, and poorer outcomes for accompanying physical diseases (Lépine, 2001).

International studies of depression may have shown that cases conforming to DSM-based definitions of MDD can be found worldwide, but they have not necessarily shown that MDD is the best way of characterising depression in every culture. These studies have certainly not established that the experience of depression is more or less the same in every culture, although this conclusion is often drawn (Kleinman, 1988). Indeed, symptomatic expression, interpretation, and social response to depression vary widely (Kirmayer, 2001; Marsella, Kinzie & Gordon, 1973; Singer, 1975; Tanaka-Matsumi & Draguns, 1997). Depression may be universally related to a loss of relationships, status, or reward incentives, as proposed by evolutionary psychiatry (Nesse, 2000), but the emotions attached to these basic predicaments are elaborated in distinctive ways in each cultural context (Shweder & Haidt, 2000). As with emotions in general, the expression of dysphoric affect is governed by cultural expectations as to the salience of particular features, the use of particular descriptive metaphors, and the appropriateness of particular displays in particular situations. The cultural context also provides lay theories of etiology and treatment, with implications for labelling, help-seeking, and the extent of stigma (Kirmayer, 2001).

Emotions are often described as 'total-system' responses that involve a wide range of features, some that are emphasised and others that recede into the background. Many, if not most, cultures use somatic metaphors to describe emotional experience, and the 'West' is no exception: the English language includes heartache, burning anger, blind panic, butterflies in the stomach, and so on. There remains a tendency in the mainstream psychopathology literature to focus primarily on the psychological features of these disorders: depression can include insomnia but it is about depressed mood and loss of interest; my loss of appetite is happening to me but my guilt is a part of me.

Nonetheless, even the North American Diagnostic and Statistical Manual of Mental Disorders (DSM-IV; American Psychiatric Association, 1994, 2000) lists a range of somatic symptoms, including changes in sleep, appetite, and psychomotor activity, as well as increased fatigue and loss of energy. Rather than being ways of masking psychological experience, somatic symptoms appear to be an integral part of both the pathophysiology and psychopathology of major depression:

> "The same neurophysiological dysregulation that gives rise to depressed mood may result in increased muscle tone, alterations in gut motility and other autonomic

symptoms either directly or through the effects of sleep disturbance. Depressed individuals' negative and pessimistic cognitive schemas foster the recall of illness-related memories, promote a negative view of their health and their future prognosis, and result in heightened awareness of unpleasant experiences. Depression directs one's attention inward, and this increased bodily preoccupation may make trivial and mild discomforts more disturbing." (Sayer, Kirmayer, & Taillefer, 2003, p. 108).

Given that somatic symptoms are almost always an important part of depression, the issue may instead be one of emphasis – why do some depressed patients have predominantly or exclusively somatic presentations while other patients place more emphasis on psychological symptoms? In the pages that follow, we will attempt some answers to this question grounded in the idea that culture and self "make each other up." The larger aim is to use a specific example to illustrate the ways in which a cultural psychology approach can contribute to our understanding of symptoms.

Five claims about culture, self, and symptoms

Having highlighted some well-established links between culture, self, and symptoms in largely general terms, we will now focus on what is perhaps the best known questions in the literature on culture and psychopathology – why do Han Chinese patients appear to emphasise somatic symptoms of depression, especially as compared with North Americans of European origin (Ryder, Yang & Heine, 2002)? The remainder of this chapter explores this question in order to illustrate our central premise: the mutual constitution of culture and self, especially its impact on emotion, can help us understand cultural differences in the presentation of psychopathology. We therefore turn to an outline of the literature on depression and somatisation among Han Chinese patients, followed by a discussion wherein this example is used to support the following five claims:

1. The mutual constitution of culture and self shapes beliefs about the meaning of symptoms.
2. The mutual constitution of culture and self shapes the personal experience of symptoms.
3. The mutual constitution of culture and self shapes the communication of symptoms to others.
4. The interrelation of culture, self, and symptom is shaped in turn by history.
5. The interrelation of culture, self, and symptom will continue changing into the future.

An example: Chinese somatisation, Western psychologisation

One of the first systematically reported cross-cultural differences in psychiatric epidemiology was the apparent rarity of depression in Chinese cultures (Kleinman, 1982). A mental health survey was undertaken in 12 regions of China in 1982, and replicated in seven of these regions in 1993 (Zhang, Shen & Li, 1998, cited in Parker, Gladstone & Chee, 2001). Of the 19,223 people surveyed in 1993, only 16 fulfilled the ICD-9 criteria for lifetime affective disorder, with lifetime- and point-prevalence estimates of 0.08% and 0.05%, respectively. Amazingly, these rates were significantly higher than those obtained from the 1982 sample, and suggest that the community rate of depression in China is several hundred times lower than in North America. National community surveys in Taiwan have also identified low depression rates when compared with other countries (Hwu, Yeh & Chang, 1989; Weissman et al., 1996).

While it is necessary to abandon the simple hypothesis that Chinese patients somatise distress while 'Western' patients 'psychologise' it, cultural variations in symptom reporting still demand an explanation. Somatisation and psychologisation occur in both cultural groups, but they do not necessarily occur with the same frequency. Indeed, Simon, VonKorff, Piccinelli, Fullerton, and Ormel (1999) note that although they find somatisation at every site, there is considerable variability in the base rates, variability that is attributed to culture without further elaboration. In order to better understand observed differences in depression, therefore, it is necessary to look at theory and evidence pertaining to whether there indeed exists a relative difference in somatisation and psychologisation.

Yen, Robins, and Lin (2000) conducted two studies in Chinese and Euro-American samples. Study 1 found that Chinese students seeking counselling reported considerably more somatic symptoms and fewer psychological symptoms on questionnaire as compared with a Chinese student control group; Study 2 found that a Chinese student sample reported significantly fewer somatic symptoms compared with Chinese-American and Euro-American student samples. The first direct comparison of clinical patients found that 60% of a Malaysian Chinese depression sample nominated a somatic symptom as their chief complaint on self-report compared with 13% of a Euro-Australian sample (Parker, Cheah, & Roy, 2001). Chinese respondents were more likely to endorse somatic symptoms, but the Euro-Australian sample had a much stronger tendency to endorse more psychological symptoms, suggesting that 'Western psychologisation' needs more attention.

Ryder, Yang and colleagues (2008) used multiple assessment methods, including clinical and structured interviews, to study symptom reporting in Chinese and Euro-Canadian psychiatric outpatients. Although there was evidence to support greater somatic symptom reporting in the Chinese sample, there was much stronger and more consistent evidence for greater psychological symptom reporting in the Euro-Canadian sample. Moreover, an externally-oriented thinking style, or tendency to focus attention away from the internal experience of thoughts and feelings, mediated the relation between cultural group and somatic symptom emphasis. This last step marks a rare occasion when explanations about the cultural shaping of psychopathology have been tested rather than offered after the fact. As we turn to our five claims about culture, self, and symptoms, we do so in hope of encouraging future studies to directly test explanatory hypotheses.

The mutual constitution of culture and celf chapes beliefs about the meaning of symptoms

Given that culture shapes both self-concept and cognitive styles, in turn influencing implicit theories of mind and behaviour, it is not surprising that people living in different cultural contexts vary in their preference for intuitive frameworks explaining distress. According to Haslam's (2005) theory of 'folk psychiatry', people process information about abnormality using four such frameworks, each of which has a distinct cognitive underpinning grounded in social psychological theory and research (Haslam, Ban, & Kaufman, 2007). The first of these frameworks, pathologising, is triggered when a normative expectation has been violated. Once pathologised, the behaviour is submitted to one or more of three explanatory frameworks: (1) medicalising, where pathology is attributed to a biological aberration beyond the sufferer's conscious control; (2) moralising, where pathology is attributed to the sufferer's poor character and conscious decision making; and (3) psychologising, where pathology is attributed to factors that are internal to the sufferer but beyond their conscious control. While held up as a universally applicable cognitive grid, there is evidence that these frameworks are differentially salient depending on the context (Giosan, Glovsky, & Haslam, 2001).

As we might expect from a cultural psychology perspective, the ways in which these frameworks are taken up depend on local norms, values, and person conceptions. What little research exists comparing East Asian and 'Western' samples suggests that culture shapes the way in which depression is or is not pathologised. Specifically, understanding the reasons why a potentially pathological behaviour took place makes it less likely to be pathologised in a 'Western' context, but makes it more likely to be pathologised in an East Asian context. Once pathologising has taken place, culture continues to influence the explanatory frame used to comprehend it. In contexts where an independent self-concept is emphasised, depression tends to be explained using a psychologising frame; in contexts where an interdependent self-concept is emphasised, depression tends to be explained using a moralising frame. Moreover, in the latter case, adherence to traditional values related to the interdependent self-concept is associated with a stronger tendency to use a moralising frame (Ban, Kashima, & Haslam, 2010).

At this point, cultural research using the folk psychiatry model is sparse and there is little work linking explanatory frameworks to specific symptoms. Haslam (2005) suggests that behaviours involved with consumption will tend to be moralised, including eating disorders, addiction, substance abuse, or sexual impulsivity. Haslam and Ernst (2002) found evidence that physical symptoms, sharp fluctuations of symptoms, or evidence of biological descent invoke explanatory principles of the medicalising framework, which in turn is associated with essentialist thinking. There is little theory and no research, however, to support a relation in the other direction, where the tendency to use specific frameworks influences the symptoms that are presented. That said, given that patients in different cultural contexts use these frameworks to understand their own behaviour, and live in a social milieu where their behaviours are observed (and framed) by others, we might expect variation in the behaviours that are focused on as problematic and the ways in which these behaviours are communicated to others. Chinese patients might emphasise somatic symptoms of depression as these can be understood within a medicalising framework, avoiding psychological symptoms that might tend instead to be seen through a moralising framework. Such possibilities await empirical investigation.

The mutual constitution of culture and self shapes the personal experience of symptoms

Although past research has offered at least some support to the idea that somatisation is especially common in Chinese patients, there is little evidence that such patients always make exclusively somatic presentations. Depression is a complex clinical phenomenon that involves both somatic and psychological features; evidence of somatisation in the Chinese suggests that the somatic symptoms are somehow more salient. In this view, different symptom presentations are more than merely strategies to obtain health care resources or to avoid stigma. Rather, patients who are somatising depression may actually be experiencing somatic symptoms to a greater degree, or at least are placing greater emphasis on these symptoms. Barsky and colleagues (Barsky, Cleary, & Klerman, 1992; Barsky, Wyshak, & Klerman, 1990) have defined the construct of somatosensory amplification as tendencies towards bodily hypervigilance, focus on weak and infrequent bodily sensations, and appraisal of sensations as symptomatic of disease. Research by Pennebaker and colleagues has confirmed that increasing self-attention increases somatic symptom reporting (Pennebaker & Brittingham, 1982) without actually affecting the accuracy with which bodily changes are perceived (Pennebaker & Watson, 1988). To the extent that such concerns trigger help-seeking, help would most likely be sought from primary care physicians as opposed to psychiatrists.

Interest has also been shown in the extent to which somatisation might be caused by difficulties in processing and expressing affect (Sayar, Kirmayer, & Taillefer, 2003). Alexithymia is a personality trait characterised by difficulty identifying emotions, difficulty communicating emotions, and externally-oriented thinking. Individuals who score highly on this trait are thought to be particularly likely to misinterpret negative emotional arousal as physical symptoms. Dion (1996) has argued that the construct of alexithymia might be unnecessarily judgmental when used as an explanation for cultural differences in somatisation, noting that externally-oriented thinking, in particular, is assessed as a set of values rather than of difficulties. Alexithymia has been shown to have a strong negative relation to emotional intelligence (Parker, Taylor, & Bagby, 2001), a construct touted as measuring the ways in which the most functional members of our society are supposed to perform (Bar-On, 2000).

Alexithymia and emotional intelligence may carry the burden of pathologising ways of engaging with emotions that are common in non-Western countries, but these constructs do have the advantage of measuring an ideal Western emotional style. Individuals in China who prefer to engage in externally-oriented thinking for culturally approved reasons are not pathological, but they would still be expected to experience physical symptoms as being more salient and more important than psychological symptoms. A culturally appropriate person from the West with depression, meanwhile, would find that psychological experiences are particularly salient and important to communicate to others. Consistent with this view, Ryder, Yang and colleagues (2008) found that externally-oriented thinking – but not other components of alexithymia – mediates the relation between cultural group and somatic symptom reporting.

The mutual constitution of culture and self shapes the communication of symptoms to others

Any consideration of differences in the extent to which certain symptoms are presented or denied must consider self-presentation biases. Many writers in this area have thus turned to stigma as a potential explanation for why psychological symptoms might be de-emphasised. Goffman (1963) has described stigma in psychiatric illness as being a sense that the people with a mental illness have a spoiled identity experienced both by these individuals themselves and by those who interact with them. People will thus be motivated to avoid stigmatising labels and will be under considerable pressure from society, particularly friends and family, not to be categorised in this way. If such labelling does take place, moreover, a vicious circle can develop where the stigma itself worsens the illness. Evidence of this effect has been found for schizophrenia, depression, and other chronic disorders (Finkler, 1985; Ritsher, Otilingam, & Grajales, 2003). Somatisation is one way for psychologically distressed individuals to inhabit the sick role in their societies without bearing the burden of stigma (Goldberg & Bridges, 1988).

Research on patterns of help-seeking among Chinese patients in Hong Kong, and also among Chinese-Canadians, has consistently demonstrated a tendency to delay help-seeking from Western mental health services (Cheung, Lau, & Wong, 1984; Kleinman, 1983; Lin, Tardiff, Donetz, & Goresky, 1978; Ryder, Bean, & Dion, 2000). However, the elapsed time is spent in the pursuit of non-medical health care and self-care of various types, with patients consulting many more health practitioners before seeking the sort of care that gets them noticed by most researchers (Cheung & Lau, 1982). Cheung (1984) studied students in Hong Kong, presenting them with hypothetical physical and mental health problems and inquiring as to the students' attributions and proposed solutions. She noted that these students were willing to make psychological attributions, but would be more likely to consult friends than physicians; the reverse help-seeking pattern was found for physical health problems. Notably, these students expressed a preference for medical rather than mental health professionals when seeking help for mental health problems. These patients would then be more likely to present with somatic symptoms because those are the symptoms that are most appropriate to a regular health care setting (Cheung & Lau, 1982).

Moreover, there is considerable work demonstrating that mental illnesses are stigmatised in Chinese societies (Lin & Lin, 1981; Shon & Ja, 1982; Ryder et al., 2000). Chinese families are particularly likely to attempt to shield the afflicted family member from the rest of the community, especially when the need for direct contact with psychiatric health service providers arises (Kirmayer, 1989). Shon and Ja (1982) outlined three reasons why mental illness reflects badly on the family: (a) physically, it is a result of heredity; (b) psychologically, it is a result of poor guidance and discipline; (c) and spiritually, it is a result of punishment for family sins. Furthermore, mental illness becomes a community issue as a result of the belief that a healthy mind contributes to social harmony (Zhi-Zhong, 1984). Family members are often seen as sharing the same problematic heredity, poor upbringing, and negative spirituality as the individual with mental illness, with serious implications for their interactions with the larger community (Lin & Lin, 1981).

The interrelation of culture, self, and symptom is shaped in turn by history

The term 'somatisation' was first introduced by psychoanalytic writers to refer to a process by which anxious affect is suppressed by defence mechanisms and allowed to reach consciousness only by means of visceral expression (Craig & Boardman, 1990). Indeed, unexplained somatic symptoms were the primary spur to Freud and Breuer's development of psychoanalytic theory (Simon, 1991). Simply put, conflicts that were defended from entering consciousness would present somatically; inability of the patient to accept this explanation was identified as resistance. The psychoanalytic view implies, therefore, that something else – a psychological problem of some kind – is being somatised. Expressing emotional problems through physical symptoms was seen as a way of avoiding anxiety-provoking content and thus, from a culture-bound and Western point of view, was usually viewed as an immature defence (Draguns, 1996). Cheung (1984) argues that such views are remnants of the West's continued adherence to mind-body dualism, in which the most important features of personal identity are situated in the mind.

The interdependent-independent and holistic-analytic distinctions can be extended to ways in which the self is experienced as being part of an integrated mind and body or part of a separated mind. In cultural contexts where independent selves and analytic thinking are the norm, body and mind are thought to exist dualistically, clearly separable and distinguishable. Most importantly, in this conceptualisation the mind is privileged over the body as the seat of the 'true self' – a distinction captured by Descartes' dictum, "I think, therefore I am". Put another way, the self might have a body, but it *is* a mind. In Western medicine, for example, physical and mental illness are differentiated (Fabrega, 1982; Lutz, 1985), with Jenkins (1994) noting that the classification of depression as a mood disorder accompanied by somatic symptoms represents a mind-body dichotomy. A contrasting example comes from Traditional Chinese Medicine, which views mind and body as being integrated with one another as well as with social context (Kaptchuk, 1983; Wu, 1982). Here, physical and psychological experiences result from a natural, simultaneous, and inseparable intertwining of mind and body, with no privileging of one over the other (Cheung, 1995).

The view of somatisation as an immature defence changed in the 1980s after Kleinman's (1982, 1986) research on neurasthenia in China. Neurasthenia was first described in the United States by the neurologist George Miller Beard as a nervous syndrome of more than 50 symptoms (1869):

> "an exhaustion of the nervous system," with "general malaise, debility of all the functions, poor appetite, abiding weakness in the back and spine, fugitive neurologic pains, hysteria, insomnia, hypochondriasis, disinclination for consecutive mental labor, severe and weakening attacks of sick headache, and other analagous symptoms..." (p. 12).

Moreover, Beard linked the emergence of this disorder to the sociocultural context - he titled his book on the subject American Nervousness – noting that the symptoms were commonly observed in 'mental workers' during periods of rapid industrialisation. Although widely used in North America and Western Europe during World War I, the neurasthenia diagnosis had a rapid decline in post-war years and by the 1930s was seldom used (Schuster, 2003).

As the neurasthenia diagnosis was all but disappearing in 'Western' settings, it was being introduced, studied, and increasingly adopted in China. Rather than being imported directly from the United States, Soviet-trained Chinese physicians after the 1949 revolution learned about neurasthenia through its prior adoption by Pavlov and consequent inclusion in standard textbooks (Shixie, 1989). Stemming ultimately from Beard's (1869) original work, the specific symptoms of fatigue, weakness, pressure in the head, poor attention span, memory loss, insomnia, easily being upset, and irritability became central to the Chinese understanding of neurasthenia. By the 1960s, as many as 80% of psychiatric outpatients in China were diagnosed as primarily neurasthenic (Lin, 1989; Yan, 1989), a figure that persisted at least until the early 1980s (Kleinman, 1982; Parker, Gladstone & Chee, 2001). A review of epidemiological studies conducted in the 1980s demonstrated that neurasthenia was by far the most frequently identified neurotic disorder in China (Cheung, 1991). The diagnosis of depression was rarely used (Lee, 1996).

In this context, somatisation is the term used to describe the tendency to present predominantly somatic symptoms, but instead of describing a defence, the term is used to describe a way of communicating distress. When this distress encounters the health care system it is given a diagnostic label that guides and shapes the ways in which this distress is dealt with by the patient, the practitioner, and the society as a whole. Starting from this perspective, Kleinman (1982) used both anthropological and psychiatric methods to assess 100 neurasthenia patients in China and concluded that 87% were suffering from some form of depression. At the same time, somatic symptoms were common chief complaints, whereas depressed mood was reported by only 9% of cases. Kleinman concluded that neurasthenia was a Chinese-specific way of presenting depression but also that neurasthenia had a sufficiently distinct symptom profile to justify continued inclusion in the Chinese and international diagnostic systems.

Although changes in scientific focus and diagnostic practice tell part of the story, Kleinman (1995) has proposed a cultural explanation for differences in neurasthenia and depression that anticipates the current shift. He argues that the climate of communist China, especially during the Cultural Revolution, rendered particular emotional experiences and particular diagnoses politically dangerous. Cheung (1991) has noted that, *"during the Cultural Revolution it was considered ideologically undesirable to be depressed"* (p. 489); core symptoms of depression could be criticised as decadent individualism, laziness, malingering, or failure to be sufficiently proletarian in outlook (ibid.). Neurasthenia served the function of providing a physical explanation for psychosocial distress, being readily understood at the time as being a product of brain dysfunction (ibid.). A field study conducted in rural China (Cheung, 1981 cited in Cheung, 1989) found that respondents were unwilling to talk about depression but had many examples of neurasthenia, including examples from their own life stories. In this conception, neurasthenia is the way that the body expresses distress that cannot be expressed in other ways (Kleinman, 1995).

The interrelation of culture, self, and symptom will continue to change

When we accept that the interrelation of culture, self, and symptom has involved shifts over time, we can no longer assume confidently that the connections we are studying now will persist into the indefinite future. For example, Kleinman's (1995) political argument about neurasthenia and somatisation in China focuses on the Cultural Revolution, a process that was halted and reversed during the leadership of Deng Xiaoping from 1978 into the 1990s. Kleinman (1986) followed up on his initial study and noted the large changes of a mere half-decade, characterising the 1980s as a period in which Chinese people were able to release previously silenced emotions. Studies ranging from content analyses of telephone helpline calls to ethnographies in rural China demonstrate that modern concerns revolve around love and money, rather than political conformity and party membership (Lee, 1999). Whereas the Cultural Revolution delegitimised the very emotional experiences central to depression, current reforms would be expected to allow greater expression of these experiences.

Several studies followed up on Kleinman's (1982) original work and reported that depressive disorders are common in patients diagnosed with neurasthenia (Lee, 1999). Moreover, the majority of patients who did not meet criteria for depression appeared to show good response to antidepressants (Zhang, 1989). Perhaps in response to this research and its implications, both community and clinical studies conducted through the 1990s have shown a dramatic reduction in the use of this diagnosis. Liu and colleagues (1992; cited in Lee, 1999) showed that, in community studies, depressive disorders had a baserate of 14% using the Chinese Classification of Mental Disorders (CCMD-2) definitions. Xu, Gao, and Xu (1993; cited in Lee, 1999) studied 2,275 inpatients discharged in Shanghai in 1990 and found 256 cases of affective disorders, including depression, again using CCMD-2. One potential explanation of this recent shift is increased exposure to Western diagnostic practices, but there may be changes in willingness to report symptoms as well. Ryder, Dere, Zhu, Yao, and Thombs (2008) have shown that the tendency for Chinese depressed patients to report lower levels of psychological symptoms relative to Euro-Canadian patients does not actually apply to 'depressed mood' itself. Not only were patients in the two groups equally likely to admit to this symptom when asked directly, they did not differ in willingness to spontaneously report it when asked in general about presenting complaints.

As culture changes over time, self-concepts shift and different symptoms may become more or less salient. Different cultural contexts in different historical periods vary in the meaning assigned to particular clusters of symptoms, and the ramifications of experiencing them and presenting them to others. At the same time, professional wisdom changes in response to both scientific evidence and current fashion, in a process that shapes and is shaped by the prevailing cultural climate. Complicating matters still further, the public and professional concerns of Western societies have an influence on the rest of the world, especially as travel and communication grow more efficient (Kirmayer, 2006). In Western cultural contexts, a concern with 'justifiable' physical illness changed to a search for 'underlying' psychological causes, as scientists grew concerned with the lack of physiological signs and increasingly left understanding of neurasthenic symptoms to psychoanalysts. In China, a similar concern with acceptable and unacceptable distress took on immense proportions during the Cultural Revolution, a trend that now appears to be reversing. Historically speaking, culture and self are moving targets, and the ways in which the predominant symptom presentation patterns in Western and Chinese societies will continue developing in the future remain to be seen.

Conclusion

Cultural variations in the self-concept set certain parameters around behaviour that constitutes normal and abnormal human functioning; symptoms of psychopathology are transformed within a culture's meaning system. The mutual constitution of culture and self shapes the interpretation, experience, and expression of symptoms, and do so in a dynamic way across persons, cultural contexts, and historical periods. This conclusion is admittedly a challenge to those scientists and clinicians who prefer to focus on supposedly well-defined and invariant constructs, rooted ultimately in neurobiology. Rather than proposing an equally rigid opposition to this deterministic view, we aspire instead to a multilevel and interactional perspective wherein phenomena such as symptoms are ultimately best understood by simultaneous appeals to multiple levels and their interrelations with one another. In combination with the psychological study of mental health, we look forward to the emergence of a cultural-clinical psychology[1] as a full partner in this ongoing interdisciplinary exploration.

Note

1 In the interval between writing and publishing this chapter, we have expressly described and advocated a cultural-clinical psychology perspective. See: Ryder, A. G., Ban, L. M., & Chentsova-Dutton, Y. E. (2011). Towards a cultural-clinical psychology. *Social and Personality Psychology Compass, 5*, 960-975.

Author's Note

Preparation of this manuscript was supported by a New Investigator Award from the Canadian Institutes of Health Research to AGR. The authors would like to thank Yulia Chentsova-Dutton for her invaluable comments on an earlier version of this manuscript.

References

Adams, G., & Markus, H. R. (2004). Toward a conception of culture suitable for a social psychology of culture. In M. Schaller & C. S. Crandall (Eds.), *The psychological foundations of culture* (pp. 335-360). Mahwah, NJ: Lawrence Erlbaum Associates.

Acton, G. (1998). Classification of psychopathology: The nature of language. *The Journal of Mind and Behaviour, 19*, 243-256.

Adeofe, L. (2004). Personal identity in African metaphysics. In L. M. Brown (Ed.), *African Philosophy: New and Traditional Perspectives*, (pp. 69-83). New York: Oxford University Press.

American Psychiatric Association (1994). *Diagnostic and Statistical Manual of Mental Disorders, 4th Edition*. Washington, DC: Author.

American Psychiatric Association (2000). *Diagnostic and Statistical Manual of Mental Disorders, 4th Edition: Text revision*. Washington, DC: Author.

Bagby, R. M., Ryder, A. G., Schuller, D. R., & Marshall, M. (2004). The Hamilton Rating Scale for Depression: Has the gold standard become a lead weight? *American Journal of Psychiatry, 161*, 2163 2177.

Ban, L., Kashima, Y., & Haslam, N. (2012). Does understanding behaviour make it seem normal? Perceptions of abnormality among Euro-Australians and Chinese-Singaporeans. *Journal of Cross-Cultural Psychology, 43*, 286-298.

Bar-On, R. (2000). Emotional and social intelligence: Insights from the Emotional Quotient Inventory. In R. Bar-On & J. D. A. Parker (Eds.). *The Handbook of Emotional Intelligence* (pp. 363-388). San Francisco: Jossey-Bass.

Barsky, A. J., Cleary, P. D., & Klerman, G. L. (1992). Determinants of perceived health status of medical outpatients. *Social Science and Medicine, 34*, 1147-1154.

Barsky, A. J., Wyshak, G., & Klerman, G. L. (1990). The somatosensory amplification scale and its relationship to hypochondriasis. *Journal of Psychiatric Research, 24*, 323-334.

Beard, G. M. (1869). Neurasthenia or nervous exhaustion. *Boston Medical and Surgical Journal, 3*, 217-220.

Beck, A. T., Rush, A. J., Shaw, B. F., & Emery, G. (1979). *Cognitive therapy of depression*. New York: Guilford Press.

Camras, L. A., Chen, Y., Bakeman, R., Norris, K., & Cain, T. (2006). Culture, ethnicity, and children's facial expressions: A study of European American, Mainland Chinese, Chinese American, and adopted Chinese girls. *Emotion, 6*, 103-114.

Camras, L. A., Oster, H., Campos, J. J., & Bakeman, R. (2003). Emotional facial expressions in European-American, Japanese, and Chinese infants. In P. Ekman, J. J., Campos, R. J. Davidson & F. B. M. de Waal (Eds.), *Emotions inside out: 130 years after Darwin's The Expression of the Emotions in Man and Animals*. New York: New York Academy of Sciences.

Camras, L. A., Oster, H., Campos, J., Campos, R., Ujiie, T., Miyake, K., Lei, W., & Meng, Z. (1998). Production of emotional facial expressions in American, Japanese and Chinese infants. *Developmental Psychology, 34*, 616-628.

Chandler, M. J., & Lalonde., C. E. (1998). Cultural continuity as a hedge against suicide in Canada's First Nations. *Transcultural Psychiatry, 35*, 193-211.

Chandler, M. J., Lalonde, C. E., Sokol, B., & Hallett, D. (2003). *Personal persistence, identity development, and suicide: A study of native and non-native North American adolescents. Monographs of the Society for Research in Child Development, 68*, 2 (Serial No. 273).

Cheung, F. M. (1984). Preferences in help-seeking among Chinese students. *Culture, Medicine and Psychiatry, 8*, 371-380.

Cheng, F. M. (1989). The indigenization of neurasthenia in Hong Kong. *Culture, Medicine, and Psychiatry, 13*, 227-241.

Cheung, F. M. (1991). Health psychology in Chinese societies in Asia. In M. Jansen & J. Weinman (Eds.), *The international development of health psychology* (pp. 63-74). Reading, UK: Harwood Academic Press.

Cheung, F. M. (1995). Facts and myths about somatization among the Chinese. In T.-Y. Lin, W. S. Tseng, & E. K. Yeh (Eds.), *Chinese Societies and Mental Health* (pp. 156-180). Hong Kong: Oxford University Press.

Cheung, F. M., & Lau, B. W. K. (1982). Situational variations in help-seeking behavior among Chinese patients. *Comprehensive Psychiatry, 23*, 252-262.

Cheung, F. M., Lau, B. W. K., & Wong, S.-W. (1984). Paths to psychiatric care in Hong Kong. *Culture, Medicine and Psychiatry, 8*, 207-228.

Choi, I., & Nisbett, R. E. (1998). Situational salience and cultural differences in the correspondence bias and actor-observer bias. *Personality and Social Psychology Bulletin, 24*, 949-960.

Choi, I., Nisbett, R. E., & Smith, E. E. (1997). Culture, categorization and inductive reasoning. *Cognition, 65*, 15-32.

Cohen, D., & Gunz, A. (2002). As seen by the other: Perspectives on the self in the memories and emotional perceptions of Easterners and Westerners. *Psychological Science, 13*, 55-59.

Chua, H. F., Boland, J. E., & Nisbett, R. E. (2005). Cultural variation in eye movements during scene perception. *Proceedings of the National Academy of Sciences, 102*, 12629-12633.

Craig, T. K., & Boardman, A. P. (1990). *Somatization in primary care settings*. In C. M. Bass (Ed.), *Physical symptoms and psychological illness* (73-103). Oxford, UK: Blackwell Scientific Publications.

D'Andrade, R. G. (1995). *The development of cognitive anthropology*. Cambridge, UK: Cambridge University Press.

Dion, K. L. (1996). Ethnolinguistic correlates of alexithymia: Toward a cultural perspective. *Journal of Psychosomatic Research, 41*, 531-539.

Draguns, J. G. (1996). Abnormal behaviour in Chinese societies: Clinical, epidemiological, and comparative studies. In M. H. Bond (Ed.), *Handbook of Chinese Psychology* (pp. 412-428). Hong Kong: Oxford University Press.

Eid, M., & Diener, E. (2001). Norms for experiencing emotions in different cultures: Inter- and intranational differences. *Journal of Personality and Social Psychology, 81*, 869-885.

Ekman, P., & Friesen, W. V. (1986). A new pan-cultural facial expression of emotion. *Motivation and Emotion, 10*, 159-168.

Fabrega, H. (1982). Culture and psychiatric illness: Biomedical and ethnomedical aspects. In A. J. Marsella & G. M. White (Eds.), *Cultural conceptions of mental health and therapy* (pp. 3-38). Dordrecht, The Netherlands: Reidel.

Finkler, K. (1985). Symptomatic differences between the sexes in rural Mexico. *Culture, Medicine and Psychiatry, 9*, 27-57.

Gecas, V. (1982). The self-concept. *Annual Review* of *Sociology, 8, 1 33*.

Geertz, C. (1973). *The interpretation of cultures*. New York: Basic Books.

Geertz, C. (2000). *Available light: Philosophical reflections on anthropological topics*. Princeton, NJ: Princeton University Press.

Giosan, C., Glovsky, V., & Haslam, N. (2001). The lay concept of "mental disorder": A cross-cultural study. *Transcultural Psychiatry, 38*, 317-332.

Goffman, E. (1963). *Stigma*. Englewood Cliffs, NJ: Prentice-Hall.

Goldberg, D. P., & Bridges, K. (1988). Somatic presentations of psychiatric illness in primary care setting. *Journal of Psychosomatic Research, 32*, 137-144.

Gone, J. P. (2008). "So I can be like a Whiteman": The cultural psychology of space and place in American Indian mental health. *Culture & Psychology, 14*, 369-399.

Greenwald, A. G. (1980). The totalitarian ego: Fabrication and revision of personal history. *American Psychologist, 35,* 603-618.

Haslam, N. (2005). Dimensions of folk psychiatry. *Review of General Psychology, 9,* 35-47.

Haslam, N., Ban, L., & Kaufmann, L. (2007). Lay conceptions of mental disorder: The folk psychiatry model. *Australian Psychologist, 42,* 129-137.

Haslam, N., & Ernst, D. (2002). Essentialist beliefs about mental disorders. *Journal of Social and Clinical Psychology, 21,* 628-644.

Hedden, T., Park, D. C., Nisbett, R. E., Ji, L., Jing, Q., & Jiao, S. (2002). Cultural variation in verbal versus spatial neuropsychological function across the lifespan. *Neuropsychology, 16,* 65-73.

Heine, S. J., Lehman, D. R., Markus, H. R., & Kitayama, S. (1999). Is there a universal need for positive self-regard? *Psychological Review, 106,* 766-794.

Hofstede, G. (1980). Culture's consequences: International differences in work-related values. Beverly Hills, CA: Sage.

Hwu, H.-G., Yeh, E.-K., & Chang, L.-Y. (1989). Prevalence of psychiatric disorders in Taiwan defined by the Chinese Diagnostic Interview Schedule. *Acta Psychiatrica Scandinavica, 79,* 136-147.

Jenkins, J. H. (1994). Culture, emotion, and psychopathology. In S. Kitayama & H. R. Markus (Eds.), *Emotion and culture: Empirical studies of mutual influence* (pp. 307-335). Washington, DC: American Psychological Association.

Jenkins, J. H., Kleinman, A., & Good, B. (1991). Cross-cultural aspects of depression. In J. Becker & A. Kleinman (Eds.), *Advances in affective disorders: Theory and research. Vol. 1: Psychosocial aspects* (pp. 67-100). Hillsdale, NJ: Erlbaum.

Ji, L., Nisbett, R. E., & Su, Y. (2001). Culture, change and prediction. *Psychological Science, 12,* 450-456.

Ji, L., Peng, K., & Nisbett, R. E. (2000). Culture, control, and perception of relationships in the environment. *Journal of Personality and Social Psychology, 78,* 943-955.

Johnson, F. (1985). The Western concept of self. In A. Marsella, G. DeVos, & F. L. K. Hsu (Eds.), *Culture and self.* London: Tavistock.

Kaptchuk, T. J. (1983). *The web that has no weaver: Understanding Chinese medicine.* Chicago: Congdon & Weed.

Kendall, P. C., Hollon, S. D., Beck, A. T., Hammen, C. L., & Ingram, R. E. (1987). Issues and recommendations regarding use of the Beck Depression Inventory. *Cognitive Therapy and Research, 11,* 289-299.

Kim, N., & Ahn, W. (2002). Clinical psychologists theory-based representations of mental disorders predict their diagnostic reasoning and memory. *Journal of Experimental Psychology, 131*, 451-476.

Kirmayer, L. J. (1989) Cultural variations in the response to psychiatric disorders and emotional distress. *Social Science and Medicine, 29*, 327-339.

Kirmayer, L. J. (1994). Is the concept of mental disorder culturally relative? In S. A. Kirk & S. Einbinder (Eds.), *Controversial issues in mental health* (pp. 1-20). Boston, MA: Allyn and Bacon.

Kirmayer, L. J. (2001). Cultural variations in the clinical presentation of depression and anxiety: Implications for diagnosis and treatment. *Journal of Clinical Psychiatry, 62[suppl 13]*, 22-28.

Kirmayer, L. J. (2006). Beyond the 'new cross-cultural psychiatry': Cultural biology, discursive psychology and the ironies of globalization. *Transcultural Psychiatry, 43*, 126-144.

Kirmayer, L. J. (2007). Psychotherapy and the cultural concept of the person. *Transcultural Psychiatry, 44*, 232-257.

Kirmayer, L. J., Brass, G., & Tait, C. (2000). The mental health of Aboriginal peoples: Transformations of identity and community. *Canadian Journal of Psychiatry, 45*, 607-616.

Kirmayer, L. J., Fletcher, C., & Watt, R. (2009). Inuit ethnopsychology and the ecocentric self. In Kirmayer, L. J. & Valaskakis, G. G. (Eds.), *Healing Traditions: The Mental Health of Canadian Aboriginal Peoples*, Vancouver, BC: UBC Press.

Kitayama, S., Duffy, S., & Uchida, Y. (2006). Self as cultural mode of being. In S. Kitayama & D. Cohen (Eds.), *Handbook of Cultural Psychology* (pp. 136-174). New York: Guilford Press.

Kitayama, S., Markus, H. R., & Kurokawa, M. (2000). Culture, emotion, and well-being: Good feelings in Japan and the United States. *Cognition and Emotion, 14*, 93-124.

Kitayama, S., Mesquita, B., & Karasawa, M. (2006). Cultural affordances and emotional experience: Socially engaging and disengaging emotions in Japan and the United States. *Journal of Personality and Social Psychology, 91*, 890-903.

Kleinman, A. (1980). *Patients and healers in the context of culture: An exploration of the borderland between anthropology, medicine, and psychiatry*. Berkeley and Los Angeles: University of California Press.

Kleinman, A. (1982). Neurasthenia and depression: A study of somatization and culture in China. *Culture, Medicine, and Psychiatry, 6*, 117-190.

Kleinman, A. (1983). The cultural meanings and social uses of illness. A role for medical anthropology and clinically oriented social science in the development of primary care theory and research. *Journal of Family Practice, 16*, 539-545.

Kleinman, A. (1986). *Social origins of disease and distress: Depression, neurasthenia, and pain in modern China.* New Haven, CT: Yale University Press.

Kleinman, A. (1988). *Rethinking psychiatry: From cultural category to personal experience.* New York: The Free Press.

Kleinman, A. (1995). *Writing at the margin: Discourse between anthropology and medicine.* Berkeley, CA: University of California Press.

Kroeber, A., & Kluckhohn, C. (1952). *Culture.* New York: Meridian Books.

Lecrubier, Y. (1998). Prescribing patterns for depression and anxiety worldwide. *Journal of Clinical Psychiatry, 62(suppl.13)*, 31-36.

Lee, S. (1996). Cultures in psychiatric nosology: The CCMD-2-R and International Classification of Mental Disorders. *Culture, Medicine, and Psychiatry, 20*, 421-472.

Lee, S. (1999). Diagnosis postponed: Shenjing Shuairuo and the transformation of psychiatry in post-Mao China. *Culture, Medicine, and Psychiatry, 23*, 349-380.

Lépine, J.-P. (2001). Epidemiology, burden, and disability in depression and anxiety. *Journal of Clinical Psychiatry, 62(suppl.13)*, 4-10

Levy, R. I. (1983). Introduction: Self and emotion. *Ethos, 11*, 128-134.

Lilienfeld, S., & Marino, L. (1995). Mental disorder as a Roschian concept: A critique of Wakefield's "Harmful Dysfunction" Analysis. *Journal of Abnormal Psychology, 104*, 411-420.

Lin, N. (1989). Measuring depressive symptomatology in China. *Journal of Nervous and Mental Disease, 177*, 121-131.

Lin, T.-Y., Tardiff, K., Donetz, G., & Goresky, W. (1978). Ethnicity and patterns of help-seeking. *Culture, Medicine and Psychiatry, 2*, 3-13.

Lin, T.-Y., & Lin, M. C. (1981) Love, denial and rejection: Responses of Chinese families to mental illness. In A. Kleinman & T.-Y. Lin (Eds.), *Normal and abnormal behavior in Chinese culture* (pp. 387-401). Boston, MA: D. Reidel.

Liu, Z. H., Yang, Q., Huang, M. S., Xiang, M. Z., Xu, M. D., Zhang, Y. H., Du, Y. Y., Hu, G. C., & Ye, L. (1992). Clinical research on neurosis – a summary report. In *Clinical Research on Neurosis* (pp. 3-4). Sichuan, China: Department of Psychiatry, West China University of Medical Sciences [in Chinese].

López, S. R., & Guarnaccia, P. J. (2000). Cultural psychopathology: Uncovering the social world of mental illness. *Annual Review of Psychology, 51*, 571-598.

Lutz, C. (1985). Depression and the translation of emotional worlds. In A. Kleinman & B. Good (Eds.), *Culture and depression* (pp. 63-100). Berkeley: University of California Press.

Lutz, C. (1988). *Unnatural emotions: Everyday sentiments on a Micronesian atoll and their challenge to Western theory.* Chicago: University of Chicago Press.

Markman, A. B., & Ross, B. H. (2003). Category use and category learning. *Psychological Bulletin, 129,* 592-615.

Markus, H. R. (1977). Self-schemata and processing information about the self. *Journal of Personality and Social Psychology, 35,* 63-78.

Markus, H. R., & Hamedani, M. G. (2006). Sociocultural psychology: The dynamic interdependence among self systems and social systems. In S. Kitayama & D. Cohen (Eds.), *Handbook of Cultural Psychology* (pp. 3–39). New York: Guilford Press.

Markus, H. R., & Kitayama, S. (1991a). Culture and the self: Implications for cognition, emotion, and motivation. *Psychological Review, 98,* 224-253.

Markus, H. R., & Kitayama, S. (1991b). Cultural variation in the self-concept. In G. R. Goethals & J. Strauss (Eds.), *Multidisciplinary perspectives on the self.* New York: Springer-Verlag.

Markus, H. R., & Kitayama, S. (1994). The cultural construction of self and emotion: Implications for social behavior. In S. Kitayama & H. R. Markus (Eds.), *Emotion and culture: Empirical studies of mutual influence* (pp. 89-130). Washington, DC: American Psychological Association.

Markus, H. R., & Wurf, E. (1987). The dynamic self-concept: A social psychological perspective. *Annual Review of Psychology, 38,* 299–337.

Marsella, A. J., Kinzie, D., & Gordon, P. (1973). Ethnic variations in the expression of depression. *Journal of Cross-Cultural Psychology, 4,* 435-458.

Marsella, A. J. (1985). Culture, self, and mental disorder. In A. J. Marsella, G. DeVos, & F. Hsu (Eds.) *Culture and self: Asian and Western perspectives* (pp. 281-308). London: Tavistock Press

Masuda, T., & Nisbett, R. E., (2001). Attending holistically versus analytically: Comparing the context sensitivity of Japanese and Americans. *Journal of Personality and Social Psychology, 81,* 922-934.

Matsumoto, D., Takeuchi, S., Andayani, S., Kouznetsova, N., & Krupp, D. (1998). The contribution of individualism vs. collectivism to cross-national differences in display rules. *Asian Journal of Social Psychology, 1,* 147-165.

Matsumoto, D., Yoo, S. H., Hirayama, S., & Petrova, G. (2005). Development and validation of a measure of display rule knowledge: The Display Rule Assessment Inventory. *Emotion, 5,* 23-40.

Matsumoto, D., Kasri, F., & Kooken, K. (1999). American-Japanese cultural differences in judgments of expression intensity and subjective experience. *Cognition and Emotion, 13,* 201-218.

Medin, D. L. (1989). Concepts and conceptual structure. *American Psychologist, 44,* 1469-1481.

Mesquita, B., & Karasawa, M. (2002). Different emotional lives. *Cognition & Emotion, 16,* 127-141.

Miller, J. G. (1988). Bridging the content-structure dichotomy: Culture and the self. In M. H. Bond (Ed.), *The cross-cultural challenge to social psychology* (pp. 266-281). Beverly Hills, CA: Sage.

Morris, M. W., & Peng, K. (1994). Culture and cause: American and Chinese attributions for social and physical events. *Journal of Personality and Social Psychology, 67,* 949-971.

Moscovici, S. (1984). The phenomena of social representation. In R. M. Farr & S. Moscovici (Eds.), *Social representation* (pp. 3-69). Cambridge, UK: Cambridge University Press.

Nesse, R. M. (2000). Is depression an adaptation? *Archives of General Psychiatry, 57,* 14-20.

Norenzayan, A., Smith, E. E., Kim, B. J., & Nisbett, R. E., (2002). Cultural preferences for formal versus intuitive reasoning. *Cognitive Science, 26,* 653-684.

Oishi, S. (2002). The experiencing and remembering of well-being: A cross-cultural analysis. *Personality and Social Psychology Bulletin, 28,* 1398-1406.

Parker, G., Cheah, Y. C., & Roy, K. (2001). Do the Chinese somatize depression? A cross-cultural study. *Social Psychiatry and Psychiatric Epidemiology, 36,* 287-293.

Parker, G., Gladstone, G., & Chee, K. T. (2001). Depression in the planet's largest ethnic group: The Chinese. *American Journal of Psychiatry, 158,* 857-864.

Parker, J. D. A., Taylor, G. J., & Bagby, R. M. (2001). The relationship between emotional intelligence and alexithymia. *Personality and Individual Differences, 30,* 107-115.

Peng, K., & Nisbett, R. E. (1999). Culture, dialecticism, and reasoning about contradiction. *American Psychologist, 54,* 741-754.

Pennebaker, J. W., & Brittingham, G. L. (1982). Environmental and sensory cues affecting the perception of physical symptoms. In A. Baum & J. Singer (Eds.), *Advances in environmental psychology, Volume 4* (pp. 115-136). Hillsdale, NJ: Erlbaum.

Pennebaker, J. W, & Watson, D. (1988). Blood pressure estimation and beliefs among normotensives and hypertensives. *Health Psychology, 7,* 309-328.

Ritsher, J. E. B., Otilingam, P. G., & Grajales, M. (2003). Internalized stigma of mental illness: Psychometric properties of a new measure. *Psychiatry Research, 121*, 31-49.

Ritsher, J. E. B., Ryder, A. G., Karasz, A., & Castille, D. (2002). Programmatic integration of qualitative and quantitative methods in the cross-cultural study of psychopathology. In P. Boski, F. J. R. van de Vijver, & A. M. Chodynicka (Eds.), *New Directions in Cross-Cultural Psychology*. Warsaw, PO: PAN.

Ryder, A. G., Bean, G., & Dion, K. L. (2000). Caregiver responses to symptoms of first-onset psychosis: A comparative study of Chinese- and Euro-Canadian families. *Transcultural Psychiatry, 37*, 225-236.

Ryder, A. G., Dere, J., Zhu, X., Yao, S., & Thombs, B. (2008). *Unpacking "psychologization": Feeling depressed versus thinking depressed in China and Canada*. Paper presented at the 19th annual meeting of the International Association for Cross-Cultural Psychology, Bremen, Germany.

Ryder, A. G., Yang, J., & Heine, S. J. (2002). Somatization vs. psychologization of emotional distress: A paradigmatic example for cultural psychopathology. In W. J. Lonner, D. L. Dinnel, S. A. Hayes, & D. N. Sattler (Eds.), *Online readings in psychology and culture* (unit 9, chap. 3). Western Washington University: Center for Cross-Cultural Research. Retrieved May 3, 2009, from www.wwu.edu/~culture.

Ryder, A. G., Yang, J., Zhu, X., Yao, S., Yi, J., Heine, S. J., & Bagby, R. M. (2008). The cultural shaping of depression: Somatic symptoms in China, psychological symptoms in North America? *Journal of Abnormal Psychology, 117*, 300-313.

Sayar, K., Kirmayer, L. J., & Taillefer, S. S. (2003). Predictors of somatic symptoms in depressive disorder. *General Hospital Psychiatry, 25*, 108-114.

Schuster, D. G. (2003). Neurasthenia and a modernizing America. *Journal of the American Medical Association, 290*, 2327-2328.

Shixie, L. (1989). Neurasthenia in China: Modern and traditional criteria for its diagnosis. *Culture, Medicine, and Psychiatry, 13*, 163-186.

Shon, S. P., & Ja, D. Y. (1982). Asian families. In M. McGoldrick, J. K. Pearce, & J. Giordano (Eds.), *Ethnicity and family therapy* (pp. 208-228). New York: Guilford Press.

Shweder, R. A. (Ed.). (1991). *Thinking through cultures: Expeditions in cultural psychology*. Cambridge, MA: Harvard University Press.

Shweder, R. A. (1995). The confessions of a methodological individualist. *Culture and Psychology, 1*, 115-122.

Shweder, R. A. (2003). *Why Do Men Barbecue? Recipes for Cultural Psychology*. Cambridge, MA: Harvard University Press.

Shweder, R. A., & Haidt, J. (2000) Cultural psychology of the emotions: Ancient and new. M. Lewis & J. Haviland (Eds.), *The Handbook of Emotions*. New York: Guilford Press.

Shweder, R., Much, N., Mahapatra, M., & Park, L. (1997). The "Big Three" of morality (Autonomy, Community, Divinity), and the "Big Three" explanations of suffering. In P. Rozin & A. Brandt (Eds.), *Morality and health* (pp. 574-586). New York: Routledge

Simon, G. E. (1991). Somatization and psychiatric disorders. In L. J. Kirmayer & J. M. Robbins (Eds.), *Current concepts of somatization: Research and clinical perspectives* (pp. 37-62). Washington, DC: American Psychiatric Press.

Simon, G. E., VonKorff, M., Piccinelli, M., Fullerton, C., & Ormel, J. (1999). An international study of the relation between somatic symptoms and depression. *New England Journal of Medicine, 341*, 1329-1335.

Singer, K. (1975). Depression disorders from a transcultural perspective. *Social Science and Medicine, 9*, 289-301.

Stipek, D. (1998). Differences between Americans and Chinese in the circumstances evoking pride, shame, and guilt. *Journal of Cross-Cultural Psychology, 29*, 616-629.

Sue, S. (1992). Ethnicity and mental health: Research and policy issues. *The Journal of Social Issues, 48*, 187-205.

Tanaka-Matsumi, J., & Draguns, J. G. (1997). Culture and psychopathology. In J. W. Berry, M. H. Segall, & C. Kagitçibasi (Eds.). *Handbook of Cross-Cultural Psychology, Volume 3: Social Behavior and Applications* (pp. 449-491). Needham Heights, MA: Allyn & Bacon.

Tesser, A., & Campbell, J. (1983). Self-definition and self-evaluation maintenance. In J. Suls & A. Greenwald (Eds.), *Social psychological perspectives on the self* (pp. 1-31). Hillsdale, NJ: Erlbaum.

Triandis, H. (1989). The self and social behavior in differing cultural contexts, *Psychological Review, 96*, 506-520.

Tsai, J. L., Chentsova-Dutton, Y., Freire-Bebeau, L., & Przymus, D. E. (2002). Emotional expression and physiology in European Americans and Hmong Americans. *Emotion, 2*, 380-397.

Tsai, J. L., Levenson, R. W., & McCoy, K. (2006). Cultural and temperamental variation in emotional response. *Emotion, 6*, 484-497.

Waller, M. (2001). Resilience in ecosystemic context: Evolution of the concept. *Journal of Orthopsychiatry, 71*, 290-297.

Wang, Q. (2001). "Did you have fun?" American and Chinese mother-child conversations about shared emotional experiences. *Cognitive Development, 16*, 693-715.

Wang, Q. (2003). Emotion situation knowledge in American and Chinese preschool children and adults. *Cognition and Emotion, 17*, 725-746.

Wang, Q. (2004). The emergence of cultural self-constructs: Autobiographical memory and self-description in European American and Chinese children. *Developmental Psychology, 40*, 3-15.

Wang, Q., & Fivush, R. (2005). Mother-child conversations of emotionally salient events: Exploring the functions of emotional reminiscing in European-American and Chinese families. *Social Development, 14*, 473-495.

Weissman, M. M., Bland, R. C., Canino, G. J., Faravelli, C., Greenwald, S., Hwu, H.-G., Joyuce, P. R., Karam, E. G., Lee, C.-K., Lellouch, J., Lépine, J.-P., Newman, S. C., Rubio-Stipec, M., Wells, E., Wickramaratne, P. J., Wittchen, H.-U., & Yeh, E.-K. (1996). Cross-national epidemiology of major depression and bipolar disorder. *Journal of the American Medical Association, 276*, 293-299.

Wu, D. Y. H. (1982). Psychotherapy and emotion in Traditional Chinese Medicine. In A. J. Marsella & G. M. White (Eds.), *Cultural conceptions of mental health and therapy* (pp. 1-38). Dordrecht, The Netherlands: Reidel.

Xu, S.-H., Gao, Z.-X., & Xu, B.-X. (1993). The application of the diagnostic criteria of the Chinese Classification of Mental Disorders. *Chinese Journal of Nervous and Mental Diseases, 19*, 59-60 [in Chinese].

Yan, H.-Q. (1989). The necessity of retaining the diagnostic concept of neurasthenia. *Culture, medicine, and psychiatry, 13*, 139-145.

Yen, S., Robins, C. J., & Lin, N. (2000). A cross-cultural comparison of depressive symptom manifestation: China and the United States. *Journal of Consulting and Clinical Psychology, 68*, 993-999.

Yuki, M., Maddux, W. W., & Masuda, T. (2007). Are the windows to the soul the same in the East and West? Cultural differences in using the eyes and mouth as cues to recognize emotions in Japan and the United States. *Journal of Experimental Social Psychology, 43*, 303-311.

Zhang, W. X., Shen, Y. C., & Li, S. R. (1998). Epidemiological investigation of mental disorders in 7 areas of China [in Chinese]. *Chinese Journal of Psychiatry, 31*, 69-71.

Zhi-Zhong, L. (1984). Traditional Chinese concepts of mental health. *Journal of the American Medical Association, 252*, 22.

Beatriz Macías Gómez-Stern
Olga A. Vásquez

Identity construction in narratives of migration

Introduction

Migration is a life changing experience in which immigrants remake their lives and identities as a result of their relocation. In recounting these experiences, individuals relive the emotional toll of displacement from their families and cultural roots, and the pain of not attaining the impetus of their migration, which in many cases, when talking of migration in the United States, is living "the American Dream." In telling their stories, immigrants recount the cultural shift that begins to take place in their lives as they negotiate entreé into the host society. This was the case for a small group of Mexican immigrants attending an adult computer literacy programme called *La Gran Dimension* (The Great Dimension, LGD), a component of a broader project called *La Clase Mágica* (The Magical Class, LCM) directed by the second author, Vásquez (Vásquez, 2002). From the first session, the self-narratives that emerged in the development of activities of a small group of around four women and two men were elaborately detailed and punctuated with emotion. These stories signalled the significance of narratives of migration in shaping the identities and lives of these participants, as well as the great potential they might have as an educative tool in adult education classes (Birren & Birren, 1996; Birren & Deutchman, 1991; Freire, 1970; Ramírez, 1995).

In this chapter we analyse some of the narratives of migration that emerged from different activities that we developed in the adult computer training group mentioned above. These narratives were elicited as tools for including culturally and personally relevant material in the class curriculum (Freire, 1970; Ramírez, 1995). We are interested in both the educational value of autobiographical stories in adult education settings such as *La Gran Dimension* and the analysis of the role that these stories play in identity formation. For the purposes of this chapter, we will focus on the second goal.

Narratives have been extensively referred to as privileged tools for the construction of identities (Bamberg, 2003). A number of studies have demonstrated the fundamental role narratives play as tools for the development of coherence and sense making in people's autobiographies and, therefore, in their identities (Brockmeier & Carbaugh, 2001; De Fina, Shiffrin & Bamberg, 2006; Linde, 1993; Redman, 2005; Smith, 2007). This approach gains special relevance in circumstances of traumatic changes in the course of everyday life (McAdams, 2006; Thomsen & Jensen, 2007) in which narratives serve as a necessary tool for the construction of a link between the former circumstances and those that result from a deep rupture. According to Crossley (2003) *"stories are particularly important when we are faced with unexpected events"* (p. 290).

Some recent studies have pointed to migration as a critical breakdown in people's lives that influences the re-construction of their personal autobiographies and identities (De Fina 2003a, 2003b, 2006; Kraus, 2006; Schrauf & Rubin, 2001; Syed & Azmitia, 2008). In these cases, narratives play a critical role in establishing fluency and coherence between the past life and the new circumstances. The individual-centred narratives of migration performed by a group of Mexican migrant participants at *La Gran Dimensión* were voluntarily generated and their content was incorporated into the instructional activities as intellectual tools—i.e., as referents and linkages between old and new knowledge (Birren & Deutchman, 1991; Birren; 1996; Clark, 2001; Dominicé, 2000; Sealey-Ruiz, 2007). Following the philosophical principles of *La Clase Mágica* we found these personal narratives were important means to incorporate the participants' previous background into the curricula both to foster learning and to validate their background experiences (Vásquez, 2002).

Narrative as a privileged tool in the construction of identity

Our conception of identity and of self-construction is based on a socio-cultural approach to the study of mind. This approach is supported by the notion of the social origins of individual higher psychological processes and the mediated nature of these processes (Vygotsky, 1987; Wertsch, 1985, 1991, 1998). Social interactions, from this perspective, are mediated by material and symbolic tools, such as computer technology and language, that embody a specific view of the world and one's role in it. In this chapter, we extend these assumptions to the study of cultural identity, a socio-culturally constructed process, mediated by cultural tools such as narratives and other means of argumentation.

A widely accepted way of concretising this situated and socially constructed idea of self is to conceive it as an action. Identity construction is used in social settings to accomplish social actions (Bamberg, 2003). We understand identity construction as an action that aims to define or characterise oneself, and often in relation to different groups of belonging (family, cultural group, gender, etc.).

Scholars such as Sarbin (1986) and Bruner (1986) propose that humans think, perceive the world, socially interact, and construct their morality based on narrative structures garnered from social interactions with members of the group. As a result, narratives are largely considered to be a privileged tool in the construction of personal and cultural identity in different disciplines (Bruner, 1986, 2004; Gergen, 1988; Linde, 1993; McAdams, 1999; 2006; Sarbin, 1986). Narratives are also "ubiquitous" instruments, because, as many scholars have found, they are employed to explain, justify, describe or interpret human actions in different moments of life, from early childhood onwards, and across different socio-cultural contexts (Bruner, 1986; Capps & Bonanno, 2000).

There is a common consensus that the defining characteristic of prototypical narratives is temporality or sequentiality (Bruner, 1986; De Fina, 2003a; Georgakopoulou, 2006; McAdams, 2001). It is through their sequential ordering of events that narratives obtain their power as interpretative and sense-making devices (Brockmeier, 2000). Labov's (1997) model of narrative structure distinguishes two main functions: the referential and the evaluative functions. The referential function relates to the ability to match temporal sequences, while the evaluative function refers to the attitude or evaluation of the narrator (either implicit or explicit) towards the narrative as a whole and the narrated "facts" in particular.

Placing stress on the evaluative function of narrative is not new in discourse analysis. In fact, the sociolinguistic and discourse-analytic definitions of narrative – as a discourse category involving an evaluation of characters and events – have been related to argumentation (Bamberg, 2003; Ochs & Capps, 2001). This idea of narrative as an argumentative mechanism links it more closely with the social contexts in which it is used, since the normative constructions of what is a tellable or good story can differ across cultural settings (Crossley, 2003; Smith, 2007; Thorne, 2004).

From a psychological perspective, Bruner (1986) conceives narrative both as a discourse mode (a way of speaking about experience) and as a way of organising experience (a way of thinking). According to this author, narratives start with an initial canonical state that has been breached in some way, recount means-ends actions by an agent attempting to restore it and end up with an implied assessment of the outcome. The story as a whole has a meaning or "gist". The comprehensibility of a narrative relies upon its mimicry of what the listener, reader or hearer accepts as possible in life. Narratives, thus, provide an interpretation of events, rather than an explanation (Bruner, 2004).

In summary, by structuring acts in sequences, exploring characters' intentions and explicitly or implicitly evaluating facts, stories help to organise the chaos of experience in a more or less sensible and coherent way. This integrative power of narratives is evident both in cultural and personal stories (Dien, 2000; Linde, 1993; Nelson, 2000; Nelson & Fivush, 2004; Schrauf, 2000; Wertsch, 2002).

Traumatic changes in people's lives are often situations in which the "expected", the normative course of actions is, in some way, compromised or disrupted. Narratives, in these cases, assume the role of making sense of the unexpected situation. As mentioned earlier, migration has been referred to in different studies as an experience that produces a turning point in people's lives that strongly influences people's identities (Bhatia & Ram, 2001; De Fina, 2003a, 2003b; Fortier, 2000; König, 2009; Shrauf & Rubin, 2001). The experience of migration implies a change in the migrants' socio-cultural context and the roles they play in their daily life. The criteria one applies to evaluate one's own personal actions changes, in addition to "the other's" gaze and, thus, it can be expected that, in some way, the foundations of the previous self-image, and especially the part of that image that is related to the cultural group of belonging, also change. In the migration experience, the person faces a different world of meanings which can produce the breaking of the expected scripts in the course of actions. This can be seen as the first condition for the emergence of narratives that aim to make sense of the new situations encountered.

Finding the self in an adult computer class

The narratives of migration performed by a group of Mexican women participating in a culturally sensitive adult computer class reveals these shifts in the construction of identity and the life they now live. Below, we describe the context in which these narratives were generated and the meanings they embody.

La Gran Dimensión at Orange Place

La Gran Dimensión (LGD) is one of the 5 developmentally designed components of a broader project called *La Clase Mágica* (LCM). The aim of LCM is to create innovative bilingual educative settings for children and adults in 4 Mexican-origin communities in and around the San Diego area using computer technology.

La Clase Mágica (LCM) targets five developmental age groups, ranging from pre-school to adulthood. Bilingualism and biculturalism form the social and intellectual foundation of all adult-child interactions and curriculum materials strategically link to the learners' prior history (Vásquez, 2002; Zentella, 1997). The program is institutionally linked to an undergraduate course offered by the Communication Department and Human Development Program at the University of San Diego, California. The students taking the course collaborate with the child participants as mentors (called *"amigos"*) in all of the LCM sites and age groups.

LGD was created to attend to the needs of LCM parents who wanted to benefit from the educational resources that their children were enjoying in the project. It was implemented at the request of the parents. In the fall of 2008, the first author of this chapter initiated the adult programme, as part of the LCM system, in the recreation room of a housing project in the city of Escondido in Southern California following the format of an earlier adult computer class which she had founded at another Mexican origin community in San Diego, 8 years earlier. At the time, LGD had already been implemented in other communities in different settings: schools, after-school clubs and recreation centres. The data presented in this chapter were collected in the community centre of a low-income housing project situated in the city of Escondido.

Escondido is a racially mixed mid-size city with 49% of the population White, 42% of Mexican origin and the rest Asian, Native American or mixed-race. At the time, many of its schools had been classified "Warning Status" under the No Child Left Behind Act, a federal law – i.e., under threat of school seizure by federal decree if scores were not raised.

La Gran Dimensión at Escondido was open to the whole adult community but typically drew in Mexican women living in the surrounding apartments. In such a community of learners as LGD, previous knowledge and experience play a special role in the learning process (Gibb, 2008; Merriam, Caffarella & Baumgartner, 2007; Mezirow, 1990,

1997; Relaño & Macías, 2003; Stein & Imel, 2002; Wilson, 1999). At LGD, the knowledge and experience garnered from the narratives produced by the participants was used to make the activities culturally relevant and personally meaningful.

Procedure

In the Fall Quarter of 2008 the first author of this paper organised, taught and studied the adult computer class in the after-hours of a very successful *La Clase Mágica* programme. At the time, the LCM site had been in operation for 7 years serving elementary school-aged children from the housing project. The programme was carried out as a participatory research action that builds on and counts upon the direct participation of the communities being studied through a dynamic research process (Burns, 2007). The aim of the present study was to elicit autobiographical narratives related to the migratory experience of participants and use these narratives as resources to generate a personally and culturally sensitive series of instructional activities. These narratives were also analysed for information regarding the authors' experiences and identities.

Ethnographic data was collected during the LGD sessions during the Fall 2008 academic quarter by two site coordinators running the programme (the first author and a staff member of the housing project). The author and the person in charge of the social activities at the Community Centre worked closely on recruiting the participants and developing an instructional curriculum that respected the site's already developed tradition of flexibility and cultural relevance in the Escondido community. The number of adults attending the programme varied across sessions, with an average of five participants throughout the quarter. However, four women were regular participants across the 10-week session.

The curriculum was designed to focus on the adults' previous knowledge and cultural background during all the activities in order to facilitate the development of computer skills which would be useful and meaningful for the participants in their everyday lives, such as using the internet to contact their families in Mexico or searching for job opportunities. Computer skills were learned through word processing

CONCEPTUAL AND APPLIED APPROACHES

programs, internet navigation, and emailing. On many occasions computer activities were also combined with group activities involving debates that exposed personal and cultural knowledge; these were later written down using computer facilities and shared among the group. Group sharing, writing, and internet posting of traditional Mexican recipes were examples of activities that built on previous experiences to teach computer skills. During these activities the group focused on writing recipes on the computer and sending them to each other.

The narratives collected during one of the first activities served as the first formative action to establish mutual knowledge between the participants in the programme, UCSD students or "amigos" and the instructors. The participants were asked to describe themselves and to narrate the story of their lives. This action served as a departure point for the programme. The activity had two main goals: to provide a "font of information" to enable the instructor to include the participants' background in the instructional activities, and to serve as an "evaluative mechanism" to establish a baseline of the participant's expressive and computer skills (Ramírez, 1995).

The session was structured in two parts. In the first part, all participants (including instructors and UCSD students) were paired off. These pairs talked to each other about themselves. An "interview script" provided by the instructor reinforced the conversations in which the partners took turns pretending to be a journalist interviewing a famous person. The script was written in Spanish and English using "code-switching" common in the everyday communicative interchanges of the U.S. Latino community (Lipski, 1985; Torres, 1992; Zentella, 1997). The script included suggestions for interview questions regarding their life stories, a question about their expectations for the course (both in relation to computer literacy and to any other aspect they wanted to learn) and their preferred leisure time activities and motivations.

In the second part of the session the participants sat in a circle for a group activity designed to introduce each person to the group. Each participant had to describe his/her partner briefly according to what she/he had said during the first part of the session. In this way, everyone in the group could hear everyone's stories.

Spanish was used by all participants with the exception of a UCSD student who was a monolingual English speaker. This individual helped others with the technical aspects of using the computer and the internet.

Eight adults (two men) participated in the activity described. Participants were all Mexican residents of the community housing where the LGD programme was taking place. All participants had a migration background and worked in the service sector including low-paying jobs in restaurants, house and childcare, retail, etc. Their level of education was variable but most of them had only elementary school education. All sessions were video recorded, and afterwards transcribed and analysed. According to the participants, in the initial stages of the programme they were reluctant to speak up and tell the truth about their life stories because of the camera. As the course advanced, they began to feel more comfortable with the presence of the camera and the instructor. The narratives described in this chapter come from one of the first activities organised, where it was obvious that they did not express themselves with complete freedom. However, the fact that they shared their experiences with the instructor shows a high motivation to collaborate and express themselves, even though some of the events narrated constituted illegal actions vis-à-vis U.S. immigration laws, such as undocumented Mexico-US border crossings. This showed a level of trust in the instructor, who was also a foreign visitor.

The expression of self

In this section we analyse the contents and structure of a narrative that is typical of the narratives garnered from these activities. We want to highlight thematic and structural features in relation to the function that these narratives perform in naturally occurring social settings. Despite the fact that the narratives were elicited in a specially-designed activity, our impression is that these narratives resemble those that are performed in everyday contexts during which identity positions are enacted and constructed interactionally.

Eight narratives were collected from the "interview" activity described above. They were all autobiographical narratives where the person told a story of their life. The length of the narratives varied from approximately 300 to 600 words, but their structure and thematic contents were very similar. We illustrate these common characteristics using two prototypical examples.

Narrative 1 (English) [1,2]

Lupe: "Ok, my name is Arsinoe Perez, but here they call me Lupe. I came here 22 years ago, I am from Oaxaca State, in Mexico. I have been working here for 22 years. I started working when I was 13 years old, in a wood sawmill, working in the kitchen, when I was very young. There were 15 girls working in the kitchen. I was there working for 10 years, and from there, I went to Tijuana with a friend. And from there, with someone I knew, I came work to San Diego. I crossed the border close to the line, walking. The first time it was very easy, it was like a walk of 15 minutes, because there was no so much patrol, but other times it was much more difficult. I have had to go back many times, when my mom was sick, and I have always crossed the border without documents. It's very hard, to leave without knowing if you will be able to return (her eyes tear up). When my mom was sick, I left everything and I went to see her, always in clandestinely (a short silence, and she recovers). Here in San Diego I met my husband, after spending two years as a single woman. I have three kids, of 18, 15 and 3 years old... almost 4. I have a 18 years old son, he is called Manuel, Manuel Jesús Albino. And ...he went to Arizona, and I always feel very sad without him. He also feels very sad for me... because ... he is far away. And we miss each other very much. Because, always ... always ... I have never given a preference to any of my kids, but, I do not know, there is something that attracts me in the way of being. And I feel ... my hearts feels very bad when there is something that he does ... I feel very bad. I don't feel like that with any other of my daughters, but he is something ... something special."

Beatriz: "Is he the only male?"
Lupe: "Yes, the only one ... and ... we miss each other very much. And he is all I have. I have two female daugh-

ters. The girl with 15 years old and the little one with 3 years old."

Beatriz: "And what do you like doing?"

Lupe: "I like cooking, preparing different foods. I like to make invents."

Beatriz: "Food?"

Lupe: "Invents."

María: "Food invents (she laughs), many recipes."

Lupe: "Many recipes ... and many other things. I would like to learn computering, more about the computer ... and I´d like to learn English ... Here in the community I am learning many useful things, to keep on fighting ... About what I like ... what I like doing ... I like to stay busy, cook, clean, give ideas, read interesting things, and to dance "grupera" music. And also romantic music."

Narrative 2 (English)

Alba: "Ah ... I interviewed Margarita. She was born in Mexico, Nayarit. She came ... and her husband came here to USA, and she ... I think you were there for two years, weren't you? (asking Margarita)."

(Margarita nods) Alba: "She was there in Nayarí for two years and she came to USA because she missed her husband" (she smiles at Margarita, who smiles back). "And ... now she is working once a week ... and one of the questions was if she likes living here, and she says that she does not like living here because there is no so much "live". She likes more Nayarit because there are many parties, a lot of culture" (smiles).

Alba: "Ah ... question number two, what she likes doing. She likes cooking, pozole and tamales, steamed. She likes dancing rancheras ... the music that ... that ... sounds in the heart?" (she looks at Margarita, they all laugh).

Alba: "One thing that she wants to learn is how to use computers. How to look for jobs and English. That's what I learned from Margarita."

Thematic characteristics of narratives of migration

The thematic analysis of these narratives revealed several key characteristics:

- The topics typically relate to migration movements and achievements.
- They intertwine personal and cultural identification factors, sometimes tracing parallels between their personal and social past and stories.
- They emphasised actual desires, activities and future goals rather than homeland nostalgia.
- Accounts of the migration movement scene and the difficulties of going back to their homeland (Mexico) typically elicited emotional response.

These excerpts illustrate common characteristics of the narratives that emerged during many of the LGD activities. For the most part, they include a segment on their homeland and related topics presented in a rather nostalgic way (as in Margarita's story). However, we found that rather than recreate the hopes and dreams about their homeland, (Macías, 2002; Macías, García & Sánchez, 2008; Macías & de la Mata, 2013) these narratives of migration focused primarily on the present time and future. They centred on what they want to achieve as migrants and how to acquire the tools to reach that position. We suggest the difference in relation to our previous studies with Andalusian (Southern Spain) migrants has to do with the fact that the two samples represent different generations and cultural groups. Most of the participants in this study were young and middle-aged women who were still active in the labour market, and had the desire to progress up the social and economic ladder. In our previous studies the average age of the target group was much higher (Macías, 2002; Macías, et al., 2008; Macías & de la Mata, 2013). Many of the participants were retired and had already reached the limit of their social and professional possibilities. We also suspect that collecting the narratives within a computer class setting, as opposed to the previous study in which they were collected in informal settings, creates a micro-social context in which the skills necessary to succeed are very present in the conversations. In terms of activity theory (Leont'ev, 1981) the migrant participants in our previous studies (Macías, 2002; Macías, et al., 2008) interpreted the situation and setting as an occasion for sharing experiences with other migrants in an informal context, displaying a very nostalgic and roots-related identity. In our present study, the setting was a non-formal educative context, where learning activities and goals were privileged (Wertsch, 1991). The focus on goals and achievements, more than recreating a missed past community, may have been influenced by the specific technology learning context. In this sense, the difference in the two research settings, as well as the difference in how the participants interpreted those settings (Wertsch, 1991), could have contributed to the differences in the narratives from the two contexts. At the institutional level, the technological orientation of the social context of Southern California could also explain these results. The participants' discourse reflected an adoption of the discourse of the "American dream", at least partially, which serves as an impetus to pursue the goals that brought them to that country.

In relation to the contents of the narratives, and in comparison to our previous findings, we did not find such constant reference to homeland landscape, food preparation and social environment in the San Diego participants' narratives as we did in Andalusian participants' ones. We inferred that this difference was due to the fact that landscape- and food-related aspects of Mexican identity are to some extent present in Southern California, especially in cities like Escondido, where the Mexican community is numerous. In Escondido one can easily find Mexican restaurants and social settings where Spanish is predominantly spoken. Nostalgia, usually nourished by the absence of such features (Bellelli & Amatulli, 1997), may be less prominent in an area such as California where these elements of Mexican cultural expression are still present.

Related to the findings above is the appearance of emotional responses, although these emerge less frequently within narratives about the homeland. They often appear within the narratives about the difficulties that immigrants suffered in crossing the border and in achieving their personal and migratory goals. The toughness of that moment seems to have made its associated meanings manifest as a prevalent feature of the migrants' life stories.

Another observed feature of the narratives of migration displayed by the participants is how they manage the connection between their cultural and personal past. This can be interpreted as a way of maintaining their ties with the hometown. The personal history of migration interweaves with the group's history and traditions, as evident in local feasts and traditional dances. We emphasise this tendency because the question that triggered the narratives was not to tell the listener about their cultural roots or home-town. However, the story of their migration movement was enriched with some home traditions and cultural details. Personal and cultural traits of identity are continuously interwoven in the personal narratives.

Structure of the narratives of migration

Overall, migrants in our study performed different collectively constructed narratives, and we were able to identify the following sequential structure in the narratives:

1 *Initial setting*. As shown in the previous examples, the starting point of the participant's narratives is the homeland. In previous studies we have found that the homeland is usually described as an idealised territory with a strong emotional charge (nostalgia). Here the homeland becomes the starting scene of the narrative and as such it is not treated as a mystified lost paradise. Rather, it is the border which seems to present difficulties in attaining their goals that triggers an emotional response. "Being in the homeland" is often presented as a kind of canonical state ("happiness in the homeland") at the very beginning of the narrative. That canonical state is then broken by something (migration), which then gives rise to the elaboration of the narrative that serves to make sense of the deviation from the canonical state.
2 *Complicating action*. We find specific sequences in the narratives that highlight actions related to having abandoned the homeland due to different personal reasons that seem very complicated. The moment

of carrying out the specific trip is experienced as a very stressful and difficult memory, and when narrated it is charged with a high emotional load. For example, in Lupe's case, remembering the many times she had to risk her life crossing the Mexico-USA borders, as well as the distance from her sick mother, caused her to choke up and fight back her tears. The narratives displayed the ways in which the participants dealt with the links between their cultural and their personal past. They relate risking their lives to maintain their ties with the hometown, in the process interweaving their personal history of migration with the group's history and traditions.

3 *Evaluation.* A common thread across the narratives is that their lives are "still in progress." Even though many of the narrators had been living in the United States for many years, they are still "luchando" (fighting) for a better future. Their own evaluation and their emotions focus on the difficulties they have had in reaching their dreams rather than how much they miss the homeland.

In summary, our analysis describes the contents and structures of the narratives of migration expressed by the participants in our study. Although we found some common features, mainly in the structure of narratives, these narratives reflect a different migrant narrative from those found in our previous studies. In our current study, nostalgia is not the central point of narratives and the focus is on the future goals concerning how participants can fit into their new lives. We also found that these narratives, like others, are highly emotional, but that emotions are attached to difficult moments such as crossing the border illegally, and not to the physical elements of the homeland, such as landscape or cuisine. A shared characteristic with other narratives of migration is the interweaving of personal and cultural traits of self construction.

Discussion

In relation to our findings, we suggest some proposals for future studies of narratives of migration. Theoretically this analysis helps us understand narratives both as a discourse mode and as a way of thinking that shapes the acts of identification performed by the individuals. By mediating the acts of identification (including the acts of cultural identification), narrative conveys a subjective dimension to self construction. This personalised nature may constitute the basis of the interweaving of the individual and cultural identity that we found in the narratives of migration. The semiotic tool of narratives draws connections between individuals and society (Bell, 2006). Our results suggest that during migration, personal stories play a relevant role in the person's cultural identity, and similarly cultural identity acquires special relevance in the tapestry that constitutes the whole identity system of an individual. The artificial limits traditionally ascribed to the different sections of a person's identities (cultural, gender, personal, etc.) (Abrams & Hogg, 1995) come into view as more flexible, fuzzy and indistinct than expected. A more thorough analysis of this issue is needed.

A second interesting topic related to the personal character of the cultural identity that is expressed through the narratives performed by our participants is their strong emotional charge. The evaluation component seen in our narratives of migration adopts a special emotional force, which is expressed in the form of vivid and clear images and elaborated descriptions of actions related to the moment of the migration movement. Our results are congruent with the ideas developed by researchers such as Meijers and Wardekker, who emphasise the essential role of emotion in identity construction (Meijers & Wardekker, 2002). These authors have developed a model of identity formation for career learning that takes as its starting point a crisis or a turning point in a person's life that generates an emotional response. This experience is then given sense by narratives, which constitute part of the person's identity. The identity process is thus conceptualised as a process in which emotions and cognitions are gradually balanced in a dialogical way. Further analysis of how the contributions of emotional, cognitive and social elements are intermingled in identity narratives is necessary, as some recent trends in narrative inquiry research have already stressed, when addressing the embodied nature of narratives.

Based on the high emotional dimension of our participants' narratives of migration we suggest that these narratives might constitute what some scholars have described as 'self-defining memories' (Blagov & Singer, 2004; Conway, Singer & Tagini, 2004; Singer & Salovey, 1993). In order to reach a better understanding of our results we set out to elaborate the idea of 'self-defining memories' in relation to our data.

Self-defining memories are memories of events that an individual believes shape "who I am" and are essential in giving meaning to the "self" (Pillemer, 2001; Singer & Salovey, 1993). They are considered to be a specific type of autobiographical memory that can be characterised as having affective intensity, vividness, reiterations (high level of rehearsal), linkage with other memories, great integrative meaning and a relationship with enduring concerns or unresolved conflicts. Many of these characteristics can be found in our narratives of migration.

The importance of self-defining memories and their integrative power in self construction have been extensively studied within personality psychology and counselling (McAdams, 2001, 2006). In relation to social variables, some studies have recently addressed possible cross-cultural and age-related differences in self-defining memories (Jobson & O´Kearney, 2008; McLean, 2008). All this research and applied work has been developed using experimental methodologies and individual data collection, usually employing personal interview techniques. However, no techniques have been developed to study how memories used in social and everyday contexts could also constitute self-defining memories; nor how experiences related to cultural identity, such as the migration experience, can become central to a person's self-system and become part of the person's set of self-defining memories.

Further analysis of migration narratives, exploring their features as self-defining memories, would be of great interest in giving us more thorough knowledge of this complex process.

Concluding Remarks

In this chapter, we have identified some common characteristics in the narratives of migration performed by the participants in a bilingual computer class. These characteristics involved both the content and the structure of the narratives. The content of the narratives of migration was usually related to socio-economic progress and the skills needed to succeed in American society. The structure of these narratives started with a canonical state (living in the homeland) that was broken by the migration movement. Within this content and structure, the narratives constitute the scaffolding that gives sense to the migratory experience in the participant's lives. Emotional display is also a salient trait of the narratives. These results have shown to be situational, and some of the narratives changed depending on the specific circumstances of migration.

However, in all cases, and to different degrees, these narratives seem to be crucial in the process of giving sense to participants' experience of migration and the construction of cultural and self-development.

As a final comment, we can argue that research on narratives of migration constitutes a rich field of study that may help us understand how personal and cultural identities interweave with each other. We consider that we have identified a relatively stable structure in the narratives of migration (although of course not generalisable to all migrants' narratives) in the same way as other authors have found stable patterns in other types of narratives (Gergen & Gergen, 1993; Linde, 1993).

Notes

1 No grammatical corrections have been made to the original transcription. As a transcription of oral discourse, the structure of speech does not always follow the rules of written texts.
2 Authors' translation

References

Bakhtin, M. M. (1981). *The dialogic imagination: Four Essays by M. M. Bakhtin*, ed. M. Holquist, translated by C. Emerson & M. Holquist. Austin: University of Texas Press.

Bamberg, M. (2005). Narrative discourse and identities. In J.C. Meister, T. Kindt, & W. Schernus (Eds.), *Narratology beyond literary criticism* (pp. 213-237). New York: De Gruyter.

Bamberg, M. (2004). Talk, small stories, and adolescent identities. *Human Development, 47*, 366–369.

Bellelli, G., & Amatulli, M. A. C. (1997). Nostalgia, immigration and collective memory. In J. W. Pennebaker, D. Páez & B. Rimé (Eds.), *Collective memory of political events. Social psychological perspectives* (pp. 209-220). Mahwah, NJ: L.E.A.

Bhatia, S., & Ram, A. (2001). Locating the dialogical self in the age of transnational migrations, border crossings and diasporas. *Culture & Psychology, 7*, 297–309.

Birren, J. E., & Deutchman, D. E. (1991). *Guiding autobiography groups for older adults*. Baltimore: Johns Hopkins University Press.

Birren, J. E., & Birren, B. A. (1996). Autobiography: exploring the self and encouraging development. J. E. Birren, G. Kenyon, J. Ruth., J. J. F. Schroots, & T. Svensson (Eds.), *Aging and biography: explorations in adult development*. New York: Springer Publishing.

Blagov, P. S., & Singer, J. A. (2004). Four dimensions of self-defining memories (specificity, meaning, content, and affect) and their relationship to self-restraint, distress, and repressive defensiveness. *Journal of Personality, 72*, 481-511.

Brockmeier, J. (2000). Autobiographical time. *Narrative Inquiry, 10*, 51-74.

Brockmeier, J., & Carbaugh, D. (2001). *Narrative and identity*. Amsterdam: John Benjamins.

Bruner, J. S. (1986). *Actual minds, possible worlds*. Cambridge, MA: Harvard University Press.

Bruner, J. S. (2004). The narrative creation of self. In L. E. Angus & J. McLeod (Eds.), *The handbook of narrative and psychotherapy: Practice, theory, and research* (pp. 3-14). Thousand Oaks, CA: Sage Publications.

Burns, D. (2007). *Systemic Action Research: A strategy for whole system change*. Bristol: Policy Press

Capps, L., & Bonanno, G. A. (2000). Narrating bereavement: thematic and grammatical predictors of adjustment to loss. *Discourse Processes, 30*, 1-25.

Clark, M. C. (2001). Off the beaten path: some creative approaches to adult learning. *New Directions for Adult and Continuing Education, 89*, 83-91.

Conway, M. A., Singer, J. A., & Tagini, A. (2004). The self and autobiographical memory: Correspondence and coherence. *Social Cognition, 22*, 491-529.

Crossley, M. L. (2003). Formulating narrative psychology: the limitations of contemporary social constructionism. *Narrative Inquiry, 13*, 287-300.

De Fina, A. (2003a). Crossing borders: time, space, and disorientation in narrative. *Narrative Inquiry, 13*, 367-391.

De Fina, A. (2003b). *Identity in narrative. A study of immigrant discourse.* Amsterdam: John Benjamins.

De Fina, A. (2006). Group identity, narrative and self-representation. In A. De Fina, D. Shiffrin, & M. Bamberg (Eds.), *Discourse and identity* (pp. 351-375). Cambridge: Cambridge University Press.

De Fina, A., Shiffrin, D., & Bamberg, M. (2006). *Discourse and identity.* Cambridge: Cambridge University Press.

Dien, D. S. (2000). The evolving nature of self-identity across four levels of history. *Human Development, 43,* 1-18.

Dominicé, P. (2000): *Learning from our lives: using educational biographies with adults.* San Francisco: Jossey-Bass.

Freire, P. (1979). *Pedagogy of the oppressed.* New York: Continuum.

Fortier, A.-M., (2000). *Migrant belongings. Memory, space, identity.* Oxford: Berg.

Edwards, D. (1997). *Discourse and cognition.* London: Sage.

Georgakopoulou, A. (2006): The other side of the story: towards a narrative analysis of narratives-in-interaction. *Discourse Studies, 8,* 235-257.

Gergen, M. (1988). Narrative structures in social explanation. In C. Antaki (Ed.), *Analysing everyday explanation* (pp. 94-112). *A casebook of methods.* London: Sage.

Gergen, M. M., & Gergen, K. J. (2006). Narratives in action. *Narrative Inquiry, 16,* 112-121.

Gibb, T. L. (2008): Bridging Canadian adult second language education and essential skills policies. Approach with caution. *Adult Education Quarterly, 58,* 318-334.

Hogg, M. A., & Abrams, D. (1998). *Social identifications: A social psychology of intergroup relations and group processes.* London: Routledge.

Hole, R. (2007). Narratives of identity. A poststructural analysis of three Deaf women's life stories. *Narrative Inquiry, 17,* 259-278.

Jobson, L., & O´Kearney, R. (2008). Cultural differences in retrieval of self-defining memories. *Journal of Cross-Cultural Psychology, 39,* 75-80.

König, J. (2009): Moving experience: Dialogues between personal cultural positions. *Culture & Psychology, 15,* 97-119.

Kraus, W. (2006). The narrative negotiation of identity and belonging. *Narrative Inquiry, 16,* 103-111.

Labov, W. (1997). Some further steps in narrative analysis. *Journal of Narrative and Life History, 7,* 1-41.

Leont'ev, A. (1981). The problem of activity in Psychology. In J. Wertsch (Ed.), *The concept of activity in Soviet Psychology* (pp. 37-71). New York: Sharpe.

Linde, C. (1993). *Life-stories: the creation of coherence.* New York: Oxford University Press.

Lipski, J. M. (1985). *Linguistic aspects of Spanish-English language switching*. Tempe: Arizona State University Center for Latin American Studies.

Macías, B. (2002). *Identidad cultural y emigración. Un estudio de la construcción del discurso identitario desde la Psicología Histórico-Cultural*. [Cultural identity and migration. A study of the identity related discourse from Historic-Cultural Psychology]. Unpublished doctoral dissertation. University of Seville..

Macías, B., García, J., & Sánchez, J. A. (2008). Cultural identity and immigration. In B. Van Oers, E. Elbers, R. Van der Veer & W. Wardekker (Eds.), *The transformation of learning. Perspectives from activity theory* (pp. 201-218). Cambridge: Cambridge University Press.

Macías, B. & de la Mata M. (2013): Narratives of migration. Emotions and the interweaving of personal and cultural identity through narrative, *Culture & Psychology, 19 (3)*, 348-368.

McAdams, D. P. (2001). The psychology of life stories. *Review of General Psychology, 5*, 100-122.

McAdams, D. P. (2006). *The redemptive self: stories Americans live by*. New York: Oxford University Press.

McLean, K. C. (2008). Stories of the young and the old: personal continuity and narrative identity. *Developmental Psychology, 44*, 254-264.

Meijers, F., & Wardekker, W. (2002). Career learning in a changing world: the role of emotions. *International Journal for the Advancement of Counselling, 24*, 149-167.

Merriam, S. B. Caffarella, R. S., & Baumgartner, L (2007): *Learning in adulthood: a comprehensive guide*. San Francisco: Jossey-Bass.

Mezirow, J., & associates (1990): *Fostering critical reflection in adulthood: a guide to transformative and emancipatory education*. San Francisco: Jossey-Bass.

Mezirow, J. (1997): Transformative learning: theory to practice. *New Directions for Adult and Continuing Education, 74*, 5-12.

Nelson, K. (2000). Narrative, time, and the emergence of the encultured self. *Culture & Psychology, 6*, 183-196.

Nelson, K., & Fivush, R. (2004). The emergence of autobiographical memory: a social cultural developmental theory. *Psychological Review, 111*, 486-511.

Ochs, E., & Capps, L. (2001). *Living narrative*. Cambridge MA: Harvard University Press.

Pillemer, D. B. (2001). Momentous events and the life story. *Review of General Psychology, 5*, 123-134.

Ramírez, J. D. (1995): *Usos de la palabra y sus tecnologías. Una aproximación dialógica al estudio de la alfabetización.* [Uses of words and its technologies. A dialogic approximation to the study of literacy]. Buenos Aires: Miño y Dávila Editores.

Redman, P. (2005). The narrative formation of identity revisited. Narrative construction, agency and the unconscious. *Narrative Inquiry, 15,* 25-44.

Relaño, M., & Macías, B. (2003). Argumentation and self-representation in everyday narratives: the logo activity. In *Proceedings of the Fifth Conference of the International Society for the Study of Argumentation* (pp.815-818). Amsterdam: Sic Sac.

Sarbin, T. R. (1986). *Narrative psychology: the storied nature of human conduct.* New York: Praeger.

Schrauf, R. W., & Rubin, D. C. (2001). Effects of voluntary immigration on the distribution of autobiographical memory over the lifespan. *Applied Cognitive Psychology, 15,* S75-S88.

Schrauf, R. W. (2000). Narrative repair of threatened identity. *Narrative Inquiry, 10,* 127-145.

Schiff, B. (2006). The promise (and challenge) of an innovative narrative psychology. *Narrative Inquiry, 16,* 19-27.

Sealey-Ruiz, Y. (2007). Wrapping the Curriculum around their lives: using a culturally relevant curriculum with African American adult women. *Adult Education Quarterly, 58,* 44-60.

Singer, J. A., & Salovey, P. (1993). *The remembered self: emotion and memory in personality.* New York: The Free Press.

Smith, B. (2007). The state of the art in narrative inquiry. Some reflections. *Narrative Inquiry, 17,* 391-398.

Stein, D. S., & Imel, S. (2002). *Adult learning in community.* San Francisco: Jossey-Bass.

Stokoe, E., & Edwards, D. (2006). Story formulations in talk-in-interaction. *Narrative Inquiry, 16,* 56–65.

Syed, M., & Azmitia, M. (2008). A narrative approach to ethnic identity in emerging adulthood: bringing life to the identity status model. *Developmental Psychology, 44,* 1012-1027.

Thomsen, D. K., & Jensen, A. B. (2007). Memories and narratives about breast cancer. Exploring associations between turning points, distress and meaning. *Narrative Inquiry, 17,* 349-370.

Thorne, A. (2004). Putting the person into social identity. *Human Development, 47,* 361-365.

Torres, L. (1992). Code-mixing as a narrative strategy in a bilingual community. *World Englishes, 11*, 183-197.

Vásquez, O. (2002): *La Clase Mágica: Imagining Optimal Possibilities in a Bilingual Community of Learners*. New Jersey: Lawrence Erlbaum.

Vygotsky, L. S. (1987). *Thinking and speech*. Translated by N. Minick. New York: Plenum.

Wertsch, J. V. (1985). *Vygotsky and the social formation of mind*. Cambridge, MA: Harvard University Press.

Wertsch, J. V. (1991). *Voices of the mind : a sociocultural approach to mediated action*. Cambridge, MA: Harvard University Press.

Wertsch, J. V. (1998). *Mind as action*. New York: Oxford University Press.

Wertsch, J. V. (2002). *Voices of collective remembering*. New York: Cambridge University Press.

Wilson, A. L. (1999). Creating identities of dependency: adult education as a knowledge-power regime. *International Journal of Lifelong Education, 18*, 85-93.

Zentella, A. C. (1997). *Growing up bilingual: Puerto Rican children in New York*. Malden, MA: Blackwell Publishers.

Zentella, Y. (2009): Developing a multi-dimensional model of Hispano attachment to and loss of land. *Culture & Psychology, 15*, 181-200.

Rashmi Singla

Intercultural family work
An inclusive paradigm for psychosocial intervention

Introduction
This chapter delineates an inclusive paradigm for psychosocial intervention work with families across cultural boundaries based on a combination of theoretical understanding and practice-based experiences.

The theoretical framework is based on constructive eclecticism in which social contextual theories such as social constructionism and sociocultural psychology are combined with life course perspective and transnationalism. Three major principles with focus on multiple identities, family inclusion and broad social context inclusion are developed in the paradigm. A case is presented and discussed to illustrate these principles. The interplay between theory, practical and empirical research in the chapter also underpins the ethical aspects of the intervention, especially in dealing with vulnerable families.

Background
Working with families across cultures is a challenge faced by an increasing number of professionals in the age of globalisation, which is

manifest in movement of people and goods across national boundaries. The identities, relationships and actions at the local context exist in a relationship with the global level context and therefore influence this challenge. In line with the broad theme of this book, I aim to develop understandings for working with families across cultural boundaries, based on a critical constructive eclectic theoretical framework combining local practices as well as practice based knowledge.

The specific basis for the practice is an NGO (non-governmental organisation) with the acronym TTT, standing for Transcultural Therapeutic Team. TTT is a psychosocial service for minority youth and their families in Copenhagen, established in 1991 (Arenas & Singla, 1995; Singla, 1997, 2003). It is inspired by intercultural psychotherapeutic perspectives (Kareem & Littlewood, 1989; Fernando, 1991) focusing on the ideology and politics of psychiatric and psychological intervention (Shashidharan, 1986). It is important to point out that in this study I perceive culture as a dynamic and complex meaning system, and not as a simplistic or static concept. Intercultural family work entails broad psychosocial intervention with families that have a different cultural background than the mainstream culture due to migration, diaspora and/or minority processes. At the same time, the structural and political dimensions of inequalities are also considered significant, and hence addressing social constraints and power differentials is also a major feature of the intercultural family work. This multi-level, inclusive paradigm constitutes a broad basis for transformations, in contrast to other narrow and exclusively individual-based paradigms.

Taking as a starting point the three basic principles that form the common denominator for the psychosocial service, the major theoretical perspectives for the intercultural family are elucidated. These principles are then illustrated through a practice-based case study dealing with a young person and family belonging to the South Asian diaspora in Denmark.

TTT was established as a grass roots organisation by a group of psychologists with ethnically diverse but academically similar backgrounds (Danish psychology degree holders) in 1991 in Copenhagen, based on the abovementioned approach. The objective was to provide a competent service to an overlooked group, namely young immigrants and refugees, inspired by the inter-cultural therapy approach developed by the treatment centre Nafsiyat in London. This approach aimed to address questions of persecution, racism and other forms of discrimination, making the centre a place in which clients feel able to talk about their experiences of exclusion without thus experiencing further persecution from their therapists (Thomas, 1995). TTT is based on the following principles, revised on the basis of ongoing practice:

- Focus on Multiple Identity
- Inclusion of Family and Network
- Inclusion of Broad Context

The next section presents these principles in detail and discusses their theoretical underpinnings.

Focus on multiple identity

Development of an identity with multiple dimensions, rejecting the simple division into identity based on the country of origin and that based on the country of residence, is one of the principles of TTT. The youth are seen not as having either/or identities but as having both/and identities combining different aspects of their complex contexts.

The presence of ethnic minority psychologists provides possible models for identification. However, prior to 1991 in the Danish context, almost all the psychologists in the relevant services had an ethnic majority background. One of the original objectives was to investigate ethnic matching, i.e. the provision of psychosocial services to young persons by psychologists with a similar ethnic background. Offering a choice of psychologists has been envisaged as an important feature of the intervention, especially as an act of empowerment in systems, which may lead to feelings of disempowerment.

Over the past two decades, this principle has been revised. The narrow concept of ethnic matching has been partly replaced by the broader concept of minority position matching, e.g. an Afghani youth and an Irani professional, who are both minorities in Danish society, though they belong to different ethnic groups. This is based on pragmatic considerations of youths from many different ethnic minority groups being referred to psychologists from a few ethnic minority groups, coupled with the absence of a language barrier for most young people, given the possibility of Danish as the common language. Other reasons include respecting the young person's gender based choice, as well as psychologists' preference for treating broader categories of young persons in order to avoid being "imprisoned" in a reductionist ethnic identity, a perceived danger if the sole criterion for matching is ethnicity. Though similar ethnic backgrounds can lead to common understandings, it can also lead to problems such as too much understanding and sympathy as well as loss of objectivity (Jalali, 1988). As Chaudhary (2008) observes, the essence of good research lies in knowing when to distance and when to close. This knowledge applies to effective psychosocial intervention as well. When there is distance between the psychologist and the client, we need to work inwards, and when one is already a part of the social reality, then one needs to step outside a little.

In accordance with the broad theoretical framework presented in this chapter, the exaggerated highlighting of 'identity' in psychological studies is probably not what we can expect to find in the real world of referrals to this service. The issue of identity/being, expressed in the query "who am I?", becomes part of the more complex and broader array of problems for the young person, and is not the dominant reason for referral to TTT.

At the same time, it is relevant to take into consideration criticism by mental health service users in the UK who complain that psychiatry and allied professions exist to suppress their feelings and behaviour (Sassoon & Lindow, 1995, p. 95). They further argue that mental health workers go through training that encourages them to diagnose or analyse instead of listening to people, even though listening should be a basic aspect of this practice.

Inclusion of family and network

It is helpful to involve the youth's family and network in the intervention in order to reach long term solutions to psychosocial problems, especially those concerning intergenerational issues. In dealing with ethnic minority youths' problems and assisting them in meeting the challenges of life, the family is seen as the psychosocial unit of operations. Continuing interdependence and fulfilment of family roles (see Kleis and Demuth, Keller, Gudi & Otto in Jensen de López & Hansen, 2011, for discussion of the concepts of independence and interdependence) are still ideals in the parts of the world that many ethnic minority parents come from (LaFromboise, Foster, and James, 1996). There can be many problems in working psychotherapeutically across cultures: for example, overlooking traditional family structures and specific family life practices can lead to major diagnostic and therapeutic errors. These errors include potentially disastrous transference in relationship interpretations, the confounding of traditional beliefs with psychiatric symptoms, etc.

An effort to establish/re-establish dialogue and compromises between the two generations is a major part of the TTT practice. Creating common understanding about the relation between the youth and family is vital. Focus is placed on the inclusion of the family, either directly by inviting the whole family into the therapy room or indirectly through a psychological plan. This proves to be an effective principle and integrates several aspects of family dynamics such as intergenerational relations and transitions in the life course.

The involvement of the family is often evaluated as positive and seen as supportive by most of the ethnic minority youth, irrespective of gender. However, there are also some cases where the relationship with the family is highly contentious and direct family involvement is not feasible as the client may consider it a form of control. All psychosocial services include aspects of support and control; the challenge is in limiting the control and expanding the support, especially for marginalised ethnic minority individuals for whom the issue of control can become still more challenging.

Inclusion of a broad context

Institutional racism and racial discrimination are considered as instances of social exclusion processes for the ethnic minority youth. In the non-inclusive paradigm, exaggerated attention is paid to the ethnic minority's culture, at the cost of broad social and intra-personal factors.

In TTT's intervention, effort is made to include societal factors, especially those related to migration as well as the minoritising processes themselves. The youth's positive contact to the majority society is also regarded as important, thus the psychologist comes to function as a bridge builder between the youth and the Danish society by establishing contact across sectors such as social, health and education. Helping the young persons understand, participate in and challenge the conditions provided by the society is also a part of the principle of the inclusion of a broad context.

Establishing contact across the borders of sectors can be difficult for several reasons, among them structural racism barriers in the society. An evaluation of the TTT indicates the shortcomings in modern mental health services described by McNamee and Gergen (1994, p. 98) are applicable to some extent. These include blaming the person, blindness to the social conditions in which the problems develop, insensitive or oppressive treatment of women and minorities, and an all-knowing professional attitude that fails to acknowledge doubts and failures.

At the same time, one must consider the classical dilemma of whether to upgrade mainstream services or establish special services. The analysis of TTT suggests that the solution lies in a combination of both approaches. This is in agreement with the conclusions of a comprehensive study about mental health in the UK as a multiethnic society (Fernando, 1995, p. 214). According to this study, the ideal is that all services will be accessible to and appropriate for all ethnic groups – multiethnic services for a multiethnic society. But in a climate where issues of race and culture are inadequately addressed, it is inevitable that services geared for specific ethnic groups must exist side by side with more general services.

These principles, applied in TTT, have been validated in work with ethnically diverse families in an intercultural context. In the following section, we discuss the theories that inform these principles.

Theories informing the principles of intercultural family work

It is imperative to remember that the abovementioned principles of TTT are intertwined in practice but separated for analytic purposes in this chapter. According to Køppe (2008), eclecticism is seen as positive in practice especially in therapy and pedagogy, as one uses the theoretical concepts that are suitable to reach the aims. These principles are embedded in a constructive eclectic framework, implying that we choose a range of theories, which are expected to encompass the phenomena involved. We turn now to the theoretical framework for these principles.

Multiple identities: Theoretical basis

The principle of multiple identities is based on social contextual theories such as social constructionism (Gergen, 2001), which question essential as well as reductionist perceptions of human beings and direct attention towards the multiple identities of family members in the intercultural family work. As an application of these theoretical understandings, we consider below some conceptualisations by McNamee and Gergen (1999) about the post-modern constructionist mental health approach.

a. Towards equalisation and co-construction

The constuctionist approach rejects the traditional status hierarchy between the therapist and the client. Instead, the professional and the client together form a community, to which both bring resources.

b. From mental to social processes

There is a move from the mental world to the social world, and constructions are seen to take place within forms of relationships. This shift invites new modes of therapeutic practice, in which the plurality of perspectives are co-ordinated into particular forms of action. There is an alternative discourse for enriching action by involving internal others in practical intervention (in line with Mead's (1934) significant others with an interactionist perspective). This generates conversations about which larger group is being represented, expanding the domain of the situation by inviting other relational configurations.

The focus on the social processes and the relational configurations for the ethnically diverse family implies inclusion of the complex multiple selves of the human beings, characterised both by continuous personal identity and by discontinuous personal diversity (Davies &

Harré, 1999). Each of these possible selves can be internally contradictory or contradictory with other possible selves in different narratives. In intervention these contradictions must be remedied, transcended, resolved or ignored.

Combination of "ethnicity in the heart "and "ethnicity in the head"

In order to understand the complex contextual factors for the families who comprise the ethnic minorities in the society of residence, it is imperative to include the concepts of ethnic identity and diaspora in the theoretical framework. Within the broad social-contextual approach, Verkuyten's (2005) ethnic identity theory directs attention towards the societal aspects such as power relations as well as emotional aspects.

Verkuyten's social-psychological delineation of ethnic identity considers both circumstantial and primordial approaches, which are considered as complementary rather than contradictory, although they pose different questions and deliver different answers (Verkuyten, 2005, p. 88). Circumstantialists would refer to the ethnicity in the head as their emphasis is on structural conditions, political strategies, and ideological determination; in other words, on the external circumstances and conditions that shape ethnic identities. These approaches are important and in particular cases they provide adequate explanations.

However, there are limitations to such approaches. There is a tendency to assume that the circumstances do the work and little attention is paid to the way individuals and groups actively, and in interaction, shape and transform their circumstances and identities. Ethnicity is viewed as an instrument that will disappear when it is no longer useful and distinctive meanings, emotions and sentiments are largely neglected in these approaches.

Conversely, primordial approaches emphasise the emotional and crucial nature of ethnicity, as the focus is on the psychological or internal dimensions of ethnicity. Primary socialisation and emotional involvement are seen as the reasons why ethnic attachments often persist. Perceived as ethnicity in the heart, these approaches try to explain why so many people attribute primary qualities to ethnic identity, even when it contradicts their interests.

However, Verkuyten points to the problems of primordial approaches, some of which include overlooking the importance of power differentials and external categorisation, ignoring the dynamic character of ethnicity and failing to account for identity variations. He argues in favour of taking both circumstantial and primordial perspectives into account, which includes social, historical and internal dimensions of ethnicity.

Accepting the significance of both the circumstantial and primordial approaches implies acknowledging the significance of the head as well as the heart in the psychosocial situation of the families who are using the services.

Diasporic identity and interconnections

An illustrative example is the identity for persons belonging to diasporic populations, which pertains to the sense of connection to the country of origin. The diaspora, defined by its Greek etymology as "a scattering" from the roots, from *dia* (apart) and *speirn* (to sow), has entered the globalising language to apply to all migrants (Guzder & Krishna, 2005). Diaspora is about dispersal and connections. Dispersion implies distance, so maintaining or creating connections becomes a major goal in dealing with that distance (Dufoix, 2008).

Drawing on sociocultural and postcolonial scholarship, the above conceptualisation is critical towards the universalistic assumptions of the predominant acculturation strategies proposed by Berry and Sam (1997). Their approach holds that similar 'underlying' operations are involved in acculturation, irrespective of geographical and historical context. In agreement with Bhatia and Ram (2000), we consider that we need to think of selfhood as firmly intertwined with socio-cultural factors such as colonialism, diasporic processes, restrictive racially based laws, and exclusion processes, in order to fully understand identity in the context of movements across borders. Issues of power and race at different levels are consequently deeply interconnected with the development of family membership, social relations and identity.

Subjective features of the diaspora, such as agency (the meanings held and practices conducted by social actors), are also included in this delineation, where diaspora is seen both as a category of analysis and as a category of practice. Our attention is directed to the multiple meanings of diaspora (Vertovec, 2000), in which it is at once a social form, a type of consciousness and a mode of cultural production/consumption. A social form is about relations, while consciousness is awareness about multi-locality, the sense of being both here and there. Kalra, Kaur and Hutnyk (2005) argue that diaspora shifts our attention away from viewing migration as a one-way process, in which people merely migrate from one place and settle in another. They pinpoint that an understanding of complex transnational identities needs new conceptual maps, and thus they conceptualise diaspora as both a positive embrace of transnational affiliation and as a defensive posture by communities to a hostile host that says they do not belong.

In practice, it is not enough to see the ethnic minority family, e.g. a family originating from India and living in Denmark, just as migrants in the host society. Attention should be paid to the family members' attitudes and relation to their country of origin, as well as to how new technologies such as the internet transform and influence this relation, especially with reference to religious affiliations (Bunt, 2009) (see chapter 7 of this volume by Macías Gómez-Stern & Vasquez).

The multiple identities of the families in the psychosocial services pertain not only to their complex contexts such as the country of residence and country of origin but also to the power structures in the world. The next section deals with the theoretical framework related to the family, which is considered a salient aspect of the life situation.

Inclusion of family: Theoretical basis

Within a socio-cultural psychological perspective, family is an important intersection between persons and society and provides a critical link between an individual and collectivity (Chaudhary, 2007). In mainstream intervention, the primary focus has been on individual treatment. Focus on the whole family has been relatively limited, but has gained increasing acceptance in the past decades and is at the core of the systemic approach.

Family therapy: Generic understanding

According to Minuchin (1974), one of the early family therapists, individual therapy is comparable to a technician using a magnifying glass, where the details are clear but the field is severely circumscribed. On the other hand, working within the framework of family therapy is comparable to working with a zoom lens. One can zoom in for a close-up whenever one wishes to study the intrapsychic field, but one can also observe with a broader lens. Working with the family thus implies approaching human beings in their social contexts. The theory of family therapy is predicated on the fact that man is not an isolate.

In working with the families, attention is paid to the family structure, which is the invisible set of functional demands that organises the ways in which family members interact. Minuchin (1974) describes two systems of constraints for the interaction. The first, the *generic* system, involves universal rules governing family organisation such as power hierarchy, family-drawing boundaries, dealing with relatives such as in-laws, relating to friends and rearing children. The second system, the *idiosyncratic*, involves the mutual expectations of particular family members and negotiations among them. The family is subject to inner pressure from developmental changes in its own members and subsystems and to outer pressure coming from demands to accommodate to the significant social institutions, which constitute the extra-familial forces.

Minuchin (1974) considers boundary drawing as a task which takes on different forms in different societies, and concludes that the diversity of culture only highlights the essential similarity of the processes involved. The extent of the so-called essential similarity is, however, challenged by social contextual theories. In the following section we shall focus on other delineations of family and therapy, as illustrated in the Asian context (specifically India and China), using a social-cultural psychological approach.

Social-cultural conceptualisation of the family and the self

Chaudhary's (2007) social-cultural conceptualisation of the family is critical towards the key myth of the family as a universal, unchanging structure without variation in time and space. The image of the family as a stable group with well-defined roles both within and outside the family persists, despite the fact that few families actually fit that image. Chaudhary maintains that the idea of the family in any cultural location is a driving force behind policy and social evaluation of individual and collective action. Family is perceived as a dynamic, ideal construction rather than an empirical fact gathered from statistical averages. Thus family is identified as a primary research theme along with others such as social class, ethnicity, and nationality.

The dominant discourse that positive family experiences are essential for well-being is challenged by the understanding of the dual form of family as both "a site of oppression and violence" (Chaudhary, 2007) and as a "haven in a heartless world" or "reservoir of intimacy" (Dencik, 2005).

Focusing on family therapeutic work across cultural borders, some of the classical delineations (Jalali, 1988) emphasise the preservation of ethnic patterns and values in different groups, which implies a simplistic, static understanding of complex concepts such as culture and ethnicity. In discussion of the family, oversimplified dichotomies should be avoided. Simplistic dichotomies, such as Easterners as collectivistic and Westerners as individualistic (Languani, 2007) are dubious, as both individualist and collectivist orientations may coexist within individuals and cultures, implying compatibility of the supposed contradictions. One example is the Indian mind. According to Sinha and Tripathi (1994, p. 136) the distinction between Indian and Western minds lies in the ways boundaries that define mental structures are displaced. In the Western mind, boundaries are perceived as stable and fixed, eg. The boundaries between self and environment, mind and matter, subjective and objective, material and spiritual, secular and religious etc.. The Indian mind, on the other hand, is governed by boundaries that are constantly shifting and variable. The self sometimes expands to fuse with the cosmos, but at another moment it may withdraw itself from it. This belief is evident in the life cycle of a person exhibiting fluctuating self-other dynamics and the notion of a person being deeply individualistic, despite the popular belief about the collectivistic self.

In congruence with Chaudhary (2007), individual existence is perceived as only one of the levels at which human dynamics operate.

The continuum of human groupings is marked by the single individual at one end and community at the other. In between are the many layers of sociality, differently organised in different contexts and times. Thus the social and personal are interdependent domains. Family is seen as a significant level of social activity, where belonging to the family has implications for the sharing of a value system, resources, space and time. These implications vary at different phases of the life course of the person and in various contexts. An illustration is an empirical study by Barn, Ladino and Rogers (2006), which emphasises the complex aspects of parenting for ethnic minorities through a study of parenting in multi-racial Britain.

Life course perspective

A life course perspective (Levy, Ghisletta, Le Goff, Spini & Widmer, 2005) pays attention to the interaction between the trajectories (models of stability and long term changes), transitions, events and family members. Furstenberg (2005) discusses how transitions may be normative and socially considered to be desirable or non-normative or even deviant. The normative aspect is contingent on the broad context.

Against a backdrop of Indian psychology, Kumar (2008, p. 24) notes that the life course is divided ideally into four *asramas* (stages). The first two, *brahmacharya* (celibate studentship) and *grhastha* (householder stage) are the preparation and fulfilment of a relational life; the third, *vanapratha* (the retiring forest dweller stage) and lastly the *sanyasa* (renunciation) loosen the bond and cremate all one's past and present relations. Thus there are transformations in the basic forms of relationship between the self and other in the different stages of the life course, making the life journey fundamentally individual in character.

The *grhastha* phase in the family is considered to be the most important because without experiencing the closeness, renunciation may not be meaningful. All the other stages are possible due to the support the household provides, and hence the family stage is highly salient in the Indian psyche. It is pertinent to point out that these psychological conceptualisations have relevance for working with the South Asian diaspora due to the psycho-historical development of the subcontinent (Kumar, 2008; Singla, 2008).

In order to work with the families, the life course in the particular context has to be taken into account as changes, especially unforeseen events, can alter its further progress and have important consequences for the persons who experience them (Levy et al., 2005, p. 19). Additionally, attention has to be directed towards the dynamics and modes of coping with intergenerational ambivalences, such as solidarity, emancipation, atomisation and captivation (Lüscher, 2005), based on the concept of linked lives. It is also relevant in working with the families to consider the points of tension in the interface between the professional and the ethnic minority family.

Family therapy across cultures

According to Lau (1986, 1990) the following areas need to be explored in intercultural family work:

1. Differences in the power position and ethnicity between the professional and the family
2. Differences in systems of symbolic meaning
3. Differences in family structure
4. Language and communication

Regarding point 1, it is important to explore the subjective placing of the experiences of discrimination and exclusion of the persons and the family, along with the historical cultural positioning of the group involved. Lau exemplifies the issue through the historical experiences of blacks related to the master-slave dynamics in the USA. Similarly, exploring the implications of British colonisation of South Asia could be relevant for families originating from India. However, it is equally imperative not to assume the meaning of this context for the unique persons and family we are working with, but rather to explore these issues.

Concerning the second point, the family professional needs to be familiar with the role of cultural materials and practices in order to deal with them. At the same time, it is important to avoid culturalism (excessive focus on a static understanding of culture) and to be aware of responses to the particular stresses in the life situation. In intercultural family work, the potentially central role of religious-philosophical beliefs should not be ignored, which is a danger given that most Western family therapy models are developed in a relatively secular context contemporary with the erosion of the authority of the Christian church. Indian psychological understandings ((Rao, Paranjpe & Dalal, 2008) and discussions of Muslim psychologists in the Western world (Badri, 1979) emphasise the meaning attached to religious beliefs and sentiments.

As to point 3, value orientations influence the organisation of the family. Lau (1986) observes that there are ideals placing the group higher than the individual in the extended family system of Asia and the Far East. An illustration is the organising principle of filial piety among the Chinese, in which loyalty to parents takes precedence over the loyalties to the spouse and children. However, one has to be aware of the changing forms of the families in the context of globalisation and movements across borders.

In intercultural family work, a useful pragmatic strategy is to locate the family on a continuum between the hierarchical and the egalitarian family structure. Concomitantly, attention should be paid to the authority and the care providing figures in the family as well as interdependence processes in the family. Authority structures and their dynamics need to be identified if the professionals want to help the family mobilise its authority. The structure and organisation has implications for parenting, life phases such as youth, as well as for intimate partnership choice leading to family formation. Especially relevant here are issues to do with individuation and separation, i.e. leaving the family (Lau, 1986).

As regards point 4, the linguistic aspect can be a resource or a hindrance in intercultural family work, depending on the matching between the family and the professional. Without linguistic matching or a competent interpreter, a proper assessment of a family's needs and strengths is almost impossible. Strategies in family therapy such as attempts to take family members beyond their normal thresholds (Minuchin, 1974) are judged to be problematic when conducted through an interpreter (Lau, 1986). Similarly there can be differences in the modes of communication such as avoidance, direct communication and confrontation: for instance, Chinese groups tend to use indirect means. Chaudhary (2007) lucidly emphasises the elaborate kin terminology used in the South Asian context, as the words chosen to address people not only suggest particular patterns of relationships but also assist in creating and sustaining patterns of social activities that constitute culture. People avoid the use of first names and feel more comfortable addressing others using a sensitively chosen kin term. This terminology is perceived as an active template for addressing and also for affiliating with other people whether they are related or not.

As mentioned earlier, the person and the family exists in the broad societal and the global context. Hence the last theoretical section of this chapter, before the case-study presentation, deals with the theories informing this principle.

Inclusion of the broader context: Theoretical basis

In order to focus on the societal context for family work, we must consider aspects of the background including theories about modernity, the individual as project manager of his/her own biography, changing ways of the family life (Beck-Gernsheim, 2002), globalisation (Castles & Miller, 2006; Stiglitz, 2002) and the current economic crisis (Stiglitz, 2010). Processes of modernisation in the risk society are responsible for social pathologies for the whole population, while exclusion processes related to racial discrimination have especial relevance for ethnically diverse populations (Anthias, 2009).

In this period of enhanced movements across geographical borders, we note, with Sherif Trask and Koivunen (2009), that many students and young professionals are highly mobile, which easily leads to romance, partnership and eventually family formation. Migrations of the heart as well as global tourism are related to the increasing number of mixed marriages, transnational families and family reunifications.

The dynamic concepts of 'interracial mixing' and 'mixed race' highlight the contested nature of 'race' as a 'scientific' idea, which attaches hierarchical meanings to physical differences. To some extent, work with these families can follow the principles discussed here, yet particular aspects are not within the scope of this chapter (see Ifekwunigwe, 2004).

The newer trends in transnational migration research consider migrants as social actors exercising agency. These processes are highly relevant for intercultural family work within this inclusive psychosocial paradigm. They interact with family members and networks, in the country of residence but also in the country of origin and potentially other countries where they have family members or professional relations.

The experiences of how the persons and families manoeuvre through changes, and what constrains them, are important issues (Castles, 2006). Although many migrants follow patterns of permanent settlement or temporary labour mobility, increasing numbers adopt transnational behaviour and consciousness: a person may work in one country, live in a second and be a citizen of a third. As earlier discussed, the diasporic ties may have been strengthened for many due to technological developments such as the internet and cheap air travel, and this should be explored in intercultural work.

However, as Healy and McKee (2004) aptly observe, while physical boundaries have become more porous due to globalisation with erosion of barriers to the movement of people, money, material goods, criminal activity and infectious diseases, the barriers between people's hearts and minds have become or remained distressingly deep. Ongoing and even widening animosity between religious and cultural groups, across social and economic classes, and between people of different skin pigmentation and gender, perpetuate human suffering on a grand scale and have to be considered in intercultural family work.

While accepting that suffering is related to the exclusion processes, Anthias (2009) invokes the concept of translocational positionality, in opposition to the focus on unitary identity and diasporic identity, as a form of hybridity based on the collective experiences of exclusion and racialisation of the Greek Cypriots, along with strong gender distinction in the sense of social place and gender placing. This approach is about not only identifications but also the lived practices as well as intersubjective, organisational and representational conditions for their existence (Anthias, 2009, p. 12). It makes us aware that complex interactions of localities can mutually ameliorate disadvantages through mutually reinforcing contradictory mechanisms.

Congruently, Brah (1996) is concerned with how research on young South Asian women reveals the differential incorporation of 'Britishness', 'Asianness' and the racialised social relations of gender and generation in post-colonial Britain. These relations are of inequality and discrimination, opposition and contestation as well as belonging. They operate in everyday life and in a variety of sites: education, labour markets, religious and political institutions, expressive cultural forms and families. Similar results are shown in a study of South Asian diasporic youth in Denmark and follow-up research on these experiences (Singla, 2008).

From these theoretical and empirical conceptualisations, we now turn our attention to the aspects of the pragmatic approach suggested by Fernando (1996). In order to make life better for people and communities by implementing relevant mental health care, he insists that social and political realities of life have to be addressed. It is thus necessary to recognise the power wielded by the law enforcement authorities, i.e. police, the influence of institutionalised 'racism', and the part played by the psychosocial system. Thus the issues of racism and experiences of exclusion have to be addressed by the professional in the intervention.

This theoretical consideration of the issues related to multiple identities, inclusion of the family and the broader context brings us to consider the significance of ethical issues in intercultural family work.

Ethical issues

The first ethical issue is to extend the services to all and especially to the vulnerable groups. These are defined as the persons who, relative to the majority society, have less power, opportunity, or freedom to determine outcomes in their lives or to make decisions that affect their situation, because of their age, physical or mental condition, ethnicity/race, economic or political position, or captive status (LaFromboise et al. 1996). We have to take into account that historically there has been underutilisation of mental health services by persons belonging to ethnically diverse groups. There is risk of endangering clients' rights when the professional lacks the knowledge and skills to work with a specific group of people, as they may fail to consider the person and family's unique frame of reference and psychosocial history before starting work. The professionals are also obligated to be alert to possible abuses of authority directed towards clients, as ethnically diverse groups are often vulnerable to human rights abuses despite laws and regulations prohibiting discrimination against such groups (ibid., p. 58). Thus it is the professional's responsibility to inform their clients about the channels for redress of grievances that extend beyond intervention.

The starting point for future directions in intercultural ethics for LaFromboise et al. (1996) is how to treat differential moral understandings in diverse cultures. Freedom, individual rights and justice are principle moral standards, and guilt is a major moral emotion, in so-called individual cultures that celebrate the unconnected individual, whereas respect for social roles and interdependence with the group are the principle moral standards and anxiety over the disapproval of others is a primary moral emotion within so-called communal cultures. These understandings imply the ethics of justice and ethics of care respectively. LaFromboise et al.'s (1996) recommendation to consider both a justice perspective and a care perspective in intercultural work seems to be highly relevant for the intercultural family. Such an approach takes into account both the autonomous and relational aspects of the situation. Factors such as world view, intergroup differences, political ramifications, and the impact of individuals' actions on the group are considered before advancing an analysis of personal liberty or rights.

Thus ethical standards in intercultural family work will be assured once the understandings of the ethnically diverse groups are ascertained through a caring perspective, and once justice comes to be understood as respect for people on their own terms. At a pragmatic level, these ethical considerations lead us to consider the issues of consent and confidentiality in intercultural work, especially with marginalised families whose voices are hardly audible in the society. The issue of informed consent underlines the professional's responsibility of making the family aware of what is being offered and the pros and cons of acceptance/refusal. A common complication for consent is when the objectives of the intervention and the organisational aspects are not made explicit. Similarly the family deserves full confidentiality, especially as there may be fear of 'gossip' when the professional and the client belong to the same ethnic minority group. The professional should assure the family that confidentiality will not be violated, and can refer to the ethical guidelines of the relevant organisation (e.g. psychological association). The greatest dilemma concerns sharing the intercultural intervention progress with the different family members. Respect for the specific family members' confidentiality and consent for sharing are the keys to dealing positively with this dilemma.

The remaining section of this chapter illustrates these principles and ethical aspects through a case presentation, in which the professional and the family have the same ethnic minority background.

Case illustration
Family intergenerational conflicts related to intimate partnership formation

The following case study from TTT's practice illustrates the importance of the principles with a concrete example, taking as its starting point the principle of multiple identities in the psychosocial intervention. Some biographical details are changed in order to assure the persons' confidentiality.

Background

Jasna is a 16-year old girl at the time of her first contact with TTT. Her paternal grandfather migrated to Denmark in 1971 from India, while her father joined him in his mid teens. Jasna's mother migrated as a reunified spouse from the country of origin when she was around 20 years old.

Jasna is the oldest of three siblings, and has two younger brothers of 11 and 9 years respectively. All three children were born and raised in Denmark. Her father is self-employed and economically well-off, while her mother has been employed as an untrained worker in a factory, with some periods of unemployment. At the time of referral, she had completed her schooling (10 years) and had started at business school.

Referral
She was referred to TTT by the social department due to serious conflicts with her parents related to her choice of boyfriend, who belonged to another ethnic and national minority from the South Asian region. She had moved out of her home for some weeks, and lived in a 'problem youth' institution, but moved back in with the family at her own request. In the period after she moved out of her home, there was contact with a Danish psychologist to prevent further conflicts, who functioned primarily as the parents' psychologist. Upon her moving back, the family was referred to TTT with the aim of psychosocial intervention for Jasna including the family.

For Jasna, the major problem was her family's lack of acceptance of her boyfriend and their degrading, excluding attitude towards her. She explained her problematic situation partly by the narrative "They don't understand me". She perceived her parents as strict, involved, as well as concerned about her well-being; nevertheless, she wished to continue staying with them. At the same time she described her younger brothers as caring but childish.

Psychosocial intervention process
The intervention lasted about a year with a follow-up session three months later. There were 24 sessions, four of which included both parents and two of which included only the mother. There were also a couple of meetings with other professionals involved in the process. Jasna was willing to cooperate with the psychologist at TTT, with whom there was gender and country of origin matching, but whose middle age and professional status were categories of differentiation contributing to a balance between proximity and distance. The sessions with the parents were in their mother tongue, while a mixture of the mother tongue and Danish was spoken with Jasna. The professional's multilingual abilities made communication possible with both generations, without involving an interpreter.

Using kin terminology, Jasna referred to the professional as "aunty", which contributed to fostering a feeling of acceptance as she felt more comfortable in addressing the older professional using a sensitively chosen kin term and avoided the use of her first name (see Chaudhary, 2007).

An in-depth assessment of Jasna's psychosocial situation cast light on her relations with the different family members and her peer group. It revealed close emotional ties with the paternal grandfather, some attachment with the siblings and a parental relationship characterised by ambivalence and unresolved conflicts. Her social network with the peer group was rather sparse, where the boyfriend had a dominant position. The family power and care relationships were also explored.

The intervention aimed at creating a reciprocal understanding between the two generations' attitudes and actions by addressing personal, interpersonal and societal changes, especially aspects related to the parental migration as well as their minority position.

At the personal level, Jasna could be characterised as having contrasting dispositions such as determination, sensitivity and vulnerability. The intervention aimed at preventing the risk factors for her self-harm and suicidal actions while at the same time supporting protective aspects such as successful completion of her education, from which she dropped out in the first phase. Additionally, it was planned to enhance her social well-being by addressing the risk of marginality related to the ethnic minority position as well as the relation to her country of origin.

Multiple identities
"Not just a young girl with a boyfriend"

An evaluation of the intervention showed that it was partly successful in strengthening Jasna's self-understandings by focusing on her multiple identities, including her ethnic identity as a member of the South Asian diaspora. The psychosocial intervention directed attention towards Jasna not only as a young girl in an intimate relation with her boyfriend but also as a granddaughter, daughter, a sister and a niece. Moreover her identity as a student and a young working girl was also brought into focus.

As these identities are related to each other, an effort was made to create a balance between her positions as girlfriend and daughter by negotiating with the parents, especially with the mother regarding the ongoing contact with the boyfriend. This action led to a reduction in Jasna's anxiety and fear about being "discovered" having surreptitious meetings with her boyfriend.

The focus on Jasna's ethnic identity using a combination of the circumstantial and the primordial approach led to an enhanced understanding of both her situation as a South Asian in the Danish society and her emotional belonging to the ethnic group. Moreover, interventional emphasis on the simultaneous attachment to Denmark and the parental country of origin contributed to Jasna's decision to travel to India for a vacation in a period marked by many intergenerational conflicts in Denmark. The trip was a sort of psychosocial moratorium for her and confirmed her multiple belongings, especially her faith in the family's religious practice. She perceived this sense of religiosity and spirituality as a positive factor. However, the intervention did not succeed in strengthening Jasna's relationship with her peer group, as she dropped out from her studies approximately 3 months after the start of school in the first phase and felt rather lonely.

Inclusion of family
"The parents are also hurt"

In the psychosocial intervention, the basic family work "zoom lens", rather than "microscope", approach made it relevant to directly involve Jasna's parents, while her grandfather, an uncle (father's younger brother) and siblings were indirectly involved. The ethnic matching between Jasna and the psychologist made it possible to use the appropriate terminology for the different members of the extended family. After consent from Jasna, her parents participated in a couple of sessions with focus on negotiations and compromises regarding the serious conflicts. Attention was paid to the authority and care-providing figures in the family with reference to the interconnections and interdependence processes in the family.

The authority structures and their dynamics needed to be identified, as the professional wanted to help the family mobilise its authority. The parental narratives about mutual expectations, power hierarchies and boundaries in the family made the differences between the paternal and the maternal attitude to Jasna's situation explicit.

There was a rather limited acceptance of Jasna's intimate relationship from her father's side while her mother indicated an openness and partial acceptance of her boyfriend. This relieved Jasna's psychological pressure to some extent, as she developed more understanding towards her mother's ambivalence to her intimate relationship through solidarity (Lüscher, 2005). The follow-up session also indicated a continued trust between the daughter and the mother.

Furthermore, the focus on the family life course and network brought out the parental obligation to Jasna's grandparents' generation and also directed her attention towards other caring adults in her extended family. This awareness resulted in an improvement of her emotional ties to a paternal uncle, who is intermarried to a Danish spouse.

The psychologist's home visit and inclusion of parents in the intervention can be seen as explanations for partial success in the improved intra-family relationships. Additionally, the family moving to another residence (to a bungalow from a modest apartment) and collaboration between Jasna and her parents regarding the interior decoration also contributed to improving their relationship. Lastly, the indirect inclusion of the grandfather and the siblings made Jasna aware of her positive emotional ties with them, which contributed to relieving her tension in everyday life as being together with them was a sort of 'oasis' for her and consequently empowered her, as did dialogues with the paternal uncle. The parents, especially the mother, were made aware of their duties and rights during the *grhastha asram* (householder stage). They expressed that they had been understood by the professional and were to some extent relieved.

Inclusion of the broad context
"My job opens doors for me"
The evaluation of the psychosocial intervention showed that the principle of inclusion of the broad context to develop a nuanced and constructive relation to the society was a success. Jasna managed to get a part-time job and restart her studies by the end of the intervention. The follow-up session confirmed the continuity of this positive development.

The focus on the late modern society, with its multiple choices and exaggerated weight on the person as one's "own manager", emphasised the significance of positive choice and action for Jasna. Focus on the experiences of exclusion and racialisation, combined with the strong distinction in the ways young men and women related to their sense of social place and gender roles, contributed to her decision to study and work at the same time. The discussions about the intersections between ethnicity and gender probably made her still more determined to complete her education while working part-time in order to increase her chances in the labour market later. The themes of minority/majority power dynamics, especially in relation to Jasna's parents' marginal position in the labour market, led to her greater comprehension of their struggles and frustrations and sympathy for them, and increased her motivation for restarting and completing her studies.

The meetings involving inter-sectorial professionals from the social department and the business school further supported Jasna and her family in continuing on the path towards the future goals of education, employment and a continued positive relationship with family. However, at the same time it is important to note that the follow-up session revealed a repetition of Jasna's self-destructive behaviour due to interpersonal conflict with the boyfriend, which she came to terms with in the follow-up intervention.

A further follow-up five years later with Jasna showed that she continued to maintain a close relationship with her biological family, especially her mother and siblings as her father had passed away due to illness. She had terminated her relationship with the earlier boyfriend and got married to a spouse belonging to her own ethnic group, with her family's acceptance. Additionally, she was successfully employed in a job corresponding to her qualifications. The long-term follow-up thus confirmed the positive outcome of the intercultural family work based on the three principles and the ethical issues articulated above, especially those addressing and strengthening intergenerational interdependence.

Discussion

A lucid presentation of a case involving intercultural family work illustrates the positive significance of constructive eclecticism as a sustainable theoretical framework for dealing with complex, intergenerational family problems.

According to this paradigm, the members of the ethnic minority family have an identity with multiple belongings, not just belonging to the country of origin (Indian) or country of residence (Danish) but to both at the same time (a diasporic identity), along with identities in relation to educational institutions, labour markets, peer groups and leisure time activities. As Ali (2005) argues, the rhetoric of 'racism' has moved into the realms of the ethnic and the cultural, and these terms, while not in common use with the families, remain potent at a fundamental level. These terms signify, make apparent or exaggerate differences and mark out the dynamics of power and conflicts. Theoretically, both the post-modern constructionist mental health approach (McNamee & Gergen, 1999) and the conceptualisation of the ethnicity of the head (Verkuyten, 2005) emphasise inclusion of the broad context, using a zoom lens instead of a magnifying glass, and turning attention from mental to social processes. Attention to the societal conditions in which the problems develop and cultural practices take place helps in avoiding the oversimplification of blaming individuals. In intercultural family work, it is essential that different family members are made aware of the structural aspects of their situations, to encourage intersubjective understanding and empathy towards each other. The case study depicts an explication of how these aspects contribute to reciprocal understanding and acceptance across generations.

In intercultural work, families are seen as active, negotiating with various categorical belongings such as gender, generation, and socio-economic position to create their own culture as a meaning system. Inclusion of the different members, the significant others, directly or indirectly in the intercultural work makes it possible to hear voices and to create dialogues and multilogues leading to compromises and long term solutions.

The theoretical conceptualisations within the life course perspective (Levy et al., 2005) directing attention to the time dimension linked lives of the different members (Lüscher, 2005), are valuable in generating both short term and long term solutions to the family conflicts. The case poignantly illustrates this, confirming the strengths of intergenerational relationships, despite conflictual dynamics in certain phases of life transition.

The combination of the ethical perspectives of care and justice (LaFromboise et al. 1996) in intercultural family work is made explicit through the case illustration. This perspective challenges the dominant discourse of individual human rights and is significant in family work as it invokes interdependence between the family members, not just the individual's rights; both autonomous and relational aspects are included.

Finally, this perspective, along with the conceptualisation of power positions and ethnicity differences between the professional and the family, emphasises the ethical issues and the moral responsibility of the professional in intercultural family work, especially when it involves vulnerable and marginalised persons.

Conclusion

This chapter has presented a comprehensive theoretical paradigm for working psychosocially with families, which belong to different cultures than the dominant one in the society. Considerations of migration, diaspora and minority processes imply structural inequalities and power differentials between the services and the family. Using the inclusive paradigm with focus on multiple identities, family/network and broad society inclusion, the chapter delineated the framework of an NGO, TTT, in the Danish context, and discussed the critical, constructive eclectic approach to intercultural family work.

It is to be noted that the principles of multiple identities, inclusion of family members and inclusion of the broad context, based on constructive eclecticism, are in fact intricately interrelated, although they have been delineated here as tools of analyses. A flexible application of this framework is an arduous process for the professionals in intercultural family work as no simplistic technique or rigid application of principles will suffice. There is still a need to develop these principles further and adapt them to changing families, time and contexts. Concurrently, there is a need to pass on this knowledge and to engage in dialogue with other relevant professionals to further improve this work. These dialogues will hopefully also lead to the broadening of our languages and our conceptualisations, making them and consequently our intercultural work still more integrative and inclusive.

References

Arenas, J., & Singla, R. (1995). *Etnisk minoritetsungdom i Danmark om deres psykosociale situation* [Ethnic minority youth in Denmark: about their psychosocial situation], Copenhagen: Dansk Psykologisk Forlag.

Anthias, F. (2009). Transnational belonging, identity and generation: Questions and problems in ,migration and ethnic studies. *Finnish Journal of Ethnicity and Migration, 4*, 6-15.

Barn, R., Ladino, C., & Rogers, R. (2006). *Parenting in multi-racial Britain*. London: National Children's Bureau.

Beck-Gersheim, E. (2002). *Reinventing the family: In search of new lifestyles*. London: Polity Press.

Badri, M. (1979). *The dilemma of Muslim psychologists*. London: MWH London Publishers.

Brah, A. (1996). *Cartographies of diaspora: Contesting identities*. London: Routledge.

Bunt, G. (2009). *iMuslims: Rewiring the House of Islam*. London: Hurst & Co.

Castles, S., & Miller, M. (2009). *The age of migration: International population movements in the modern world (4th Ed.)*. New York: Guilford Books.

Chaudhary, N. (2007). The family: Negotiating cultural values. In J. Valsiner & A. Rosa (Eds.), *The Cambridge handbook of sociocultural psychology* (pp. 524-539). Cambridge: Cambridge University Press.

Christensen, C. C. (2006). Intersektionalitet (Intersectionality). *Kvinder, Køn & Forskning nr. 2-3*, [Intersectionality in women, gender and research].

Crenshaw, K. (1994). Mapping the margins: Intersectionality, identity politics & violence against women of color. In M. A. Fineman & R. Mykitiuk (Eds.), *The public nature of private violence: The discovery of domestic abuse* (pp. 93-118). New York: Routledge.

Davies, B. & Harré, R. (1990). *Positioning: The discursive production of selves.* Journal for the Theory of Social Behaviour, 20, 43-63.

Dencik, L. (2005). *Mennesket i postmoderniseringen – om barndom, familie og identiteter i opbrud* [Human beings in postmoderisation- about childhood, family and identitiesunder uprising]. Værløse: Billesø & Baltzer.

Dufoix, S. (2008). *Diasporas*. Berkeley: University of California Press.

Fernando, S. (1991). *Mental health, race and culture.* London: Mind Publications.

Fernando, S. (1995). *Mental health in a multi-ethnic society: A multi-disciplinary handbook.* London: Routledge.

Gergen, K. (2001). Psychological science in a post-modern context. *American Psychologist*, 56, 803-813.

Guzder, J., & Krishna, M. (2005). Mind the gap: Diaspora issues of Indian origin women in psychotherapy. *Psychology and Developing Society, 17,* 121-138.

Ifekwunigwe, J. O. (2004). *'Mixed Race' studies: A reader*. London: Routledge.

Jalali, B. (1988). Ethnicity, cultural adjustment, and behaviour: Implications for family therapy. In L. Comas-Diaz & E. E. H. Griffith (Eds.), *Clinical guidelines in cross-cultural mental health* (pp. 9-32). New York: Wiley.

Jensen de López, K., & Hansen, T. G. B. (2011). *Development of self in culture,* Self in Culture in Mind Series, Vol I. Aalborg: Aalborg University Press.

Kalra, V., Kaur, R., & Hutnyk, J. (2005). *Diaspora and hybridity*. New Delhi: Sage.

Kumar, K. (2008) Indian thought and tradition: A psychohistorical perspective. In K. R. Rao, A. C., Paranjpe & A. K. Dalal (Eds.), *Handbook of Indian psychology* (pp. 19-52). Delhi: Foundation Books.

Køppe, S. (2008). En moderat eklekticisme [A moderate eclecticism]. In *Psyke & Logos, 29,* pp 15-35.

LaFromboise, T. D., Foster, S. L., & James, A. (1996). Ethics in multicultural counseling. In P. B. Pedersen, J. G. Draguns, W. J. Lonner & J. E. Trimble (Eds.), *Counseling across cultures* (pp. 47-72). New Delhi: Sage.

Languani, P. (2007). *Understanding cross-cultural psychology.* New Delhi: Sage.

Lau, A. (1986). Family therapy across cultures. In J. Cox (Ed.), *Transcultural psychiatry* (pp. 234-252). London: Croom Helm.

Lau, A. (1996). Family therapy and ethnic minorities. In K. N. Dwivedi (Ed.), *Meeting the needs of ethnic minority children: A handbook for professionals* (pp. 91-107). London: Jessica Kingsley Publishers.

Levy, R., Ghisletta, P., Le Goff, J.-M., Spini, D. & Widmer, E. (Eds.) (2005). *Towards an interdisciplinary perspective on the life course*. Amsterdam: Elsevier.

Lüscher, K. (2005). Looking at ambivalences: the contribution of a "new-old" view of intergenerational relations to the study of life course. In R. Levy, P. Ghisetta, J le Goff, D. Spini & E. Widmer (Eds.) *Towards an interdisciplinary perpsective of the life course* (pp. 95-131). Amsterdam: Elsevier.

Healy, J., & Mckee, M. (2004). *Accessing health care: Responding to diversity*. Oxford: Oxford University Press.

Minuchin, S. (1974). *Families and family therapy*. Cambridge MA: Harvard University Press.

Rao, K. R., Paranjpe A. C. & Dalal, A. C. (Eds.) (2008). *Handbook of Indian Psychology*. New Delhi: Cambridge University Press/Foundation Books Imprint.

Sassoon, M., & Lindow, V. (1995). Consulting and empowering black mental health system users. In S. Fernando & F. Keating (Eds.). *Mental health in a multi-ethic society: A multi-disciplinary handbook* (pp. 89-106). London: Routledge.

Shashidharan, S. P. (1986). Ideology and politics in transcultural psychiatry. In J. Cox (Ed.), *Transcultural psychiatry* (pp. 158-178). London: Croom Helm.

Sherif Trask, B., & Koivunen, J. (2007). Trends in marriage and cohabitation. In B. Sherif Trask & R. R. Hamon (Eds.), *Cultural diversity and families* (pp 80-99). New Delhi: Sage.

Sinha, D., & Tripathi, R. (1994). Individualism in a Collective Culture: A case of Co-existence of Opposites (pp. 123-136). In Kim, Triandis, Kagitcibasi, Choi & Yoon (Eds.), *Individualism and Collectivism: Theory, method and appplications*. New Delhi: Sage.

Singla, R. (1997). Etnisk minoritetsungdom og psykologisk intervention. [Ethnic minority youth and psychological intervention] In J. Arenas (Ed.), *Interkulturel Psykologi* (pp. 124-142). København: Hans Reitzels Forlag.

Singla, R. (2003). Ungdom og etnicitet, Udfordringer i modernitetens landskabet. (Youth and ethnicity: Challanges in Landscape og Modernity) *Psykologisk Set*, 20 pp. 1-9 www.tttdanmark.dk

Singla, R. (2004). *Youth relationships, ethnicity & psychosocial intervention*. New Delhi: Books Plus.

Singla, R. (2008). *Now & then – Life trajectories, family relationships and diasporic identities: A follow-up study of young adults*. Copenhagen: University of Copenhagen.

Stiglitz, J. (2002). *Globalisation and its discontents*. London: Penguin.

Stiglitz, J. (2010). *Freefall: Free markets and the sinking of the global economy.* London: Allen Lane.
Verkuyten, M. (2005). *The social psychology of ethnic identity.* Hove: Psychology Press.
Vertovec, S. (2000). *The Hindu diaspora: Comparative patterns.* London: Routledge.

Manuel L. de la Mata Benítez
Mercedes Cubero Pérez
Andrés Santamaría Santigosa
Francisco Javier Saavedra Macías

Self-positionings and voices in identity reconstruction of women after suffering gender violence

9

In this chapter, we propose the notions of positionings and voices as analytical tools that may help us understand how a woman that has been abused by her partner or ex-partner proceeds, through an autobiographical interview, towards the reconstruction of her identity. For this purpose, we will start by approaching the concept of positionings to undertake the analysis of their relation to the notions of narrative and identity. We propose a dynamic and discursive view of personal identity, enhancing its situated character, expanding upon essentialist perspectives that underline continuity and stability. After that, we will pause to consider the notions of *positionings* and *voices* as analytical tools for the study of identity in the context of gender violence. We will conclude with the presentation of the analysis conducted, including the instruments: an autobiographical interview with a woman who has been abused by her ex-partner.

A glimpse into the notion of positioning

Positioning theory is based on Foucault's concept of *subjective positioning*. Starting from that notion, Davies and Harré (1990) have developed a consideration of human thinking in terms of *discursive positioning*. These authors proposed a definition of positioning as *"the discursive process whereby selves are located in conversations as observably and subjectively coherent participants in jointly produced story lines"* (ibid., p. 48). This concept points to the way in which people *take* positions in relation to discourse as they produce utterances in a conversation, interview or any communicative exchange. As a theoretical tool, the notion of positioning emphasises the links between the discourses that permeate the social world and the particular interchanges in which meanings are constructed. And this is the main advantage of this theory, as it allows the detailed study of how discourse operates in communicative exchanges between people (Harré & Langenhove, 1999). Positioning theory foregrounds cultural influences on the discourse here-and-now, as well as the way in which individuals resist and reject dominant discourses in everyday conversations.

But when people speak, they are not only positioning themselves though conversation, interview, narrative, etc. in relation to other people, but also in relation to the utterances of other conversations (Bakhtin, 1986). At the same time, they themselves are positioned by the interlocutors. Beyond that, every utterance provides (whether explicitly or implicitly) positionings to respond from. As we can see, positioning theory is, in some ways, a theory about the development of a sense of the self in discourse. The analysis of sexist language, for instance, has offered many examples of exclusive positionings in relation to women, as we shall see below.

We can identify two axes that articulate the main assumptions of positioning theory. First, the *people* in interaction, and second, the *narratives* they construct in these interactions. These axes give coherence and meaning to positioning, conceived as the construction of narratives that make action understandable for the person and for the others, and in which the participants in narration take specific positionings. In other words, they help to identify how the person positions her/hisself in a specific situation, how she locates the others and how the others position her. Smith (1988) refers to this when he distinguishes between the *individual agent* and the *subject,* the latter being understood as the set or the cluster of positionings, provisional and not necessarily immovable, in which a person is momentarily located by discourse in the world s/he inhabits.

Davies and Harré (1990), on the other hand, point out that positioning does not coincide with the notion of role, but is related to the way in which an individual positions herself and is positioned by the others in specific dialogical situations that include not only conversational exchanges, but also narratives produced by the individual. In these narratives, the voices of others are also present (Bakhtin, 1986). Moreover, positionings is, in this sense, the origin of subjectivity, since taking a position in discourse necessarily implies taking a specific point of view: that is, a concrete perspective about the world and about ourselves. The latter is closely related, as we will see below, to one of the key concepts in this chapter, *voice*.

For Harré and Langenhove (1999), episodes are the fundamental units that shape social reality and provide structure for the social encounters that derive from them. They put the different sequences of interaction together into a unified and meaningful whole. In every episode, two essential elements can be highlighted:

1. The first is *position*. This is a relationship between a *self, another* and an *audience*. Moreover, this notion is not static, but is negotiated, changing and adapting to others' opinions. In sum, it moves with and is transformed in interaction.
2. The second element is *positioning*. The complex interplay of positions and its negotiation unavoidably produces a positioning. This is just a plane that gives meaning to the interaction developed in each episode. Positioning is contextualised, i.e., it has no rationale beyond the episode itself; it unfolds as it flows forth from ongoing action. The notion of positioning is characterised, above all, by its relevance for understanding the positions as relational processes, which constitute themselves in interaction and negotiation with others. The positionings are like the threads that weave the fabric of

social interaction together. They are the fabric of our interactive situations, the fabric of our positions.

From all that has been said above, it follows that it would be a mistake to consider positioning as the result of an intentional game or the sum of the normativity established by a set of pre-defined roles. Rather, from this perspective, intentions emerge *in situ*, in the simple game of positionings and re-positionings the other, which takes place in every interaction or, as in our case, throughout an (auto)biographical interview that elicits a personal narrative.

In our view, therefore, positioning theory is a conceptual and methodological apparatus that is particularly suitable for studying the construction and reconstruction of identities in the context of personal narratives. This holds firstly because it is assumed that every interaction is, by definition, discursive or narrative, and secondly, because for this theory positioning is a changing phenomenon, fragmented and absolutely contextual. Many authors in varied disciplines and with diverse methodological approaches have defended the usefulness of this notion in the study of identity construction (Bamberg, 2004, 2007; Wortham, 2000).

Narrative identity, discourse and positionings

To be consistent with the ideas presented in the previous section, we adopt a constructivist, discursive, social and cultural view of identity, in which this phenomenon is regarded as a multiple and continuously negotiated reality. Identity is understood as a process by which individuals, through the social and cultural practices in which they are involved, discursively establish who they are in their relationship with other individuals and with social contexts and settings. In other words, identity is the result of what people do and say in their daily practices, not a monolithic or purely psychological concept.

Over the last fifteen years, research has shown that the construction of identity can be achieved through narration, more specifically by considerations of what is narrated, to whom, and in what way. Schiffrin (1996) conceives narrative as a linguistic lens through which to discover people's own (somewhat idealised) views of themselves as situated in a social structure. Georgakopoulou (1997) affirms the close relation between narrative and self-presentation and, in a similar vein, de Fina (2003) stresses the central role of narrative to the construction of identities when she argues that, through narration, people enact and negotiate personal and social roles, relationships, and their membership in specific communities. It is important to note here that narrative discourse is not considered as a simple reflection of a person's inner world (although we are not denying the existence or the importance of psychological aspects of identity) (Block, 2006).

Accordingly, identity does not consist of appropriating or using elements with a pre-established meaning. On the contrary, it is within discursive practices that those elements acquire their precise social and identificational significance. That is because the social meanings associated to linguistic units are not unique or stable outside of the discursive practices where identities are materialised. It is precisely in this context, in our opinion, we must understand the concept of positioning as previously presented. This indicates that identity is not shaped by the individual affiliation to certain pre-determined social groups; these categories only acquire their identity significance from the *relationships* established between the individual and other social actors in interactions.

In discussing the construction of identity through narrative, the social constructionist paradigm claims that "*social reality is not uniform and objective, but it is created by human beings that are conceived as agents rather than passive organisms*" (Sarbin & Kitsuse, 1994, pp. 2, 8). A similar view is put forth by Schrauf (2000, p. 128), who argues that "*personal and social identities are proffered, contested and negotiated in discursive practices*".

In other words, identity is relational and depends on the positionings the individual takes with respect to other individuals, positionings that is the product of discourse and not of pre-assigned roles. Put more simply, we could say that a white person can be identified as such because there is a group of non-white people, with respect to whom a positioning in a specific interaction is taken. In this sense, it is especially relevant not to forget that the positionings which take place in communicative interactions are not always conscious or voluntary, since taking a position towards other social actors is something inherent to interaction itself. In this vein, Davies and Harré (1990) point out that positioning do not need to be intentional or linear and that the positionings adopted can be stable, or they can be ephemeral and changing.

It is also noteworthy, as Davies and Harré have stressed, that positionings are sometimes the result of a self-choice or *reflective*, while in other occasions they are imposed by other social actors, or *interactive*. At the same time, the identities formed in communicative interactions are not independent, butare related to each other. It is only for analytical purposes that we can separate them.

In relation to the latter, it is necessary to distinguish between *being positioned*, which attributes a sort of determinist force to the narratives, and the more active notion of the subject as *self-positionings*. Being positioned and self-positioning are two metaphoric constructions for two different relations between the world and the agent: in the first case the direction goes from the world to the agent and in the second from the agent to the world (Bamberg, 2004). The social strength of an action and the positionings of the actor(s) mutually determine each other. The positions people take in conversations are connected to the scripts that structure that conversation (Harré & Langenhove, 1999).

In the previous paragraph we have introduced a critical element, very closely related to identity, narrative and positionings, which plays a central role in our analysis: *agency*. One of the aspects that changes in a remarkable way along and across personal narratives is the way in which people express *social agency* through narration. Emirbayer and Mische (1998) claim that social agency consists of three components: an *iterative* component, focused on the past, a *projective* one, focused on the future, and a *practical-evaluative* component, focused on the present. In this model, the authors see narrative as one of the instruments of the projective component, since along the life-span agency is manifested in people's capacity to incorporate different future trajectories, which may influence their personal narratives. As a consequence, this proposal could suggest that, as the life-span continues, human beings lose their agentive capacity, to the extent that their personal narratives progressively reduce their projective components and focus more on the revision and re-interpretation of past experiences. However, the evaluative component is a central aspect of narrative activity, both related to present and past experiences (Hermans, 1992). Taking this as the starting point, Grob, Krings and Bangerter (2001) have shown that evaluative resources develop and change their form and function throughout the adult life-span. Accordingly, we may consider that what changes is the way in which agency is expressed through narration, as we shall see in the interview presented below.

Voices involved in narratives

Some ideas and concepts proposed by the philosopher and semiologist Mikhail Bakhtin (1986) will be applied in our analysis. These concepts let us examine the process by which the women that participate in the study construct personal narratives about their history of abuse.

Among the key notions in Bakhtin's theory, we shall focus on *voice/voices*, as it can be especially useful for the analysis of personal narratives. Personal narratives can be understood as a meeting place between voices and positionings.

Bakhtin proposes a theory of language that is constructed in social exchanges. For Bakhtin, an *utterance* is always produced from a particular point of view, from the specific perspective of an axiological belief system. This perspective is called voice. Moreover, voices are linked to a specific social, cultural and historical context. The communication act is constituted as an exchange of voices that human beings reproduce, manipulate, quote, etc. On this view, meaning only exists when two or more voices make contact. The voice of a speaker responds to the voice of a listener. Understanding an utterance involves a process in which other utterances get into contact and confront it. Thus, understanding consists of linking the speaker's word to a counter-word (the hearer's alternative word). To understand someone else's utterance means to orient towards it, to find a place for that utterance in its context.

Thereby, Bakhtin rejects the conception of an individualist and private self: the self is essentially social. Every individual is constituted as a collection of numerous *selves* that s/he has assimilated along his/her life, in contact with the different *voices* that, in some way, conform to our ideology. Therefore, it is the social subject who produces a text that is precisely the intersection between ideological and linguistic systems. For this reason, discourse analysis, in our view, leads to *polyphony*: that is, to the analysis of the set of voices that populate our utterances and are put into contact with the *others*' positionings and utterances. Polyphony, in Bakthin's terms, is a feature of narratives, which include a diversity of points of view and voices (Wertsch, 1991).

Our discourse is polyphonic: it is populated by other voices, as internalised dialogues, so that the voices of others are incorporated into our own discourse. Utterances arise as responses to previous utterances and are oriented to those in the future (Bakhtin, 1999). The self is set up, therefore, at the other's request and this other is installed in our territory. This leads to the conclusion that the self is, by nature, polyphonic and communicates in a set of mixed voices from diverse origins.

Besides taking into account the voices of individuals in his sociohistorical context, Bakhtin postulates that the human exchanges that happen in a novel are nothing but the interplay between the voice of the author and the voice of the characters (Bakhtin, 1999). For him, the discursive experience of any person becomes possible as it is constituted in terms of a permanent assimilation of others' utterances. Bakhtin considers this process as the creative assimilation of others' words with different degrees of alterity.

A concept that is closely connected to that of voices is *ventriloquation*, which is central in the process of appropriation (internalisation) of other voices. Ventriloquation involves the process "*whereby one voice speaks through another voice or voice type in a social language*" (Wertsch, 1991, p. 59). The voices of the others are integrated in our discourse and resonate in our mind. They transport us to past contexts and experiences that are projected to the present and, in turn, facilitate representation in the future. This process of ventriloquation and interanimation of voices is a key for the shaping of personal, social, cultural and gender identity. Interanimation involves the process by which different voices are put in contact with each other.

In our view, the notion of position(ing), together with voices, may allow us to articulate the relationship between a *micro* plane of analysis (the analysis of the different positionings that women adopt during the course of their narratives) and a *macro* plane (the analysis of the social, cultural, institutional and historical contextualisation of those positionings). We think that the analysis of the voices that, in many occasions, these women bring to their discourse, or that in other cases 'populate' their narratives, can be a valuable instrument. This approach allows us to observe how others' perspectives and points of view (persons, groups, institutions, generic voices, etc.) articulate the positionings adopted in the here-and-now of discourse in an autobiographical interview and, in so doing, contribute to the narrative (re)construction of personal identity.

Positionings as a tool for the study of identity development through narrative

As a tool for the study of identity development through narrative, Bamberg and colleagues (Bamberg, 1997, 2004; Korobov, 2001) have developed a three-step procedure to identify participants' positioning during narrative activity. As explained above, *positionings* are understood as discourse spaces in which participants make sense of each other, themselves and the nature of the events reported.

From this perspective, narratives are not the reflection of an identity that is hidden in the text, but functional elements for creating characters in time and space within an interactive context: *me in front of my father, me against my group of friends,* or *me against my boss.* In our case, the interactive context includes *me in front of an interviewer* in a research context (although the interviewer positionings herself as an ally of the interviewed woman). As discussed above, these tools have been primarily applied to the study of identity. The work on positioning analysis thus focuses on what narrative positionings can say about individual actors or the social categories (e.g. adolescents, male, etc.) that they appropriate and construct through narratives. It is necessary to take into account that construction processes are always bidirectional. That is, while constructing my identity, I am creating a context that accompanies and limits identity construction.

Obviously, a self-positioning, for instance in the context of a chess game (*I am an excellent player*), explicitly or implicitly implies an other-positioning (*my opponent is afraid*). The discursive acts of positioning can be personal attributes or motives (*do not worry, I am a good person*), roles or social rights (*as a father, I told you to shut up*) or based on the adoption of moral rules (*a friend does not do that*). Moreover, positionings are structured in different levels that can be very complex. For instance, someone that is telling an autobiographical narrative can position him/herself in the past as an innocent person and, at the same time, in the present as a suspicious person (*when I was young, I was too good a person, but now I have learnt my lesson*).

From this perspective, we can say that positioning analysis (Archakis & Tzanne, 2005; Bamberg, 2004, 2011; Bamberg & Georgakopoulou, 2008; Georgakopoulou, 2000; Korobov, 2001; Wortham, 2000) provides analytical procedures especially suitable for examining (auto)biographical interviews such as those in our study. Some authors in this field, like Bamberg (2004) or Lucius-Hoene (2002), have systematised those procedures by successively focusing on different levels of narrative activity. Their main field of application has been the study of identity through narration, especially in relation to the dimensions of gender, age, socio-cultural context and especial life experiences (Bamberg, 2004, 2011; Bamberg & Georgakopoulou, 2008). So, for instance, the analysis of positionings has been used to study the narratives of people with serious mental problems in their process of recovery (Saavedra, Cubero & Crawford, 2009; Saavedra, Santamaría, Crawford & Lucius-Hoene, 2012). The proposal of this analysis arises from the evidence that any interactive process must be situated in a wide social context where the interpretation of facts and behaviours takes place. This idea is particularly important for the highly complex decision-making processes of abused women.

In this chapter we shall use an adaptation of these strategies for examining the experience of abuse of a woman to try to understand how she positionings along her personal narrative, and how this narrative is embedded in a particular social, cultural, individual and family history.

Among the indicators that may help us analyse the positionings in the narrative, we can point to the use of pronouns, verb tenses, the use of reported speech, social categories, the identification of voices and social discourses, pauses, prosody, etc. In sum, we consider any semantic, syntactic or pragmatic indicator that lets us determine the positionings adopted by the woman through the interview. All the positionings identified are based on the transcription of the interview selected for the chapter.

We have applied a procedure of group analysis. This can be considered as a procedure to achieve reliability in analyses conducted by several researchers (Cohen & Crabtree, 2008). Specifically, after the individual analysis of the interviews, these analyses were presented in seminar sessions with the whole research group. The positionings that were not sufficiently justified and based on empirical data were discussed and discarded, and ultimately a synthesis of results was elaborated.

A study of identity re-construction through self-positionings

The analysis presented in this section is part of a larger study entitled "Recovering the control of our lives: identity reconstruction and empowerment in women victims of gender violence"[1]. One of the aims of that study was to contribute to constructing an active and positive image of battered women (Crawford, 2006). For that purpose, we focused on studying recovered women. We wanted to make them visible, to know about their achievements and how they live this through, starting from their experience, and contributing to the creation of positive models that may help other women in their process of recovery.

We focus on the analysis of an autobiographical interview to examine the positionings through discourse analysis. We will consider both self-positionings (reflective, according to Davies & Harré, 1990) and other-positionings (interactive, according to the same authors), that is, we are interested both in how the woman positionings herself and how she is positioned by others. In the same vein, we will consider positionings with different degrees of explicitness, those expressed by using direct speech and those expressed though reported speech. Complementarily, we will also analyse the voices that may articulate the different positionings, voices that reflect the main characters of the stories narrated. These voices have different levels of generality, from particular and concrete voices (e.g. the voices of the participant women, the voices of the ex-partners, etc.) to generic voices (voices of friends, women, the neighbours, etc.) or even institutional voices (family, religion, etc.).

The case of Rosa

Selected from a total of six women, we present the analysis of the interview of a woman that we have called Rosa. Rosa is 41 years old at the time of the interview. She seems very cheerful, energetic and a little nervous. Rosa got married when she was eighteen and she has been married for 23 years. She has two daughters, the elder daughter is 20 years old and the younger one, who is living with Rosa, is 13 years. In 2006 Rosa took a job in a bakery, as a delivery worker. One year later she went to the Women's Information Centre, where she had been referred to by the Social Services. Her lawyer explains that she was very scared and had to leave her home quickly as she feared for her life. She states that she has been suffering a situation of violence for more than 20 years, and that insults, humiliations, beatings and threats (including death threats) from her husband were continuous. After some "rather strong" episodes that occurred during a feast in her town, she says she could not stand it anymore. As she did not want to hide anything from her husband, she asked for a divorce attorney to assist her for a divorce. However, she wanted an agreed divorce, so that her husband would not get angry, because she was frightened of how he would react. She says that once the husband realised that she was leaving he became extremely aggressive and she felt, more than ever, that he was going to kill her. So, she felt "the impulse" to leave in order to save her and her daughter's life. In that situation, she called her sister and left home, bringing nothing with her, in order to move to the flat of a relative. Finally and after many difficulties, Rosa and her husband signed an agreement that established that he continued living in the house that used to be the family home while she and her daughter moved to live in a rented flat.

When we met Rosa she expressed that she felt more relaxed since she moved from her ex-husband. Sometimes he insists that they should get back together and she still feels guilty, however, her anxiety has decreased. Rosa claims that she has now re-established friendships after a long time without these during her marriage, and she has found someone who makes her feel loved for the first time.

The interview was conducted by a female member of the research group. It took place in the "Instituto Andaluz de la Mujer" (Andalusian Women Institute), a regional government institution for the promotion of gender equality. It was conducted in May 2008 and lasted for approximately 1 hour.

Rosa - a strong and resolute woman

The story of abuse told by Rosa is characterised by the existence of nine positionings, of which the four major ones were:

1. Victim:
   "Because the beatings, you know, they do not hurt so much as the humiliations and violations; when we were in bed he used to say that I looked like an inflatable doll and then he kicked me out of the bed."
2. Strong and resolute woman:
   "…if this family goes on, it is because I am getting on with it alone."
3. Responsible mother:
   "…he didn't care that I never had money, that my sisters had no money, I had to make good use of all money.
4. Working woman:
   "I work at the bakery, right? Delivering bread…I wake up very early in the morning and work hard and …"

These positionings can be found throughout the whole interview and let Rosa tell her story of abuse, as well as presenting the arguments, reflections and life-events that led to her taking certain decisions that concluded in *"a need to break up with my husband and leave everything behind"*. When adopting these positionings Rosa is elaborating some reflections, but that does not mean that this narrative is characterised by the predominance of a reflective self. Rather, we could say that what characterises the interview is the predominance of a re-lived self, thanks to the pervasive use of direct speech to enact the voices of the main characters in the story. Voices such as hers (*"I told myself' I live because I have to live, because I have a daughter and have to fight for her'"*) or that of her ex-husband (*"… I told him about any problem and he didn't know anything 'For that I come home …?!!' He opened the door and left again. I couldn't talk to him"*) or her sister (*"My sister was the one who knew and told me 'I can't force you, but he is going to kill you if you don't leave, And also I can't tell you what to do, sister', that's what she said"*), constantly appear in her discourse, whether as direct agents of the utterances (subject of enunciation) or as characters involved in the utterances (subject of the utterance). In Rosas's case, that reflective self seems to focus on the less frequent positionings, such as that of recovered (*"Now I regret not having done it much earlier, the very day he raped me and got me pregnant of my eldest daughter"*) and beloved woman (*"… now I am living, I am living and still when I get near him I get very happy … because I didn't know what this is"*) that we will analyse below.

One of the most significant aspects in the interviews with battered women in general, and with Rosa in particular, is that the voice of the ex-husband is always present. The predominance of this voice can be understood as it is used in different ways. One is to recreate and exemplify the violence suffered and Rosa's positioning as victim:

> *"…he said 'I'm gonna cut your neck. Nobody escapes from where you are going, but I will be free in three or four years'"*.

In this case it is the only voice that articulates a negative positioning about her: "slut", incompetent woman, bad mother.

> *"…I was useless, I did everything wrong"*.
> *"…I was a slut and I was with my colleagues, I was with all men"*.

The voice of the ex-husband is also brought to discourse as the voice to react to in order to adopt different, and often opposite and more positive positionings. These opposite positionings convey a higher control of Rosa's life and a high level of agency, such as those of a strong and resolute woman or a responsible mother.

> "...I'm not useless, nor a bad mother, because, I, I was pregnant and raise his child."
> "I am strong and he said that I can't go on and I can".

The voice of her sister is the most significant voice in Rosa's story. This voice is frequently used in discourse as representing an alter for the construction of her arguments:

> "When I left, my sister said, 'child, I'll buy all the groceries', because I had no money at all".

Moreover, this is the only voice which appears at the moments that Rosa refers to social support throughout the years of violence and on the specific day she decided to escape with her daughter.

> "At that moment I was very badly nervous, very scared, ... I called my sister and asked her to get the key of my cousin's house, the house was not fixed, dirty, without anything, and my sister got it."

It is important to highlight that Rosa always refers to her sister with gratitude. Against her decision of not having support from "psychologists" or medication, her sister was her only support.

> "My sister helped me very much, very much, very much, I can't thank her enough."

Besides these specific and particular voices, more generic voices also appeared, including those of the "people" ("*I think that it was because people told him 'Oh, your wife is so capable'. And he got jealous*"), or even

CONCEPTUAL AND APPLIED APPROACHES

"institutional" or the "family's" voice ("… *the family never knows, until they know and help you*"), to articulate the different positionings adopted.

Although they were not so frequent, we may point to the existence of other positionings, which are also important to understanding Rosa's story of abuse and how she overcame it.

Such positionings consist of the following five categories:

1 Recovered woman
 "*Now I'm fine, every day I feel happier to have done so.*"
2 Daughter
 "*…he beat me hard, my mother had a heart surgery and the doctor didn't want her to get worried … and I put makeup on my face. She realized and said 'You have black eyes'. 'That's painting, mom'.*"
3 Frightened woman
 "*I wanted to divorce since a long time ago, but I was frightened, I was…He said he'll skip the restraining order and send me to the.*"
4 Submissive wife
 "*I didn't say anything. I was quiet…*"
5 Beloved woman
 "*I didn't know what a caress was, I didn't know anything. He is a person who is always taking care of me; even now he calls me every morning to see how I am.*"

In these positionings we also find the voice of her sister and especially the voice of the ex-husband, although there are also other voices, such as those of her new partner or her mother.

With regard to Rosa's adoption of positionings, the analysis of the interview has revealed an especially significant fact. Articulating the positionings that give a greater agency to Rosa, there is another voice that, in some way, we could say helped or even was responsible for the positionings adopted by Rosa. This is the voice of the interviewer. In the interview we can see how the interviewer empathises with the interviewee in a way that not only supports and reinforces the view of Rosa as a recovered woman ("… *I would like you to tell me how did you come to get recovered"*), as a responsible mother (*"Then the children, everything was for them, right?"*), as a strong and resolute woman (*"...I took everything, the house, the children and also my work"*) or as a beloved woman (*"...I'm convinced that you have learnt so much, you are a very strong woman I, I know, and everything is going to be great with this man that loves you and respects you so much..."*). In some cases the interviewer positionings Rosa way before Rosa even positions herself (see the first and the last example). The interviewer does this by elaborating a conclusion from certain statements uttered by Rosa, which evaluates and generalises the meaning of the signs in Rosa's discourse (as in the second and last example), or through the way in which the interviewer formulates her own questions to include the positioning that Rosa is ascribed later (as in the first case). In this sense, the interview itself could be considered as a therapeutic act, and as a setting that facilitates the process of recovery or reconstruction of Rosa's personal identity.

In relation to the voices through which the different positionings are articulated, we must point out that in all the positionings already mentioned, there are other voices which refer to the social network that witnessed the acts of violence, (colleagues, the daughters, ex-husband's friends, neighbours) or became Rosa's social support in her process of recovery (the mother, the father, the new partner). Thus, in Rosa's case, as well as in other interviews with battered women, there is a complex process of interanimation of voices (Wertsch, 1991) involved in the dialogical reconstruction of the identity of these women.

Towards conclusions

Thanks to the analysis of the positionings adopted by Rosa to define herself and to those conferred by others, as well as to the voices through which all these positionings are re-created and exemplified in discourse, we are able to elaborate a first picture of the history of abuse narrated in the interview.

Positionings and the conflicts between them

What we have said so far leads us to describe the above interview in relation to the conflict between positionings that characterises it. In this case we could say that the story narrated by Rosa, as well as many others, exemplifies an identity conflict between a vision of herself as a "bad woman", "incompetent" and "frightened", as she is positioned by her ex-husband (other-positionings), and another view of her as a "working woman", "strong and resolute", which arises as a reaction to the former, by which Rosa positions herself (self-positionings, mostly). This conflict, that goes along the whole "journey" from her past as a "victim", to her present as a "recovered and beloved woman", reported in the interview, sustains the rest of the positionings, which are aligned along the poles of the conflict. This conflict between positionings seems to be at the core of the identity construction and self construal of our participants.

The conflict between positionings or positive views of Rosa, where she usually self-positionings, and negative positionings (in most cases, other-positionings), is also evidenced in terms of more or less agentive positionings. However we must warn against a frequent misinterpretation. In many cases, the lack or the reduction of agency is associated with passivity. Far from that, the interviews analysed here provide evidence how this lack of agency often involves *resistance* and the use of *tactics* (cf. de Certeau, 2000). Although the term "resistance" is widely used in the social sciences, our employment of this is related to Wertsch's (1998) reading of Bakhtin. According to Wertsch, the way individuals appropriate any mediational means (such as a specific voice or social language) may reflect different attitudes towards it, ranging from a complete acceptance to a complete rejection. Resisting other's voices, for instance by producing a "counter-word", is a way of preserving some individual agency even when using someone else's discourse.

The notion of tactic, together with strategy, was developed by Michel De Certeau (1984) to point out that individuals or groups act with different degrees of control (and power) over the situations in which they act. De Certeau uses a spatial metaphor to distinguish between the cases in which they have the capacity to set a "proper" place, a scenario for their actions. Conversely, when they have to act in someone else's scenario (in other words, in a situation defined by someone else) they are using "tactics".

In the case of Rosa, for instance, when she positioned herself as a victim, a positioning that can be characterised as having low agency, she tells how she avoided or tried to escape abuse by doing things such as: *"To work I woke up at 4, barefoot, so that he didn't hear me"* or *"We went to bed dressed, with my bag under the bed, the keys and the mobile under the pillow"*. They are clear examples of active resistance and her actions are examples of tactics. Only when a battered woman is able to break up with the offender and create a new "scenario" for her life we can say that her action is strategic. And, following De Certeau, we can say that both strategies and tactics involve agency on the woman's side. Put in Bakhtin's terms, the capacity to resist and respond to other voices with a "counter-word" (Bakhtin, 1986, Wertsch, 1991) seems to be critical for these women to overcome the situation of violence and reconstruct their identities. This shows us again the complex process of interanimation of voices that underlies the narrative reconstruction of identity in our participants.

Emotions

As it has been reported in other autobiographical interviews with women who have suffered gender violence, in the case of Rosa we see an emotional conflict directly associated with the identity conflict mentioned above. Despite emotions not being at the centre of our analysis, we do not want to close the discussion without mentioning the existence of a strong feeling of injustice and anger. At different moments of the interview, Rosa expresses these feelings by saying *"I don't deserve this"*. The anger and desperation she experiences over that injustice could explain that, as a consequence, the positionings of "working woman" and "strong and resolute" are constantly elicited and, moreover, are presented with a very high emotional load and many details. We consider that these are the basis for the construction of Rosa's new positioning, her new identity as a "recovered woman", associated with feelings of security and happiness.

Turning points and triggering events

In this story of more than twenty years of humiliations and aggressions, there is a *turning point* (cf. McAdams, 1999, 2001, 2003; McAdams and Olson, 2010), triggered by life events that mark the person's life-trajectory. That is, there is a moment of breaking up with that life, a day on which, according to Rosa, she *"think[s] nothing...only feel[s] panic for [her] life and for [her] daughter's"*. She experiences a *"great impulse"*, an internal state which mandates action and which, together with her *"great strength"*, led to her saying *"Lidia, put your clothes into garbage bags; we are leaving home. Your father could kill us"*. Thus, these ideas and feelings (the fear of dying, the safety of her daughter and, above all, her impulse and great strength) become the transcendent facts that, together with the existence of a social network, led Rosa to escape home and thereby start the process of recovery or identity reconstruction. This event was a key in the strengthening of the positionings associated with a greater control of her life (such as those of "recovered" or "resolute woman") and the weakening of other positionings (such as "victim", "bad" and "incompetent" or "submissive woman") that did not help and maybe even inhibited the process of change and transformation.

In summary, in this interview, as in others, we can find events that serve as triggers for breaking up with the offender, usually situations in which the women felt particularly humiliated and threatened (both themselves and/or their children). But in addition to referring to these special situations of violence, women talk about their strength and about the support from others as a key to breaking up with the abuser. Interestingly, the positioning of "mother" appears in Rosa's interview (and also in other cases), combined with other positionings that involve a high degree of empowerment and agency.

We can conclude that these turning points are characterised by the existence of:

- *The triggering events*: situations experienced by these women that made them (or their children) felt especially threatened and humiliated.
- *The social network*: the existence of relatives, friends and institutions that support them is a key to breaking up with the offender.
- *An internal state that drives to action*: they tell of an immediate necessity to act, an impulse.

- *Activating feelings*: strength, bravery, fear, empowerment and control.

To summarise the arguments, figure 1 represents Rosa's journey as well as a brief interpretation of this.

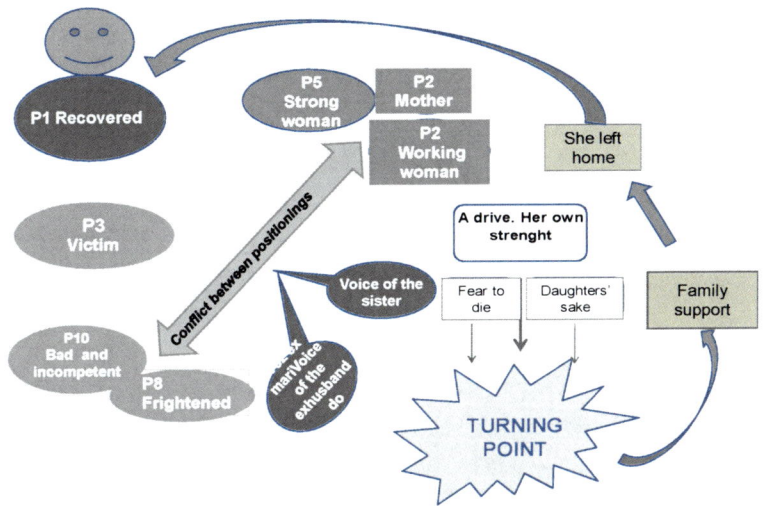

Figure 1. Rosa's journey

We can conclude by saying that after the journey Rosa considers herself a recovered woman. To reach this point she has lived through a strong conflict between seeing herself as an incompetent and frightened women, and through different positionings mostly articulated by the voice of the ex-husband, and on the other hand seeing herself as a strong and responsible working woman and mother, articulated by the voice of her sister, and the counterpoint of the voice of her ex-husband. These conflicts appear as a turning points elicited by a strong fear of dying and the need to take care of herself for the good of her daughters. Conflicts could be resolved because of Rosa's great strength. Such situations, thanks to her family support, produced the new positioning, that were articulated through the voice of her sister resulting in her leave her husband. This in turn signified the end of the positioning of herself as a victim and the beginning of a new positioning as a woman in the process of recovering her identity.

Note

1   This research was granted by the Plan Nacional de I+D+I of the Spanish Ministerio de Educación y Ciencia (2004-2007) (National Plan for R+D+I).

References

Archakis, A., & Tzanne, A. (2005). Narrative positioning and the construction of situated identities: Evidence from conversations of a group of young people in Greece. *Narrative Inquiry, 15*, 267-291.

Bakhtin, M. M. (1986). *Speech genres and other late essays*. C. Emerson, & M. Holquist (Eds.). Austin: University of Texas Press.

Bamberg, M. (1997). Positioning between structure and performance. *Journal of Narrative and Life Story, 7*, 335-342.

Bamberg, M. (2004). 'I know it may sound mean to say this, but we couldn't care less about her anyway'. Form and functions of `slut bashing' in male identity constructions in 15-year-olds. *Human Development, 47*, 331-353.

Bamberg, M. (2007). Stories: Big or small – Why do we care? In M. Bamberg (Ed.), *Narrative– State of the art* (pp. 165–174). Amsterdam: John Benjamins.

Bamberg, M. (2011). Who am I? Narration and its contribution to self and identity. *Theory and Psychology, 21*, 3-24.

Bamberg, M., & Georgakopoulou, A. (2008). Small stories as a new perspective in narrative and identity analysis. *Text & Talk, 28*, 377–396.

Block, D. (2006). *Multilingual identities in a global city: London stories*. London: Palgrave.

Brescó, I. (2009). La construcción narrativa de los eventos del pasado. Una propuesta teórica ["The narrative construction of past events: a theoretical proposal"]. *Estudios de Psicología, 30*, 215-230.

Cavanagh, K. (2003). Understanding women's responses to domestic violence. *Qualitative Social Work, 2*, 229-249.

Cohen, D. J., & Crabtree, F. (2008). Evaluative criteria for qualitative research in health care: Controversies and recommendations. *Annals of Family Medicine, 6*, 331-339.

Crawford, M. (2006). *Transformations. Women, gender and psychology*.Boston:McGraw-Hill.

Davies, B., & Harré, R. (1990). Positioning: The discursive production of selves. *Journal for the Theory of Social Behavior, 20*, 43-63.

De Certeau, M. (1984). *The practice of everyday life*. Berkeley, CA: University of California Press.

De Fina, A. (2003). *Identity in narrative. A study of immigrant discourse*. Amsterdam: John Benjamins.

Emirbayer, M., & Mische, A. (1998). What is agency? *American Journal of Sociology, 103*, 962-1023.

Georgakopoulou, A. (1997). *Narrative performances. A study of Modern Greek storytelling*. Amsterdam: Benjamins.

Georgakopoulou, A. (2000). Analytical positioning vis-à-vis narrative positioning. *Narrative Inquiry, 10*, 185-190.

Grob, A., Krings, F., & Bangerter, A. (2001). Life markers in biographical narratives of people from three cohorts: A life span perspective in its historical context. *Human Development, 44*, 171-190.

Harré, R., & Van Langenhove, L. (Eds.) (1999). *Positioning theory: Moral contexts of intentional action*. Malden: Blackwell.

Hermans, H. (1992). Telling and retelling one's self-narrative: A contextual approach to life-span development. *Human Development, 35*, 361-375.

Korobov, N. (2001). Reconciling theory with method: From conversation analysis to critical discourse analysis to positioning analysis. *Forum: Qualitative Social Research, 2* (3). Online at http://www.qualitative-research.net/fqs.

Lucius-Hoene, G., & Deppermann, A. (2002). *Rekonstruktion narrativer Identität* [Reconstruction of narrative identity]. Opladen: Leske+Budrich.

McAdams, D. P. (1999). Personal narratives and the life story. In L. Pervin & O. John (Eds.), *Handbook of personality: Theory and research* (2nd ed., pp. 478-500). New York: Guilford Press.

McAdams, D. P. (2001). The psychology of life stories. *Review of General Psychology, 5*, 100-122.

McAdams, D. P. (2003). Identity and the life story. In R. Fivush & C. A. Haden (Eds.), *Autobiographical memory and the construction of a narrative self. Developmental and cultural perspectives*. (pp. 187-207) Mahwah, NJ: Lawrence Erlbaum Associates.

McAdams, D. P., & Olson, B. D. (2010). Personality development: Continuity and change over the life course. *Annual Review of Psychology, 61*, 517-542.

Saavedra, J. (2009). *Narrativas de vida en contextos socio-culturales: Explorando narrativas de vida de personas con esquizofrenia que viven en Casas Hogares* [Life narratives in socio-cultural contexts: Exploring the life narratives of persons with schizophrenia living in care homes]. Universidad de Sevilla. [Doctoral thesis published online at: http://fondosdigitales.us.es/tesis/tesis/1128/narrativas-de-vida-en-contextos-socio-culturales-explorando-narrativas-de-vida-de-personas-con-esquizofrenia-que-viven-en-casas-hogares/]

Saavedra, J., Cubero, M., & Crawford, P. (2009). Incomprehensibility in the narratives of individuals with a diagnosis of schizophrenia. *Qualitative Health Research, 19,* 1548-1558.

Saavedra, J., Santamaría, A., Crawford, P., & Lucius-Hoene, G. (2012). Auditory hallucinations as social self-positions: A theoretical discussion from a single-case study. *Journal of Constructivist Psychology, 25,* 1-22.

Sarbin, T. (1986). *Narrative psychology: The storied nature of human conduct.* New York: Praeger.

Schiffrin, D. (1996). Narrative as self-portrait: Sociolinguistic constructions of identity. *Language in Society, 25,* 167-203.

Sarbin, T., & Kitsuse, J. I. (Eds.) (1994). *Constructing the social.* London: Sage.

Schrauf, R. W. (2000). Narrative repair of threatened identity. *Narrative Inquiry, 10,* 1-19.

Wertsch, J. V. (1991). *Voices of the mind.* Cambridge, MA: Harvard University Press.

Wortham, S. (2000). Interactional positioning and narrative self-construction. *Narrative Inquiry, 10,* 157-184.

Qi Wang
Jessie Bee Kim Koh
Yang Yang

The cultural self in mind and action

10

Children, regardless of culture, come to acquire a sense of "who I am" by the toddler age. This early cognitive sense of self continues to develop and evolve into self-representations, self-concepts, and self-theories. The father of modern cognitive psychology, Ulric Neisser, conceives of the self as comprising five kinds of self-knowledge defined by different forms of information (Neisser, 1988). The ecological self and the interpersonal self are both based on online perception, with the former specifying our physical existence with respect to the environment and the latter establishing a state of inter-subjectivity as we are engaged in immediate social interaction with others. They are situated in the here-and-now and are apparent in very early infancy. In contrast, the private self involves internal, reflective representations of our conscious experiences that are only accessible to ourselves, such as thoughts, dreams, and imaginations. It develops during the preschool years when children come to recognise the privacy of their mental life. Most pertinent to this volume, there is the extended or remembered self that is built on the memory of significant personal experiences from our lives, that is, autobiographical memory; and the conceptual self that is our conceptual representation of who we are, including our knowledge of our bodies, our minds, our traits, and our roles in society. It is these two kinds of self-knowledge that are most susceptible to social-cultural influences as they develop in a myriad of daily exchanges between individuals and their immediate and distal cultural contexts. They together make up a self that integrates the framework of the culture, which has been referred to as the 'cultural self' (Wang, 2006; Wang, Shao & Li, 2010).

This volume is a wonderful collection of essays on empirical research that provide unique theoretical, methodological, and practical insights into the development, expression, and maintenance of the cultural self and its consequences for well-being. The chapters address the remembered self (i.e., autobiographical memory), the conceptual self (also referred to as self-concept or self-construal), the interplay between the two, and their respective implications in clinical, family counselling and immigration contexts. A number of messages strongly and clearly conveyed in the studies are critical to the understanding of the cultural self:

a. Both the remembered self and the conceptual self are inherently cultural.

b. The self is dynamic, flexible, and adaptive to the ever-changing cultural and historical conditions in which we reside.

c. The self is resilient; it actively, although not necessarily wittingly, adopts strategies appropriate to one's culture to cope with trauma and life disruptions.

d. There is no better way to study the cultural self in the changing world than by the combination of a variety of methods and the use of both quantitative and qualitative analyses.

e. The self takes the form of both internal representations and external behaviours; it is both how we view ourselves, in our mind, and how we act upon the physical and social world, through our actions, including discursion actions as shown in narrative.

The beginning of the remembered self

The study reported by Abels, Mortazavi and Keller addresses a number of new issues in relation to cultural influences on the remembered self. Conceptually, it looks beyond the usual contrast between individualism and collectivism and considers various dimensions of culture, including uncertainty avoidance, power distance, and masculinity, that may impact on self-construal, and the related consequences for autobiographical memory of childhood experiences. The data from Iran and the corresponding cultural analysis in contrast to German culture are particularly valuable; this is the first study that we know of to examine early childhood memory in this population. Empirically, the study investigated the autobiographical self as constructed in the process of remembering versus knowing, and comparing narratives of participants' own experiences and narratives of what they heard from others. It further compared fragmentary memories of smells and emotional sensations versus coherent memories of events. Methodologically, the combination of quantitative and qualitative analyses makes the results richer, more contextualised, and more firmly culturally rooted.

Many interesting questions arise from the study. For example, how does the cultural self-construal variously influence the different types of memory, be they remembered or heard, fragmentary or coherent? Would a particular dimension of the cultural self-construal be more likely to result in, for instance, fragmentary memories? Pertaining to the non-remembered events, such events may be further categorised as vicarious events, that is, events that happened to other people, or events of the participants' early experiences of which they do not have memory, such as their birth. This distinction is important as the two subgenres involve different protagonists – the self versus others – and may therefore exhibit different contents, styles, and narrative stances across cultures. A further question concerns the specific functions that each type of memory may serve in cultural self-construal. While autobiographical memories – memories of one's own significant experiences – are generally considered self-defining in the Western psychological literature, the function of vicarious memories in building a self-identity is largely an uncharted area in empirical research. Family conversations about vicarious events appear as early as those of children's own experiences (Fivush, 2008). These family stories carry rich cultural messages about the ethnic heritages of parents and grandparents, about the historical background of the family and the community, and about the cultural beliefs and expectations to be imparted into children. Different forms of reminiscing may be exhibited in families across cultures and these may further play a critical role in the construction of the cultural self (Wang, in press). Systematic theoretical analysis and empirical investigation are required to address these questions.

The self in development

Spaten conducted an in-depth analysis of self-narratives and self-reports in Danish children from middle childhood through adolescence, to trace the development of self-understanding in social and ecological contexts. In addition to examining developmental changes, the study also looked at the influence of gender and social-economic status (SES) on the self-concept, which yielded some interesting and unique findings. The lack of interaction between time and gender in children's self-representations is particularly intriguing. Such an interaction, previously found in North American children of European origin, is usually taken to reflect the consequences of gendered ideologies, expectations, and concerns in which children become increasingly immersed as they grow older. The lack of the interaction may reflect the particular characteristics of gender socialisation in Danish culture. Furthermore, the in-depth analyses of a small group of children's self-narratives provide unique access to the variables and factors embedded in a variety of ecological systems (school, family, teacher, peers, the larger society) that play critical roles in children's self-development. Tracing children's narratives over time further reveals the constructive and adaptive nature of the self in line with specific cultural circumstances and contexts. Perhaps most importantly, the quantitative and qualitative analyses together demonstrate that the process of self-making in culture unfolds in children's activities and their narrative interpretations of these activities: that is, in both mind and action.

The overall pattern of age differences in self-concept revealed in the study are consistent with the general findings concerning the development of self-representations, which move from being observable and concrete to intangible and abstract, from being general and decontextualised to differentiated and context-specific, and from concerning physical to social and psychological attributes (Harter, 1998). In addition to these well-documented self-dimensions, what other dimensions of the self-concept may emerge in the study of the self in cultural contexts? The examination of the independent and interdependent self-construals may be the first step. How these cultural self-construals emerge and develop with age and social-cultural experiences (Wang, 2006) and whether and how demographic factors such as gender and SES and ecological variables such as peers and neighbourhood influence such development are important questions to further pursue in a variety of cultural contexts. Methodologically the pursuit of effective ways to empirically test different culture dimensions as causal contributors and mediators for self-development is a task that all self researchers must undertake.

The biased self

Self-serving bias, and self-serving attributional bias (SSAB) in particular, has been commonly observed in North American populations of European origin, where individuals perceive and interpret life situations in ways that help maintain a favourable self-image. Such a positive bias is generally considered beneficial or even necessary for individuals' well-being (Taylor & Brown, 1988). While SSAB is believed to be associated with individualistic cultures that encourage self-enhancement and value self-esteem, Sanjuán found its existence in a Spanish sample, whose culture is traditionally considered collectivist. Her study further replicated the positive connections between SSAB and psychological well-being measures frequently found in North American samples. These findings are important in demonstrating that psychological phenomena, and the self in particular, need to be understood not only in relation to specific cultural contexts, but also from a historical perspective. With the many cultural and economic changes taking place in Spain during the past decades, the culture is moving towards greater individualism, accompanying which are the changing selves, cognitions, and behaviours.

One follow-up question concerns the relation between SSAB and well-being in cultures where SSAB tends to be weak and is generally discouraged. Would a positive bias in favour of the self be equally beneficial for individuals in such cultures, or would the health benefit be attenuated or even reversed? Also, apart from SSAB, are there other types of attributional bias, such as group-serving bias, and how do they influence individual well-being as a function of culture? Furthermore, is SSAB a cause or consequence of well-being? Correlational data is unable to answer this question. Intervention approaches may help to provide a causal link between SSAB and health outcomes. Finally, if cultural variables (e.g., individualism, cultural self-construal) indeed play a role in producing SSAB, there should be within-culture and individual differences in SSAB as well. The cultural variables can be included in research design, and even manipulated in experiments to test their causal influences.

The self at play

Jensen de López conducted an insightful set of case studies of children's spontaneous play activities as a process in which the construction and socialisation of the self take place. And by comparing child play in different cultural communities, the study reveals that play is culturally framed, as is the self. Furthermore, the self is once again construed as mental representations of oneself in relation to the physical and social reality, and enacted in concrete actions of, in this context, pretend play. The theoretical framework and the findings are much in line with the 'developmental niche' model that underscores the contribution of three main subsystems of the environment to developmental processes (Super & Harkness, 2002): caregiver psychology (e.g. parental values and beliefs), the customs and practices of childrearing (e.g. parents' behaviours and attitudes towards play), and the physical and social settings in which children live (e.g. cultural artifacts, time, ecological space). Thus, while *"culture structures the environment for development"* (ibid., p. 270) culture structures the environment for play. Furthermore, the findings reveal that children are not passive learners mechanically imitating or reproducing adult roles and activities in their pretend play; instead, they are active producers of their own play and bring their cultural knowledge, self-motivation, and prior experiences into the play activities.

While analysing the cultural meaning and ecology of the child's environment in shaping play activities, it is useful to include such cultural dimensions in the measurement. It is also important to quantify different types, dimensions, components and functions of play and link them to the development of self. Play as a re-enactment of activities in the adult world, such as weddings and funerals, serves as a critical forum for cultural transmission. Apart from adult activities, children also often re-enact activities in their own lives that may be unfamiliar to adults, such as a school game, a karate class, and an observed peer conflict. The latter has not been well studied. What functions does this type of pretend play serve in constructing the self? While reinforcing existing cultural knowledge, it may also generate cultural elements, rules and conventions unique to the younger generation. Finally, although pretend play is traditionally considered in Western psychology to be a unique or even primary pathway for children's cognitive and social development, a recent review suggests a lack of causal connection between pretend play and any developmental outcomes, including language, emotion regulation, executive function, social skills, reasoning and problem solving, creativity, intelligence, and theory of mind (Lillard et al., 2012). Further research that intends to clarify the role of play in child development will benefit from the process approach of the current study and should situate play activities in specific cultural contexts.

The cultural self in psychopathology

Psychological disorders are not free from culture. Although the self, both conceptual and autobiographical, has been a focal topic in clinical psychology, empirical studies of the cultural self in relation to psychopathology, diagnosis, and treatment are fairly recent (e.g. Jobson, 2011). The chapter by Ryder, Ban, and Dere represents this emerging approach. The authors provide an impressive synthesis of the literature to illustrate the various ways by which the cultural self is associated with mental disorders and symptoms, particularly elaborating on the cultural meaning and expression of emotion and the cultural meaning and subjectivity of illness in the context of depression. The cultural self is again manifested in mind to shape the interpretation and experience of emotional distress and symptoms. It is further enacted in actions of communication, help-seeking, and coping behaviour as well as in actions demonstrated in the forms and expressions of symptoms. The analysis further reveals the cultural self as a transient, dynamic construct influenced by traditional beliefs, political ideologies, and the changing cultural contexts, which in turn affects the expression, diagnosis, and treatment of emotional disorders specific to time and place.

Much empirical research is needed to test the ideas proposed in the chapter, as the authors have noted. In addition to examining why and how *known* depressive symptom presentations vary as a function of culture and self, another critical question is to explore *unknown* culture-salient symptoms to further unveil the complexity of the depressive phenomenon. For example, as relationships are a salient aspect of the Asian self, depressive symptom presentations may entail interpersonal concerns. Indeed, studies conducted with Singaporean Chinese children and adolescents have found a cluster of previously undocumented depressive symptoms, labelled as Negative Social Self, in addition to known clusters of depressive symptoms such as negative affect, loss of interest, and somatisation (e.g. Koh, Chang, Fung, & Kee, 2007). It is also important to examine why and how culturally salient symptoms develop so as to delineate the mechanisms involved. For example, the way in which parents discuss emotional experiences with their children varies across cultures, which is directly implicated in children's self-concept development (Wang, Doan, & Song, 2010). During such conversations, European American mother-child pairs tend to focus on the emotion itself, whereas Chinese mother-child pairs tend to highlight social concerns related to the emotion (Wang, 2001). This difference corresponds to the finding that psychological depressive symptoms tend to be salient in Westerners, whereas interpersonal depressive symptoms tend to be salient in Asians. Early socialisation may play a critical role in shaping individuals' explanatory framework of symptoms and coping behaviour in culture-specific ways.

The self as migration narrative

Migration narratives have become increasingly important in our transcultural world. The chapter by Gómez-Stern and Vasquez articulates the idea that narrative is both a mental process and a communicative action via which individuals discern meaning from life experiences, in this case migration experiences, and further acquire continuity and coherence in their autobiography and self-identity. To some extent, narrative is the synonym of the self. It is the self in making. The researchers collected self-narratives from a small group of working-class immigrants, mostly women, in an educational setting. One particularly interesting finding is the parallel between personal stories and the familial and cultural past, where *"the personal history of migration interweaves with the group's history and traditions"*. This echoes the idea that vicarious memories of important others and of the family, community, and culture are just as important as personal memories in constituting the autobiographical self and identity (Wang, 2013). In addition, the use of emotion in the migration narratives is particularly significant in providing an evaluative stance to life circumstances, especially obstacles and disruptions, and the hopes and dreams that emerge in the process of adapting to a new life.

When studying migration narratives for self-making, one important factor to consider is the changes in socio-cultural contexts before and after immigration. Oftentimes, the self-identity of immigrants reflects a dynamic fusion of old and new personal experiences and cultural ideologies. Kağitçibaşi (2012) has argued that in the face of increasing globalisation and immigration, especially in the case where individuals cross borders from a collectivistic context to an individualist context, adopting an autonomous-related self is perhaps the most adaptive option. Furthermore, different socio-cultural contexts often require different competences for survival and success. Thus, while social competence such as sensitivity to the needs of others, taking responsibility for others, and being respectful to others may be critical in the former collectivistic context, cognitive competence that emphasises specialised skills and knowledge may be required in the new individualistic context to allow oneself to be competitive in society (ibid.). The Mexican immigrants in the study were precisely trying to enhance their skills by enrolling themselves in an adult computer class. Their narratives that featured themes of socio-economic progress and skills needed to succeed in the American society may further amplify their understanding of the changing cognitive demands.

The multifaceted self at work

The chapter by Singla highlights the multifaceted, dynamic nature of the self. Focusing on ethnic minority youths in Denmark, the author provides an elegant illustration of an intervention programme that, drawing upon a wide range of theories of human development, aims to help the youths adjust to their environment and the mainstream culture. A critical feature of the programme is to take into consideration the characteristics of the youths both in terms of their self-identity as shaped by experiences and ideologies of the host and home countries and the complex contexts of their lives, and in terms of their family structures, practices, and expectations for interdependence and fulfilment of roles. The inclusion of the youths in the larger culture and society through a deliberate effort to create contacts between the youths and various organisations and to empower the youths with cultural knowledge further underpins the success of the programme. The construction of the self from the mental world to the social world, from mentality to action, from conflict to resolution, and from ethnic confusion to ethnic pride is achieved through the delicate guidance of the therapist who serves as an equal partner and who is aware of and sensitive to the cultural characteristics and experiences of the ethnic minority youths.

Systematic translational research is a growing field of scientific inquiry whose significance cannot be neglected. Such research is indispensable to the evaluation and implementation of evidence-based clinical practice and public health programmes like the one described here. In dealing with real world issues, researchers need to be mindful in the design, testing, and dissemination of programme models that best reflect the accumulated knowledge from basic behavioural research. Evaluative data should be gathered from the programs to further inform future practices. In addition to qualitative descriptions of programme outcomes, quantitative assessments can be developed, as in the case study of how Jana came to develop a coherent, balanced, multifaceted self-identity and the resulting attitudes and behaviour towards her family, so that the results can be more generalisable. It is also essential to situate the programs in specific cultural contexts, adopting the strategies and practices most appropriate to the target population.

Self-redemption through narrative positions and voices

The final chapter by de la Mata, Pérez, Santigosa, and Macías examines the "survival" narrative of a battered woman to understand the reconstructive process of the self. The use of position and voice as the narrative tools is especially effective in this context, revealing the dynamic, changing, and adaptive nature of the self as both mental representations and concrete, discursive actions and interactions in the daily life, as exemplified in the self-redemption of the battered woman. The positions and voices embedded in the narrative help to demonstrate the multiple identities the narrator assumes, the important people who had made an impact, positive or negative, on her life, as well as her emotions, attitudes, and agency. The timeline and the change of positions and voices from being negative to positive in the narrative further help to reveal the process of overcoming violence and self-recovery. Mirroring the findings by Gómez-Stern and Vasquez, emotion is again a defining feature and a driving force of the narrative. The change of emotional tone leads to the change of positions and voices, which eventually gives rise to a reconstructed, new identity.

Although the postmodern view of the self as language may not be shared by all self researchers, language and narrative lend flexibility, and therefore adaptability, to the self. This function of language is particularly important when the self is considered in a cultural context. Importantly, apart from the narrative construction of the self, individuals' presumptions about themselves as well as their affiliations with certain pre-determined social groups are also a critical part of their self-identity, which then guide and shape their narrative activities that, in turn, reconstrue or give new meaning and significance to the self-presumptions and social affiliations. Furthermore, in addition to the qualitative analysis, quantitative analysis of the narrative positions and voices, particularly in relation to other psychological theories, will make possible the study of representative samples to produce generalisable knowledge and to identify individual differences. For instance, the multiple narrative positions may reflect self-complexity, which has been found to be a cognitive buffer against stress and depression (Linville, 1987). The model of self-complexity assumes that self-knowledge is represented in multiple aspects, called self-aspects. Individuals with high self-complexity represent the self in a great number of self-aspects and maintain a great distinction between the different self-aspects; as a result, they are less prone to depression, perceived stress, and other psychological illnesses and symptoms. By creating multiple self-representations for herself though the different positions in her narrative and by pulling apart the negative and positive positions in order to focus on the positive ones, Rosa could be said to be demonstrating high self-complexity that is beneficial to her recovery process from the abuse.

Conclusion

This collection of essays deserves applause. The studies reported are provocative, tapping many issues and, in the meantime, raising many questions concerning the multifaceted self in our changing world. As diverse as the topics covered in the chapters are, culture is always held central in the analysis. The message is unequivocal: the self is cultural in nature, be it the remembered self or the conceptual self. The cultural self is as dynamic as the methods used to study it, as the chapters eloquently demonstrate. Most importantly, the self is not constituted by mechanical neural connections or networks. It comprises dynamic mental representations developed through our making sense of our psychological, social, and cultural experiences; and it enacts and takes shape in our actions and interactions, through both behaviour and language, as we participate in the cultural activities of our time.

References

Fivush, R. (2008). Autobiography, time and history: Children's construction of the past through family reminiscing. In N. Galanidou & L. H. Dommasnes (Eds.), *Telling children about the past: Interdisciplinary approaches* (pp. 42-58). Ann Arbor, MI: International Monographs in Prehistory.

Harter, S. (1998). The development of self-representations. In W. Damon (Series Ed.) & N. Eisenberg (Vol. Ed.), *Handbook of child psychology: Vol. 3. Social, emotional, and personality development* (5th ed., pp. 553-617). New York: Wiley.

Jobson, L. (2011). Cultural differences in levels of autonomous orientation in autobiographical remembering in posttraumatic stress disorder. *Applied Cognitive Psychology*, 25, 175-182.

Kağitçibaşi, Ç. (2012). Sociocultural change and integrative syntheses in human development: Autonomous-related self and social-cognitive competence. *Child Development Perspectives*, 6, 5-11.

Koh, J. B. K., Chang, W. C., Fung, D. S. S., & Kee, C. H. Y. (2007). Conceptualization and manifestation of depression in an Asian context: Formal construction and validation of a children's depression scale in Singapore. *Culture, Medicine and Psychiatry*, 31, 225-249.

Lillard, A. S., Lerner, M. D., Hopkins, E. J., Dore, R. A., Smith, E. D., & Palmquist, C. M. (2012). The impact of pretend play on children's development: A review of the evidence. *Psychological Bulletin*, doi: 10.1037/a0029321.

Linville, P. W. (1987). Self-complexity as a cognitive buffer against stress-related illness and depression. *Journal of Personality and Social Psychology*, 52, 663-676.

Neisser, U. (1988). Five kinds of self-knowledge. *Philosophical Psychology*, 1, 35-59.

Super, C. M., & Harkness, S. (2002). Culture structures the environment for development. *Human Development*, 45, 270-274.

Taylor, S. E., & Brown, J. D. (1988). Illusion and well-being: A social psychological perspective on mental health. *Psychological Bulletin*, 103, 193-210.

Wang, Q. (2001). "Did you have fun?": American and Chinese mother-child conversations about shared emotional experiences. *Cognitive Development*, 16, 693-715.

Wang, Q. (2006). Culture and the development of self-knowledge. *Current Directions in Psychological Science*, 15, 182-187.

Wang, Q. (2013). *The autobiographical self in time and culture*. New York: Oxford University Press.

Wang, Q., Doan, S. N., & Song, Q. (2010). Talking about internal states in mother-child reminiscing influences children's self-representations: A cross-cultural study. *Cognitive Development, 25*, 380-393.

Wang, Q., Shao, Y., & Li, Y. J. (2010). "My way or Mom's way?" The bilingual and bicultural self in Hong Kong Chinese children and adolescents. *Child Development, 81*, 555-567.

Author list

Monika Abels • mabels@orn.mpg.de
Max Planck Institute for Ornithology, Germany

Lauren M. Ban • lm.ban@hotmail.com
Concordia University, Canada

Manuel de la Mata Benítez • mluis@us.es
Universidad de Sevilla, Spain

Peter Berliner • peer@dpu.dk
DPU, University of Aarhus, Copenhagen, Denmark

Jessica Dere • jdere@utsc.utoronto.ca
University of Toronto Scarborough, Canada

Beatriz Macías Gómez-Stern • bmacgom@upo.es
Universidad Pablo de Olavide, Spain

Tia G. B. Hansen • tia@hum.aau.dk
Aalborg University, Denmark

CONCEPTUAL AND APPLIED APPROACHES

Heidi Keller • hkeller@uni-osnabrueck.de
University of Osnabrück, Germany

Jessie Bee Kim Koh • bk94@cornell.edu
Cornell University, United States

Kristine Jensen de López • kristine@hum.aau.dk
Aalborg University, Denmark

Francisco Javier Saavedra Macías • fjsaavedra@us.esk
Universidad de Sevilla, Spain

Shahrenaz Mortazavi • 1937-2012

Mercedes Cubero Pérez • cubero@us.es
Universidad de Sevilla, Spain

Andrew G. Ryder • andrew.ryder@concordia.ca
Concordia University and Jewish General Hospital, Canada

Pilar Sanjuán •psanjuan@psi.uned.es
Universidad Nacional de Educacíon a Distancia, Spain

Andrés Santamaría Santigosa • asantamaria@us.es
Universidad de Sevilla, Spain

Rashmi Singla • rashmi@ruc.dk
Roskilde University, Denmark

Ole Michael Spaten • oms@hum.aau.dk
Aalborg University, Denmark

Olga A. Vásquez• ovasquez@ucsd.edu
University of California San Diego, United States

Qi Wang • ovasquez@ucsd.edu
University of California San Diego, United States

Yang Yang • yy472@cornell.edu
Cornell University, United States